Issues in Religion and Theology

5

The Kingdom of God
in the Teaching of Jesus

Issues in Religion and Theology

Titles in the series include:

Issues in Religion and Theology 5

The Kingdom of God in the Teaching of Jesus

Edited with an Introduction by

BRUCE CHILTON

FORTRESS PRESS | SPCK
Philadelphia | London

First published in Great Britain 1984
SPCK
Holy Trinity Church
Marylebone Road
London NW1 4DU

First published in the USA 1984
Fortress Press
2900 Queen Lane
Philadelphia
Pennsylvania 19129

Library of Congress Cataloging in Publication Data
Main entry under title:

The Kingdom of God in the teaching of Jesus.

(Issues in religion and theology; 5)
Bibliography: p.
Includes index.
1. Kingdom of God—Biblical teaching—Addresses, essays, lectures.
2. Eschatology—Biblical teaching—Addresses, essays, lectures.
3. Jesus Christ—Teachings—Addresses, essays, lectures.
I. Chilton, Bruce.
II. Series.
BS2417.K5K56   1984   231.7′2   83–20569
ISBN 0–8006–1769–X

British Library Cataloguing in Publication Data

The Kingdom of God in the teaching of Jesus—
(Issues in religion and theology; 5)
1. Jesus Christ—Teachings
I. Chilton, Bruce   II. Series
232.9′54   BS2415

ISBN 0–281–04091–5

Filmset by Northumberland Press Ltd, Gateshead
Printed in Great Britain by Richard Clay (The Chaucer Press) Ltd,
Bungay, Suffolk

Contents

Acknowledgements

Rudolf Otto, "The Kingdom of God Expels the Kingdom of Satan", is reprinted by permission from *The Kingdom of God and the Son of Man* (London: Lutterworth, 1938, rev. 1943) 97–107, a translation of *Reich Gottes und Menschensohn: Ein religionsgeschichtlicher Versuch* (Munich, 1934). Copyright © Lutterworth Press 1938.

Werner G. Kümmel, "Eschatological Expectation in the Proclamation of Jesus", was translated by Charles E. Carlston from "Die Naherwartung in der Verkündigung Jesu", in *Zeit und Geschichte*, ed. E. Dinkler (Tübingen: Mohr, 1964) 31–46, for J. M. Robinson (ed.) *The Future of our Religious Past* (London: SCM, 1971; New York: Harper & Row, 1971) 29–48, and is reprinted with the author's permission. Copyright © W. G. Kümmel 1964, 1971.

Erich Grässer, "On Understanding the Kingdom of God", is translated by permission of the author from "Zum Verständnis der Gottesherrschaft", first published in *ZNW* 65 (1974) 3–26. Copyright © E. Grässer 1974.

Michael Lattke, "On the Jewish Background of the Synoptic Concept, 'the Kingdom of God' ", is translated by permission from "Zur jüdischen Vorgeschichte des synoptischen Begriffs der 'Königsherrschaft Gottes' " in P. Fiedler and D. Zeller (ed.) *Gegenwart und kommender Reich* (Stuttgart: Katholisches Bibelwerk, 1975) 9–25. Copyright © Katholisches Bibelwerk 1975.

Norman Perrin, excerpts from *Jesus and the Language of the Kingdom: Symbol and Metaphor in New Testament Interpretation* (Philadelphia: Fortress, 1976; London: SCM, 1976) 16–32, 127–31, 197–9, are reprinted by permission. Copyright © SCM Press 1976.

T. Francis Glasson, "Schweitzer's Influence – Blessing or Bane?", is reprinted by permission from *JTS* 28 (1977) 289–302. Copyright © Oxford University Press 1977.

Bruce Chilton, "God in Strength", is reprinted by permission from *God in Strength: Jesus' Announcement of the Kingdom* (Linz: Plöchl, 1979) 277–93. Copyright © Bruce Chilton 1979.

Hans Bald, "Eschatological or Theocentric Ethics?", is translated by permission of the author from "Eschatologische oder theozentrische Ethik? Anmerkungen zum Problem einer Verhältnisbestimmung von Eschatologie und Ethik in der Verkündigung Jesu", first published in *VF* 24 (1979) 35–52. Copyright © H. Bald 1979.

The Contributors

BRUCE CHILTON is Lecturer in Biblical Studies at the University of Sheffield, and the author of *God in Strength* (1979) and *A Galilean Rabbi and his Bible* (1984).

RUDOLF OTTO (1869–1937) was Professor of Systematic Theology at the University of Marburg from 1917 to 1929, and wrote widely on the history, philosophy and phenomenology of religion, including Indian philosophy, mysticism, and above all *The Idea of the Holy* (1917).

WERNER G. KÜMMEL is best known for the English translation of his *Introduction to the New Testament* (1975), his *New Testament Theology* (1974) and *History of Research* (1973).

ERICH GRÄSSER is Professor of New Testament at the University of Bonn. In addition to his monographs on the delay of the parousia (1959) and the imminent expectation of Jesus (1973), he has written books on faith in Hebrews (1965) and Albert Schweitzer (1979).

MICHAEL LATTKE studied in the Roman Catholic theological faculties of Tübingen, Freiburg and Augsburg, and is now lecturer in Religious Studies at the University of Queensland. His dissertation on love in the fourth Gospel (*Einheit im Wort*) was published in 1975, and he has edited the Odes of Solomon (1979).

NORMAN PERRIN (1921–76) was Professor of New Testament at the University of Chicago. *The Kingdom of God in the Teaching of Jesus* (1963) and *Rediscovering the Teaching of Jesus* (1967) were followed by some significant studies of Mark.

T. FRANCIS GLASSON taught at New College, University of London, until his retirement. His published works include *The Second Advent* (1945), a commentary on the Book of Revelation (1965), *Jesus and the End of the World* (1980) and several articles on the same subject.

HANS BALD is Professor of New Testament at the University of Munich.

Series Foreword

The Issues in Religion and Theology series intends to encompass a variety of topics within the general disciplines of religious and theological studies. Subjects are drawn from any of the component fields, such as biblical studies, systematic theology, ethics, history of Christian thought, and history of religion. The issues have all proved to be highly significant for their respective areas, and they are of similar interest to students, teachers, clergy, and general readers.

The series aims to address these issues by collecting and reproducing key studies, all previously published, which have contributed significantly to our present understandings. In each case, the volume editor introduces the discussion with an original essay which describes the subject and its treatment in religious and theological studies. To this editor has also fallen the responsibility of selecting items for inclusion – no easy task when one considers the vast number of possibilities. Together the essays are intended to present a balanced overview of the problem and various approaches to it. Each piece is important in the current debate, and any older publication normally stands as a "classical" or seminal work which is still worth careful study. Readers unfamiliar with the issue should find that these discussions provide a good entrée, while more advanced students will appreciate having studies by some of the best specialists on the subject gathered together in one volume.

The editor has, of course, faced certain constraints: analyses too lengthy or too technical could not be included, except perhaps in excerpt form; the bibliography is not exhaustive; and the volumes in this series are being kept to a reasonable, uniform length. On the other hand, the editor is able to overcome the real problem of inaccessibility. Much of the best literature on a subject is often not readily available to readers, whether because it was first published in journals or books not widely circulated or because it was originally written in a language not read by all who would benefit from it. By bringing these and other studies together in this series, we hope to contribute to the general understanding of these key topics.

The series editors and the publishers wish to express their gratitude to the authors and their original publishers whose works are reprinted or translated here, often with corrections from living authors. We are also conscious of our debt to members of the editorial advisory board. They have shared our belief that the series will be useful on a wide scale, and they have therefore been prepared to spare much time and thought for the project.

DOUGLAS A. KNIGHT
ROBERT MORGAN

Abbreviations

BZ	*Biblische Zeitschrift*
BZNW	*Beihefte zur ZNW*
CBQ	*Catholic Biblical Quarterly*
EvT	*Evangelische Theologie*
ExpT	*Expository Times*
FRLANT	*Forschungen zur Religion und Literatur des Alten und Neuen Testaments*
HTR	*Harvard Theological Review*
JBL	*Journal of Biblical Literature*
JSNT	*Journal for the Study of the New Testament*
JSOT	*Journal for the Study of the Old Testament*
JTC	*Journal for Theology and the Church*
JTS	*Journal of Theological Studies*
LTK	*Lexikon für Theologie und Kirche*
NovT	*Novum Testamentum*
NTS	*New Testament Studies*
RB	*Revue Biblique*
RGG3	*Religion in Geschichte und Gegenwart* 3rd edn 1959–65
SBL	Society of Biblical Literature
SBT	Studies in Biblical Theology
SJT	*Scottish Journal of Theology*
SNTS	Societas Novi Testamenti Studiorum
Str-B	H. Strack and P. Billerbeck, *Kommentar zum Neuen Testament*
SUNT	Studien zur Umwelt des Neuen Testaments
TDNT	G. Kittel and G. Friedrich (ed.), *Theological Dictionary of the New Testament*
TLZ	*Theologische Literaturzeitung*
ThR	*Theologische Rundschau*
VF	*Verkündigung und Forschung*
ZNW	*Zeitschrift für die neutestamentliche Wissenschaft*
ZTK	*Zeitschrift für Theologie und Kirche*

Introduction

BRUCE CHILTON

"The kingdom of God" was the burden of Jesus' message. Each of the Synoptic Gospels makes this clear early on in passages of a summary nature which suggest that the evangelists saw Jesus' primary purpose in terms of preaching the kingdom (Matt. 4:12–17; 4:23; 9:35; Mark 1:14–15; Luke 4:43; 8:1; 9:11). Their presentation is justified when we consider that the kingdom is mentioned in many sayings ascribed to Jesus. In the passages already cited, Jesus is portrayed as announcing the kingdom, and in several other sayings also (Matt. 8:11,12/Luke 13:28–9; Matt. 11:12–13/Luke 16:16; Matt. 16:28/Mark 9:1/Luke 9:27; Luke 12:32) Jesus appears to proclaim the imminence of God's kingdom. The majority of kingdom sayings in the Synoptic Gospels seem more concerned to offer teaching about the kingdom than to proclaim it. In many such sayings, the kingdom is compared to another entity in order to illuminate some aspect of it, as in the parables. All of the synoptic evangelists present a considerable amount of parabolic material in respect of the kingdom (Matt. 13:24–50; 18:23–35; 20:1–16; 22:1–14; 25:1–13; Mark 4:26–34; Luke 13:18–20). Logia (from the singular *logion*, a technical term which refers to a saying of Jesus both as presented by an evangelist and as handed on prior to the writing of our Gospels) may also be described as catechetical which qualify the kingdom with reference to time (Luke 21:31, cf. 12:32) or possession (Matt. 5:3, 10; Luke 6:20; Matt. 19:14/Mark 10:14/Luke 18:16). A large number of sayings speak of entry into the kingdom; here the fact, quality or condition of entry is at issue (Matt. 5:20; 7:21; Mark 9:47; 10:15/Luke 18:17; cf. Matt. 18:3; Matt. 19:23–6/Mark 10:23–7/Luke 18:24–7), and to this extent teaching about the kingdom is offered. The only definite reference to the kingdom of God in the Gospel according to John (3:3, 5) also belongs to this category. Matt. 12:28/Luke 11:20 has, as we shall see, played an important role in the history of discussion concerning whether the kingdom should be seen as present or future in Jesus' preaching. As it stands, however, the logion qualifies the kingdom

1

with regard to Jesus' own activity as an exorcist. Insofar as the saying contradicts the assertion of Jesus' hearers that he acts on behalf of Beelzebul (Matt. 12:24, 27/Luke 11:15, 19), it may be regarded as controversial rather than catechetical. The same can be said of logia which dispute the possession (Matt. 21:31, 43; cf. 23:13) or the time (Luke 17:20–1; 19:11–27) of the kingdom.

The assignment of sayings here made under the categories of proclamation, teaching and controversy is, of course, open to discussion and in any case applies only to the texts of the Gospels as we can read them today, not to any hypothetical reconstruction of how the logia stood before the evangelists handed them on. We may not assume that they record Jesus' preaching of the kingdom with anything like stenographic accuracy; occurrences of the phrase "kingdom of God" are far from consistent among the Gospels. The nearly complete absence of the phrase from John poses a major difficulty in understanding the origin, development and purpose of that Gospel. The synoptic presentation is only relatively harmonious, and notably varied in matters of actual wording. Matthew typically prefers the periphrasis "kingdom of the heavens" to "kingdom of God", but "kingdom" by itself also appears here (4:23; 6:33; 9:35; 13:19,38; 24:14). Matthew has more uses of the term "kingdom" than does any other New Testament writer, even to the point that he ascribes such preaching to John (3:2), and yet at 5:29 and 18:9 he has no mention of it in sayings which are very similar to Mark 9:47, which concerns entry into the kingdom. The Matthean (4:12–17) and Marcan (1:14–15) portraits of the beginning of Jesus' kingdom teaching are quite different, and Luke does not even have Jesus refer to the kingdom in his presentation of the inaugural sermon of Jesus at Nazareth (4:16–30, but cf. vv. 43 and 15). These significant differences suggest that the evangelists were active in shaping the material handed down to them, and that the traditions before them were already divergent.

There is, then, no question of a unanimous testimony among the Gospels to a stenographically recorded preaching of Jesus. Nonetheless, the impression given by the synoptic evangelists that Jesus was first and foremost concerned with the kingdom is in full accord with the various traditions available to them. A further observation leads to the same conclusion. In many cases, "kingdom" appears in a saying of Jesus in order to explicate something else. That is, the kingdom is not the subject at issue, but is used to identify or explain another entity, such as the "mystery" of the kingdom (Mark 4:11, cf. Matt. 13:11; Luke 8:10), the "word" of the kingdom (Matt. 13:19), the "sons" of the kingdom (Matt. 8:12; 13:38), the "keys" of the kingdom (Matt. 16:19) and the "gospel" of the kingdom (Matt. 4:23; 9:35; 24:14). Nothing is said about the kingdom in these cases; Jesus is rather portrayed as assuming that the hearer or reader knows enough about the kingdom for it to shed light on the subjects actually at issue. The situation is similar at Matt. 6:33/Luke 12:31, where we are simply told, in a discussion about anxiety, to seek the kingdom. In all of these instances, the impression is confirmed that Jesus spoke of the kingdom consistently, and that it was a basic element in what he preached, taught and entered controversy over.

In some cases, incidental references to the kingdom leave us puzzled. What can it mean when a scribe is told he is not far from the kingdom (Mark 12:34), or when Jesus promises he will drink wine "new in God's kingdom" (Mark 14:25, cf. Matt. 26:29; Luke 22:16, 18)? Until one knows basically what the kingdom is, such sayings (cf. Matt. 5:19; 11:11/Luke 7:28; 11:12/Luke 16:16; 13:43, 52; 18:1, 2; 19:12; Luke 9:62; 18:29) will remain opaque. That does not imply that Jesus deliberately spoke in an obscure manner about the kingdom. Luke (14:15) even has an unnamed dinner guest speak of eating in the kingdom, which suggests that Jesus was understood by his original hearers when he used such imagery (cf. Mark 15:43/Luke 23:51 for evangelists' reference to the kingdom as if it were self-evident in its meaning). Indeed, the twelve are sent to preach the kingdom (Matt. 10:7/Luke 10:9, cf. v. 11 and 9:2, 60); in sending them, Jesus assumed they would be understood, if not welcomed. Lastly, the prayer handed down in Jesus' name presents the kingdom as a natural part of devotion, not an esoteric entity (Matt. 6:10, cf. v. 13; Luke 11:2).

The Gospels clearly demonstrate that Jesus was possessed of a message concerning the kingdom. He proclaimed it, acted upon it (cf. Matt. 12:28/Luke 11:20), called disciples to help preach it, explained it in parables and other catechetical sayings, and disputed its meaning with those with whom he disagreed. The confrontational aspect of his message, in which the kingdom was a basic element, brought him into such conflict with the religious and secular authorities of his day that he was finally crucified. With the terrible clarity that the resurrection accounts vividly convey, his followers came to believe after his death that the man and his message had been vindicated by God, that Jesus had lived and died for a truth no power on earth could destroy. Whether or not one shares the faith in Jesus' preaching, and his disciples' response to him, which the New Testament affirms, simple historical interest requires a rational account of Jesus' message – and particularly his conception of the kingdom – which is based on the evidence of his own words. Nothing less will permit us to understand the New Testament as a whole, especially the synoptic tradition, and the religious movement in Galilee and Jerusalem which gave rise to its documents.

It has been a hallmark of biblical scholarship since the Enlightenment to explicate "the kingdom of God" against the background of contemporary Jewish usage. At the same time, generations of contributors have not lost sight of the overall aim: so to understand the kingdom in Jesus' preaching that his ministry and the movement he began become explicable. A sensitive reading, that is to say exegesis, of the Gospels involves putting them in their historical contexts; equally, it requires that the text be permitted to speak its particular message, not reduced to generalizations about ancient religious thought or the nature of Christian faith. This approach is determined, not by an *a priori* decision to let the Gospels regulate faith, but by the intellectual desire to appreciate their literary individuality. Once they have been better appreciated, of course, the critical reader may well find himself awakened or challenged – most likely both – in respect of faith, but this volume is concerned with the preliminary question, as posed and answered by ordinary historical and literary technique: What did Jesus mean by "the kingdom of God"? The purpose of this introduction is to orient the reader in the terms in which the investigation has been conducted and to explain the significance of the articles and extracts from books which have been selected for presentation.

Essentially, critical enquiry into the meaning of the kingdom has been a modern (that is, post-Enlightenment) phenomenon. Historical factors before that time largely directed the focus of Western theology to questions such as justification and afterlife. Above all, Christology was treated as if it were the paramount concern in Jesus' preaching. Christianity was distinctive because of its concentration on the person of Jesus, and it was natural that this should be at the centre of concern in the patristic period, and that the New Testament should be used to explain who Jesus was in relation to God. Once Jesus was seen primarily as a Person within the Trinity, his sayings were regarded not so much as those of a historical figure as words which needed to be explained within the Trinitarian faith. The concentration on natural and philosophical theology during the medieval period represented a vigorous response to the challenge of developing a Christian philosophy of life and society, but it also resulted in the relative neglect of specifically historical issues. During the Reformation, despite the appeal to the biblical text as authoritative and the consequent growth of biblical criticism as a distinctive discipline, the problem of salvation outweighed the nascent concern to understand Jesus as a historical figure. The Enlightenment brought with its appeal to rationality a desire to escape the dogmatic controversies of the past by means of a historical treatment of the biblical text. But the question of Christology continued to be dealt with as the central issue in Jesus' teaching by such influential writers as H. S. Reimarus, F. D. E. Schleiermacher and D. F. Strauss (cf. Kümmel, 1973). By the end of the nineteenth century, however, the kingdom in Jesus' preaching was brought to the centre of theological interest, largely as a result of the work of Albrecht Ritschl.

At the time Ritschl wrote, liberal theology in Western scholarly circles was in the ascent. Its basic programme was to use critical exegesis in order to free one's approach to Jesus from dogma, and its consistent tendency was to see Jesus primarily as a moral teacher. Ritschl cannot be compared directly with such writers as Ernest Renan, who deliberately avoided recourse to the supernatural in his account of Jesus' ministry. Indeed, Renan's overall project was to offer a new system of dogma (cf. Schweitzer [1910], 181), and in this he typifies the course of liberalism. What began as the attempt to free believers from dogma became by the end of the century a new dogmatic rationalism which was at war with conservative circles. As Albert Schweitzer rightly complained (180–92), Renan simply ignored the aspects of John's Gospel (his base text) which did not please him. He is an excellent example of how rationalism can become uncritical by putting texts under the authority of its own view of the world. Ritschl's interest, at Tübingen and Bonn, was at first in the area of church history, but from 1864 he was Professor of Systematic Theology at Göttingen. His work is characterized by careful critical enquiry and great powers of synthesis. His overarching moral concern, however, and his attempt to offer a fresh account of the Christian teaching of justification and atonement (1870–4) show how far he was influenced by the liberal programme.

Ritschl defined the kingdom as the greatest benefit offered by God to men, and, at the same time, their common task of realizing this benefit in active obedience ([1900], 30). God, in essence, shows the correct ethical way through Jesus, and it is up to men to enact it. Notably, this definition occurs in a section of Ritschl's book devoted to showing the similarity between the concept of the kingdom and that of justification, so that his synthetic interests are here manifest. Moreover, it has been repeatedly pointed out that Ritschl's formulation is indebted to that of Immanuel Kant, for whom the kingdom was a morally ordered society (cf. Lundström [1963], 3). Such an ethical emphasis certainly predominates in Ritschl's thesis, although he excluded any notion of independent human activity. His enduring achievement consisted in relating the preaching of Jesus to systematic theology. His work succeeded in making the kingdom central in subsequent discussion, in showing that the kingdom concept in itself could be investigated both as preached by Jesus and as a fruitful element in contemporary theology. Despite the criticism to which his work has legitimately been subjected, his understanding of the kingdom as the source of ethical behaviour, albeit in a revised form, can still be defended.

Ritschl's influence reached far outside Germany, and is discernible, for example, in the work of H. C. King (*The Ethics of Jesus,* 1910). His formulation was taken up by one of his students, Wilhelm Herrmann, but applied in a much more individualistic way to refer to the rule of God in one's own heart (*Systematic Theology* [1927], 46), and a similarly conservative conception is to be found earlier, in the work of Adolf von Harnack, *What is Christianity?* (1901). On another front Ritschl's influence was felt in the "Social Gospel" movement, which flourished in America from the end of the last century until the stock market crash of 1929. The societal dimension of the kingdom was emphasized by such leaders of the movement as Shailer Mathews (*The Social Teaching of Jesus* [1897], 58) and Walter Rauschenbusch (*A Theology for the Social Gospel* [1912], 131). The ideology of the "Social Gospel", however, diverged from Ritschl's understanding of the kingdom. It was held that people had only to attend to and act upon the principles of Jesus in order to transform the world. The consideration that the kingdom comes from outside human society, which Ritschl had tried to protect, was largely lost on adherents of this movement. Even today, talk of "building" or "spreading" the kingdom – along with the notion that the Church is to be identified with the kingdom – is current, and stems from the belief that Jesus preached an ethical cause rather than a divine reality. The transcendent aspect of the kingdom in Jesus' teaching was ignored by many of Ritschl's successors, whether the ethics they pursued were of an individual or societal nature. But they did succeed in relating the kingdom to what people might actually do in and about the world they live in, in marked contrast to those who were to hold that Jesus' conception of the kingdom was altogether other-worldly.

The other-worldly aspect of the kingdom, the extent to which it should be regarded as eschatological in Jesus' preaching, has dominated scholarly discussion in the period since Ritschl wrote. "Eschatology" is the name given to belief in God's final intervention in human affairs, his last word (*eschaton*) to history. An urgent expectation of God's imminent and ultimate vindication of his people is characteristic of early Judaism. This has increasingly been accepted over the past hundred years. The typical feature of this expectation is its immediacy: God was believed to be about to act decisively in the near future. Wilhelm Baldensperger argued that the phrase "Son of Man" was used in Jewish circles to designate the messianic figure of the last time, and he held that this understanding was crucial in Jesus' conception of himself (*Das Selbstbewusstsein Jesu*, 1888). As Lundström ([1963], 29–34) had demonstrated, however, Baldensperger reverted to a Ritschlian conception when he came to the kingdom, and it was left to others (notably O. Schmoller, *Die Lehre vom Reiche Gottes in den Schriften des Neuen Testaments,* 1891) to explicate the kingdom eschatologically. The classic eschatological account of the kingdom was written by Johannes Weiss. The first edition of his work appeared in 1892; the revision, published in 1900, is renowned for the vigour of its style and the economy of its argument.

Weiss was not only Ritschl's student, but his son-in-law as well, and he admitted in his preface that it was difficult for him to write the book ([1900], v). But his inner struggle was by no means of a purely personal nature: Weiss continued to believe that Ritschl's definition of the kingdom was of value for systematic theology. He could not disabuse himself of the suspicion, however, that Ritschl and Jesus spoke of different things when they referred to "the kingdom of God". Weiss realized that for Jesus the kingdom was no moral cause, but a reality soon to break in on the world from God. His certainty of the kingdom, according to Weiss, led Jesus to announce salvation and judgement ([1900], 176) in the certain expectation that his heavenly father would act (178). Weiss used the word "apocalyptic" to describe Jesus' expectation. This term has been and is used of Jewish and Christian documents similar to the Book of Revelation ("The Apocalypse") in that they purport to disclose the details of God's last intervention in history. An "apocalyptic" writing typically conveys a "revelation" (*apokalypsis*) concerning the "end" (*eschaton*), sometimes by providing a calendar of occurrences leading up to and even including God's final acts. Apocalyptic is therefore eschatological, but eschatology need not be as detailed in respect of the final events as apocalyptic is. Weiss recognized that there was nothing calendrical about Jesus' teaching, and only called it 'apocalyptic" because it involved Jesus' special revelation, as Messiah, of God's final design (175, 176). He openly acknowledged (11, 19) that apocalyptic literature did not provide the key to Jesus' kingdom usage, and perhaps would have done better to use the term "eschatological" in respect of Jesus' preaching, rather than try to qualify the use of "apocalyptic" for this purpose. In any case, his qualified usage of specialist language proved susceptible of serious misinterpretation: the word "apocalyptic" as applied to Jesus' announcement of the kingdom was, perhaps, bound to be taken up by some to suggest that an eschatological timetable was involved. Writing in the second edition of his book, Weiss lamented the "unfruitful debate" his work had occasioned as to whether the kingdom was only future or already present in Jesus' understanding (69). Weiss' fundamental concern was to emphasize that the kingdom Jesus announced was not this-worldly moral improvement, but the miracle of God's intention for the world. It is one of the ironies of contemporary scholarship that his work in fact incited a debate regarding the time of the kingdom, which he regarded as a side issue.

Responsibility for the temporal preoccupation in much recent discussion of the kingdom belongs principally to Albert Schweitzer, whose *The Quest of the Historical Jesus* was first published in 1906. In form, the book is a history of previous discussion; in substance, it is a passionate indictment of the liberal attempt to understand Jesus as a moral teacher of timeless truths. Schweitzer's prose is much more forceful than is usually found in theological writing, and his treat-ment of his predecessors is not infrequently acerbic. With unmatched mastery, he demonstrated and pilloried the persistent tendency to minimize the eschatological dimension of Jesus' preaching. He in-sisted that only a "consistent eschatology" – that is, eschatology as reconstructed from apocalyptic writings ([1954], 365–6) – could make sense of Jesus' preaching. He saw implied in Jesus' kingdom usage an apocalyptic timetable of events, including cosmic tribulation, leading to the end (359–62): he expected the end of the present age to come during his ministry in Galilee (356–7), and he sent his disciples to preach to this effect (cf. above all Matt. 10:23). When the disciples returned from their mission, Jesus' hopes were disappointed: the kingdom had not come (362). From this time on, he sought to take the final tribulations on himself by means of his own suffering (386–8). In effect, Jesus attempted by the means appointed by God to force God to disclose the kingdom, and the man who died on the cross was a complete failure, even in terms of his own religious expectations. It is in this sense that Schweitzer could describe Jesus as an offence to religion (399).

Schweitzer's radical thesis, which he had already developed some five years earlier (1901), has seldom been defended in detail. It owed a great deal to the work of H. S. Reimarus, an eighteenth–century historian, who, as Schweitzer acknowledged, was scornful of biblical revelation ([1954], 13–26, 15). Indeed, Schweitzer considered that the significance of Weiss' work lay in its support of the purely eschat-ological portrait of Jesus pioneered by Reimarus (239–40). Be that as it may, Schweitzer himself was motivated by a deeply religious sense.

He believed that the historical Jesus was alien to us, but that this only underscored the necessity of focusing on what he called the spirit of Jesus as it transforms our lives (399–401). If he was imprecise in explaining just how such a focus was to be achieved, the power of his conviction is demonstrated by his career as a whole. The weakness of Schweitzer's scheme as an exegetical account of Jesus' preaching must nonetheless be acknowledged. Apocalyptic literature simply does not evidence the conception of the kingdom which Schweitzer held was Jesus' starting-point. More particularly, the elaborate account of Jesus' belief that the messianic tribulations prior to the kingdom's coming could be transferred into his own suffering is unsupported by the evidence. Yet in spite of the general agreement that he did not establish the positive suggestions he attempted to make, the current characterization of the kingdom as "apocalyptic" and/or "eschatological" is probably best ascribed to the influence of Schweitzer.

In Germany, August von Gall pressed the case for a futuristic interpretation of the kingdom in a work which attempted to set "the kingdom of God" in the context of the development of ancient religion as a whole (*Basileia tou Theou*, 1926). He especially emphasized the Zoroastrian origin of the kingdom idea. Von Gall's eschatological emphasis is fully consistent with a growing trend in studies after Schweitzer (cf. S. J. Case, *Jesus*, 1927; W. Michealis, *Täufer, Jesus, Urgemeinde*, 1928; M. Goguel, *The Life of Jesus*, 1933), but its appeal to the ancient religion of Iran in order to define the kingdom was both innovative and influential. A similar, history of religions approach was taken by Rudolf Otto in *The Kingdom of God and the Son of Man* (German 1934, English 1938). By means of an appeal to Zoroastrian sources Otto was able powerfully to convey the impression that Jesus' conception of the kingdom was dualistic and other-worldly. The chapter made available in the present volume illustrates this, and it also shows that the kingdom in Otto's view must be seen as the force behind Jesus' ministry: the kingdom is the in-breaking power of God which focuses on Jesus so as to make his messianic claims possible.

Otto's reference to Iranian religion in order to explain Jesus' teaching is typical of the weakness of the history of religions approach: the broad similarity between the two beliefs, despite the fact of their cultural and temporal distance from one another, is used to claim that there is a relationship of direct dependence (cf. C. Colpe, 1961). Research since the time of Otto has shown that the Zoroastrian sources are in any case far too late to use as evidence for the understanding of pre-Christian religion (cf. E. M. Yamauchi, *Pre-Christian*

Gnosticism, 1973). With deftness of style, however, Otto relates Jesus' conception of the kingdom to his understanding of himself, and he speaks of the kingdom as an active force in Jesus' faith. In the extract, Otto selects a passage (Matt. 12:28) which is susceptible of discussion along these lines. His selection was by no means governed by purely exegetical considerations. Otto had been a student of Albrecht Ritschl's, and his overall interest was systematic. In an early work (*Kantisch-Fries'sche Religionsphilosophie,* 1909), he had devoted himself to the philosophy of Jakob Friedrich Fries, a follower and critic of Kant. Fries viewed the kingdom above all as aesthetically perceived, in the rule of eternal beauty and of holy love (*Sämtliche Schriften,* 12, 144). The ground of religious perception lies in the presentiment ("Ahnung") of eternal ideas according to Fries (198), and in Otto this perception is seen as a felt experience of the eternal ([1909], 105, 110, 122, 198f.) as it conditions being. The influence of Fries on Otto's most famous work, *The Idea of the Holy* (1917), is obvious. There is nevertheless an experiential emphasis in Otto which is absent in Fries, whose philosophy of religion is merely a byway in his discourse on aesthetics. Otto understood the kingdom preached by Jesus as a mysterious power, miraculous and transcendent, yet at the same time experienced and acted upon by Jesus. Otto therefore presented an eschatological view of the kingdom which allowed of a present aspect. He was able to do so on the strength of his systematic understanding of religious experience; for precisely that reason, his ideas have not found much support among exegetes. But Otto offered a comprehensively eschatological, but non-apocalyptic, understanding of the kingdom which did justice to the sayings which refer to the kingdom as having come, the very thing exegetes have rightly complained that Schweitzer failed to explain. (Cf. Kümmel, 1957, for an attempt to accommodate the present aspect within an eschatological understanding.) Albeit indirectly, Otto pointed the way in which future discussion was to move.

Dodd's *The Parables of the Kingdom* first appeared. Dodd was critical of the approach to the kingdom in Jesus' preaching by means of Iranian eschatology ([1965], 24 n.2), although he fully approved of Otto's insistence upon the dynamic character of the kingdom. The most extensive critique he offered, however, was of Schweitzer's position. As Weiss before him, he observed that "the kingdom of God" is not a stock usage in apocalyptic literature, and he also emphasized that Jesus on occasion (cf. Matt. 12:28/Luke 11:20 above all) referred to the kingdom as having already come (30). Such passages contradicted Schweitzer's "consistent eschatology" in Dodd's view (55), and he sought to establish the use of the phrase "realized eschatology" as an overall characterization of Jesus' message (35). The latter phrase was intended by Dodd to exclude an understanding of the kingdom in apocalyptic terms, and to assert that the kingdom was held by Jesus to be experienced in his own ministry (30, 35, 37, 159). As the title of his work suggests, Dodd sought to explain the meaning of the kingdom in Jesus' preaching with particular reference to the parables. He found that the kingdom is here compared to processes of nature in a manner quite unlike that of apocalyptic Judaism. From this observation he inferred that the essentially divine quality of the natural order is the premise of the parables (10–11), and that Jesus spoke of a power which was released in the world by his own ministry. In his criticism of Albert Schweitzer, Dodd was representative of a growing tendency among English theologians to highlight the present aspect of the kingdom (cf. A. T. Cadoux, 1930, and T. W. Manson, 1931). Exegetically, however, he proceeds in an inductive manner: without reference to – indeed, in spite of – the marked eschatological element in the religion of Jesus' day, Dodd asks us to infer that Jesus' message was an almost philosophical assertion about the natural world. Where Otto had too easily assumed the mutual influence of religions in the ancient world, Dodd has rightly been taken to task for offering a portrait of Jesus which does not take adequate account of the world in which he actually lived.

The keen interest in the parables of Jesus during the pre-war period inspired Joachim Jeremias, whose work is the classic expression of a modern historical approach. The first edition of *The Parables of Jesus* was published in 1947; there have been eight subsequent German editions, and two translations into English. Jeremias was influenced by A. T. Cadoux and C. H. Dodd ([1963], 21 nn. 60, 62), and took up their attempt to place the parables in the concrete context of Jesus' ministry. The distinctive feature of his book lies in the care of its historical exegesis. His programme, pursued in a detailed but relatively non-technical way, reflects the critically established judgement that our sources contain both the sayings of Jesus themselves and church interpretation of those sayings, and that they do so sometimes without making a formal distinction between the two. As Jeremias showed, the interpretation provided in Mark 4:14–20 to the parable of the sower (vv. 3–8) departs from Jesus' normal practice in allegorizing the individual elements in the parable so that they are no longer part of a single, coherent image, but rather more like a series of preaching points (77f., 81f.). The parable itself, on the other hand, is true to ancient Palestinian agricultural practice in its description of the sower's activity, and is designed to convey in vivid imagery the certainty that the kingdom is "in the process of realizing itself" (11–13). His use of the last phrase shows, as he openly acknowledged (230 n. 3), that Jeremias is in Dodd's debt. But he wisely rejected Dodd's "realized eschatology" as a description of Jesus' preaching because he believed that it proceeds on the basis of an *a priori* definition of the kingdom. Jeremias insisted on a more systematic procedure in reading the sources, one under which we isolate dominical material from ecclesial interpretation and refer methodically only to the former in explicating the theology of Jesus himself.

Jeremias' method relies a great deal on "form criticism", which is the attempt to characterize material in the Gospels according to its function before it was written down (that is, during a period of oral transmission), in its "setting in (the) life" (of the early Church). In the example already cited, the allegorizing interpretation of a parable was held to reflect its setting in the teaching of the Church, while the parable itself was seen to serve Jesus' own more immediate aim of calling men to recognize their predicament in the face of God's self-realizing kingdom. By such analysis, form critics distinguish between traditions – that is, the materials used by the gospel writers. Although the precise shape of the traditions before the Gospels remains a matter of dispute, there is general agreement that these traditions were circulated and interpreted, orally and/or in writing, before they were assembled by the evangelists. The evangelists, then, collected this material as an editor of an anthology might. From the German word for editing (*Redaktion*), we have the technical name, "redaction criticism", for the attempt to explain how the evangelists assembled, shaped and interpreted the traditions available to them. Jeremias was also a pioneer in this field. His analysis of Mark 4:11–12 brilliantly exemplifies how the evangelists provide an old saying with a new context (14). At the same time, Jeremias showed how it was possible to describe traditions without recourse to the necessarily hypothetical form-critical category, "setting in life". A certain circularity always attends the use of this category: a text is said to imply a "setting", which in turn is taken to lead to the correct interpretation of the text. But when he came to treat of Mark 4:12, Jeremias did not first of all make a guess as to its setting; following T. W. Manson, he proved that the Jewish "Targum", that is, Aramaic paraphrase, to the book of Isaiah is actually quoted here (15). He thereby opened the door to a more exacting method of tradition criticism which cites actual evidence of contact in a passage with the material contained in other documents whose historical background is known, and thus does not require us to invent "settings in life" in which to locate hypothetical "forms".

12

Subsequent discussion has, however, revealed two weaknesses in Jeremias' contribution. Methodologically, he does at least occasionally seem to equate "Aramaic" or "Palestinian" with what is authentically dominical, and "Greek" or "hellenistic" with church interpretation (cf. Marshall, 1972–3). But his own analysis of Mark 4:11–12 suggests that a Greek redactor might have had access to primitive tradition, and any student of Jewish literature knows Jesus was not the only preacher in the first century who spoke Aramaic and used vivid images from daily life. The distinction between dominical and ecclesial simply cannot be reduced to the distinction between Aramaic and Greek. When we conclude that a saying is authentically dominical, this is a historical judgement, taken in the light of all the evidence available: linguistic considerations are clearly important, but they are not solely determinative. Jeremias himself usually exercised the full range of his immensely well-informed historical judgement to defend the supposition that Jesus preached self-realizing eschatology, that is, God's inception of his final acts. This conception of the kingdom has won wide support, in that it allows of the emphatically future element of eschatology while claiming that in Jesus the hour of fulfilment has come (230). But, as in the case of Dodd's argument, this account of Jesus' eschatology remains suppositious in the absence of a contemporary Jewish document which understands the kingdom in this fashion. Although Jeremias contributed most importantly to the general understanding of early Judaism, the search for evidence of this kind has had to continue, and the suspicion remains that his understanding of eschatology owes as much to systematic considerations as to exegesis (cf. already Jeremias *Jesus als Weltvollender,* 1930).

W. G. Kümmel offered findings similar to those of Jeremias, and by two years (1945) anticipated to some extent the idea that Jesus' eschatology was self-realizing. His method differed strongly from that of Jeremias, being synthetic rather than analytic. Kümmel sought to develop an overview of Jesus' eschatology, and so to place the kingdom in the context of sayings about the second coming and the final judgement. To his mind, it was plain that Jesus expected an emphatically future kingdom to arrive within the life of his generation ([1957], 49f.), and also that Jesus thought of the kingdom as active in his own person (107, 154). Just as Jesus' reference to the kingdom's nearness gives his message immediacy and certainty (152f.), so his emphasis on the kingdom's futurity forces us to conceive of the kingdom as a historical, or actually tangible, act of God. In both aspects, he held, Jesus' authority comes to expression (155), and his authority must have both present and future (that is, historical) dimensions in order to be complete. The temporal nearness of the kingdom therefore acquires systematic importance in Kümmel's thesis, which is why he so vehemently defends it in the article here presented, even though it involves him in saying that Jesus was wrong about when the kingdom would come (below p. 44).

Kümmel defends the futuristic understanding of the kingdom with reference first of all to Jesus' assertion that the kingdom of God has drawn near (*ēngiken*, cf. Mark 1:15; Matt. 4:17; Matt. 10:7; Luke 10:9, 11). In *The Expository Times* (1936–7) an article had appeared which aroused extensive discussion. In this essay, J. Y. Campbell attacked Dodd's view that Jesus meant to say the kingdom had already come. Campbell produced evidence that *ēngiken* renders the Aramaic verb *qrb*, not *mṭ'*, and so that we must understand Jesus' preaching in the sense that the kingdom is "near", but not realized or "come". Dodd replied rather weakly that he took *ēngiken* in the sense of *ephthasen* (which appears in Matt. 12:28/Luke 11:20). Although *ephthasen* does pose difficulty for any consistently eschatological understanding of Jesus' preaching, Dodd certainly pressed the evidence beyond reasonable limits in trying to make the verb normative for the meaning of sayings in which it does not in fact appear. In any case, K. W. Clarke (1940) provided more detailed support for Campbell's position, and his article has been very influential in the post-war period. The derivation of *engizō* from *qrb* was generally accepted, although the tense of the verb in Jesus' sayings (perfect) has continued to cause perplexity. Even if the meaning of the term in the present tense merely indicates nearness, rather than arrival, the perfect, it has been held, must in some sense support Dodd's view (cf. Hutton, "The Kingdom of God has come", *ExpTim*, 64, [1952–3] Fuller [1954], 25). The position had been further complicated by an article by Matthew Black, "The Kingdom of God has come", *ExpTim*, 63 (1951–2) which observed that *qrb* might in any case refer to actual coming, and not merely approach. A more thorough survey of the Semitic data by R. F. Berkey (1963) similarly found that a precise distinction between proximity and actual contact could not be made on the basis of the evidence to hand (187). It is indeed noticeable that in Daniel 7:13 forms of the verbs *qrb* and *mṭ'* are used in respect of the same event. Kümmel cites some of this discussion in coming to the conclusion that *engizō* refers to approach, and only rarely to actual arrival, although he wisely does not pretend that the matter can be settled by etymological considerations alone.

Turning from questions of etymology and syntax, Kümmel seeks to place the sayings concerned in the context of Jesus' preaching as a whole. Once this is done, he claims that Jesus' futuristic understanding of the kingdom is obvious. In his article, he cites in particular the parable of the fig tree (Mark 13:28–9 and parallels), the parable of the unjust judge (Luke 18:2–8) and three short sayings (Mark 9:1; 13:30; Matt. 10:23). At this point, the overtly synthetic nature of Kümmel's argument becomes apparent. As Schweitzer before him, he makes the teaching about the Son of Man (notably 10:23) determinative for understanding the kingdom. In fact, Mark 9:1 is the only saying in the list given which actually mentions the kingdom. Mark 13:28–9, 30 is a collection of sayings organized around the theme of the Son of Man's coming, and is widely agreed to contain interpretations added in the course of tradition and redaction.

Kümmel oversynthesizes, in assuming that one concept in Jesus' message (the Son of Man, a very difficult phrase anyway) will immediately shed light on another, and in supposing that we have direct access to Jesus' words in material which is probably secondary. The first failing is particularly manifest when Kümmel cites the parable of the unjust judge in connection with the kingdom, the second when he cites Mark 13:30, which even in its present context is followed by sayings which soften the temporal emphasis (13:31–2). The evident fact that the strata of the Gospels are not uniformly eschatological in outlook puts attempts to synthesize a single perspective from them into serious question. Even Mark 9:1 may not be as straightforwardly futuristic as Kümmel would have it; it has been suggested that "those who will never taste death" refers to angelic figures such as Moses and Elijah (cf. Mark 9:4, 5), who in Jewish tradition were held to be immortal (cf. Chilton [1978]; [1979, 251–74]; [1980]). In that case, Jesus in Mark 9:1 would mean that the certainty of the kingdom, the fact that God willed it for men, was attested by the likes of Elijah and Moses, who already knew God's power in an intimate way. A discussion of the linguistic issues involved in this question cannot detain us here; our point is merely that Kümmel's article does not take full account of the complexity of the evidence. The enduring strength of his contributions lies in their insistence that a range of temporal conceptions is implied in Jesus' preaching, including his message of the kingdom. But it remains problematic to suppose that sayings which deal with different subjects, reflect distinctive backgrounds, and have undergone various degrees of interpretation, permit us immediately to infer an overarching eschatology into which the kingdom fits neatly.

Along with Joachim Jeremias' contribution, Kümmel offered an account of the kingdom which represented, and helped to develop, the post-war consensus. The important place of eschatology in Jesus' preaching has been almost universally accepted, even to the point that it can be admitted that Jesus was somewhat misguided in respect of the time of the kingdom. R. H. Hiers (1973) has even championed Schweitzer's thesis in its undiluted form. But in the main, scholars have tended to concede that Schweitzer too confidently placed Jesus' preaching in a rigidly apocalyptic context, and that he persistently ignored Jesus' manifest assertion that the kingdom was already active, at least in his own ministry. In addition to the influential contributions already mentioned, we would cite from the Catholic side the highly respected work of Rudolf Schnackenburg (1963) and from Evangelical circles G. E. Ladd's readable introductory monograph whose evocative title in the second edition (*The Presence of the Future*, 1974) sums up in a phrase a great deal of what has been said to date.

But Schweitzer has influenced not only the substance, but also the form, of recent contributions. In 1963, two books were published in English bearing the same title: *The Kingdom of God in the Teaching of Jesus*. One was written by Norman Perrin, and the other was a translation of Gösta Lundström's 1947 doctoral thesis; both discuss the history of research on Jesus' understanding of the kingdom and confirm a qualifiedly eschatological approach. If Schweitzer's powerful rhetoric provided a tombstone for liberalism, Lundström's and Perrin's more measured prose amounted to a carefully built pedestal for the new form of the Weiss–Schweitzer consensus. In both books, the extent to which contributors were able to do justice to the eschatological aspect of Jesus' message became the criterion on which their work was judged, although the need to appreciate the present activity of the kingdom in Jesus' understanding was also emphatically acknowledged.

Kümmel's article in this volume shows how deeply important an eschatological understanding of Jesus can be to modern theologians. The essay of 1974 by Erich Grässer, also presented here, is even more explicitly theological.

In this admittedly sometimes elliptical article Grässer shows clearly how disciplined exegesis can be used to evaluate theological claims about the meaning of the kingdom. His treatment of Matt. 12:28/Luke 11:20 is in form a critique of a contribution from Theodor Lorenzmeier. Lorenzmeier defends a political understanding of the kingdom by means of theses that appear problematic to Grässer. Lorenzmeier holds that the demonological content of the saying is meaningless, and should be taken to refer to the aggression, illness, totalitarian ideologies and social oppression to which human beings are subject. The kingdom opposes these, but not directly: it requires men who are fellow workers with God. As such, it will always be revealed in opposition to the powers of inhumanity. From this reading, Lorenzmeier concludes that Christian existence is essentially a matter of understanding human existence, as threatened by what is inhuman and as liberated by the kingdom. The difficulty with this argument, as Grässer sees it, is that at each step the transcendent aspect of the kingdom is given over to a consistently generalized humanitarianism in a way which contradicts the clear import of the text. The overthrow of the demonic powers in Jesus' saying is a sign of God's own intervention, which challenges the reader as something from outside his usual experience, but by no means the mere victory of one human force over another. Along the same lines, Grässer observes that the kingdom does not need men; Jesus announces it rather as coming to needy men without being conditioned by their acceptance of it. In the case of the saying under consideration, it comes – as grace – to the individual, not to the collective humanity which Lorenzmeier has in view. Grässer considers that such grace, pointing forward to a future revelation, is the proper object of Christian faith.

Grässer's article is important for several reasons. Lorenzmeier's position represents a recent renewal of the tendency, documented by Grässer, to equate the kingdom with human ideals, institutions, or movements. However worthwhile such causes may be, Grässer reminds us that Jesus' preaching is fundamentally an assertion in respect of God, and that we cannot do justice to the evidence at hand if we pretend otherwise. The debate between Lorenzmeier and Grässer also illustrates how ordinary exegesis, the simple attempt to specify what a text is saying and how it says it, can illuminate theological discourse. Christians sometimes speak subjectively about the kingdom without recourse to a definition derived from Jesus' words. For one person, the kingdom is a movement of liberation; for another, the institutional Church; for yet another, the experience of grace in Christ. But unless we can say clearly how our cherished notions are defensible as understandings of what Jesus meant by the kingdom, we will be unable convincingly to claim them as aspects of his preaching or to communicate them to others on the basis of commonly accepted evidence. Exegesis is necessary to the understanding of what biblical faith meant, and is therefore relevant to what it might mean today. Grässer reminds us of this, and of the importance of identifying the areas of disagreement with one's disputant so as to clarify the issues at stake.

Grässer makes it clear that the kingdom for him is essentially a matter of grace; his debt to Karl Barth is explicitly acknowledged, and is also apparent in his emphasis on the individual as the object of

Jesus' preaching. Eschatology is taken to represent the transcendent future hope which is implicit in the promise of individual grace. This is fairly typical of the way in which Schweitzer's claims about eschatology have been taken up in modern theological discussion. Obviously, however, basic questions are begged by such expositions. On what grounds, for example, can the kingdom be equated with grace? Is the emphasis on individual assurance more a feature of Jesus' preaching, or of the individualizing tendency in Protestant theology? We are brought back by these questions to the foundational task of defining what Jesus, as a Jew of the first century, meant when he proclaimed the kingdom of God. Moreover, Lorenzmeier's strong assertion of the ethical component in Jesus' preaching, especially in view of Grässer's relative silence on this matter, raises the further issue: how was Jesus' ethical teaching related to his announcement of the kingdom? Or, put another way: did his preaching concern only his hearers' attitude to an eschatological event? This question will recur in our discussion of Hans Bald's article, but should be kept in mind as we proceed to speak of the more basic task of defining "the kingdom of God".

From what has been said so far, the importance of contributions such as Michael Lattke's will be apparent: he returns to the basic question of what a Jew in the time of Jesus would have understood by the phrase. Although he accepts the consensus that the kingdom in Jesus' preaching is eschatological, his careful consideration of ancient Jewish usage is an eloquent warning against the assumption that the kingdom in Jesus' day was defined in a rigid manner. The relative paucity of references to the kingdom in Jewish sources underlines this point and, in Lattke's judgement, requires that we consider divine kingship language generally, not only explicit references to "the kingdom of God". Even by broadening his brief, however, Lattke is unable to characterize the kingdom as an essentially apocalyptic category, in that it does not feature as an element in a calendar of the last things. (When he refers to the kingdom in the *Ascension of Moses* as "apocalyptic" in the last sentence of III.1, he is not using the term in its strict or literary sense, but only generally, in order to say the kingdom comes by revelation, as in Weiss.) Faith in God's kingdom, as presently effective and soon to be consummated, does not seem to have been the peculiar property of the apocalyptic seers. In one sense, such faith is at least as old as Exodus 15:18, and is shared by documents which are not apocalyptic. By the time rabbinic literature achieved recognizable form, one could speak of taking on the yoke of the kingdom when one confessed the one God and his Torah by reciting, "Hear, O Israel, the LORD our God, the LORD is one ..."

(Deut. 6:4–9). As Lattke clearly realizes and rightly stresses, however, our sources for rabbinic Judaism are in fact more recent than the NT, so that we cannot assume that everything we read in them was part of the "background" of the New Testament. In making this assertion, Lattke corrects the impression given by T. W. Manson (1931), who pioneered the approach Lattke adopts.

There is yet another, and more basic, question which Lattke's survey raises. If kingship imagery can be used apocalyptically and non-apocalyptically, as well as to refer to God's eternal dominion and to the recitation of a biblical passage, does it have any concrete meaning in itself? When Jesus announced "the kingdom of God", did he intend only to allude to the various things his hearers already may have known about God being king? Lattke successfully demonstrates that the kingdom is not a component in a systematically apocalyptic scheme, but he is so successful that we are led to wonder how Jesus could have been intelligible to his hearers if they understood the kingdom only as it is presented in the sources Lattke discusses. As a particular instance of the problem Lattke's contribution poses, we mention Jesus' consistency in using the precise phrase, "the kingdom of God", which is all but inexplicable on the assumption that variety in phrasing prevailed in the contemporary usage of kingship imagery.

Lattke's analysis represents the increasing difficulty experienced by scholars in arriving at a clear understanding of what "kingdom of God" means, or even at a framework, such as "apocalyptic", within which it might be understood. We have already noted the tendency, particularly in the work of Dodd and Kümmel, to move too quickly from the text to a theologically acceptable synthesis; in the absence of clear definition and a demonstrable context, one is thrown back on inference, and the danger of inferential exegesis is always that one will be as influenced by factors in one's own culture as by the text in question when articulating an interpretation.

In *Jesus and the Language of the Kingdom* (1976) Norman Perrin boldly sets out a framework with which the kingdom in Jesus' preaching might be understood. His approach owes a great deal to the phenomenonological method of Mircea Eleade, in which texts are used to reconstruct the belief systems which lie behind them. That is, the text is seen as a phenomenon of belief, not an object of study in itself. Perrin paints on a broad canvas, portraying a "myth" of God's kingship with reference to the Old Testament, intertestamental literature, Rabbinica, and other ancient Near Eastern documents, as well as the New Testament. The myth, according to Perrin, was that God had acted in the creation and in the history of Israel, and would continue to do so; it made sense of Israel's experience as a people under God. "The kingdom of God" is the symbol which evokes this myth, and is only meaningful insofar as it evokes the myth. Symbols can be of two kinds: those which point, as signs, to only one particular referent, and those which, as symbols in the proper sense, are not to be identified with any single referent. Perrin conceives of the kingdom as a symbol in the latter sense; it relates Israel to the myth of God as king through the whole range of his experience, not in any one event or circumstance. If there was a tendency in apocalyptic literature to reduce symbols to signs, by making them ciphers for particular persons or things, this was not Jesus' procedure. Drawing on the contribution of Amos Wilder (1971) – who has had an extraordinary influence on parables research since Jeremias – Perrin shows that, just as Jesus' preaching was symbolic, so his parabolic teaching was essentially metaphorical. The intention behind the parables is not to point as a sign to some particular feature of human experience, but to convey Jesus' vision of God as king.

Quite consciously, Perrin is using "myth", "symbol" and "metaphor" as key categories for an essentially modern representation of Jesus' teaching. Recent discussion of how human beings interpret and understand reality by means of language (hermeneutics) has provided the framework within which the kingdom is set, and on that basis it is defined. The goal of Perrin's exposition is to speak of the faith of the New Testament, not merely to understand its text. Perrin understood very well that his own programme, based on a hermeneutical system, was a response to the existentially based programme of Rudolf Bultmann. Such bold syntheses succeed or fail according to their adequacy in two directions: (1) as historically tenable accounts of the texts to which they refer, and (2) as philosophically tenable accounts of life as the reader experiences it. The latter point cannot concern us here, but the former demands our attention. Although "myth", "symbol" and "metaphor" are hardly categories in which we would expect Jesus and his hearers to have explained his message, Perrin's synthesis suggests that kingdom language was designed, not so much to express an idea or concept as to convey a vision of God active in the world. That suggestion might be tested exegetically.

Perrin's major works on the kingdom reflect a developing dissatisfaction, or at least an unease, with the eschatological consensus. He himself contributed to the development of that consensus (1963), and takes it as axiomatic along with a form-critical method (1967). In both respects, *Jesus and the Language of the Kingdom* represents, if not a turn about, then an attempt to move into new territory. Perrin, by the philosophically based method already described, sought to express an understanding of the kingdom which might be future oriented and eschatologically transcendent, but not univocally futuristic. He realized that it was not enough to say that the kingdom was eschatological, but proleptically present, in Jesus' ministry. That is the essence of the eschatological consensus; although it may sound like a solution, it is really only a statement of the problem. The evidence is quite clear that the kingdom cannot be pinned down to a single temporal dimension. But stating that only begs the question: just what are we dealing with when we hear of a kingdom which presents itself so flexibly as both future and present? Perrin's later work, some of the most creative and insightful he ever produced, implies that the eschatological consensus needs to be replaced by another framework within which the kingdom might be understood. Unfortunately he did not have occasion before his death to defend his proposed framework as an actual exegesis of Jesus' sayings.

The need for an alternative framework to the eschatological consensus has been underlined by T. Francis Glasson's argument that Schweitzer's understanding of the kingdom as apocalyptic was erroneous. In the article reprinted here Glasson argues vehemently that the eschatological interpretation of Jesus' teaching, insofar as it assumes the validity of Schweitzer's position, is disastrously flawed. The Jewish documents cited by Schweitzer do not demonstrate that the phrase "kingdom of God" would have evoked an apocalyptic calendar of eschatological events in the mind of Jesus or his hearers. There is much more variety in the documents than Schweitzer's reconstruction of apocalyptic would allow, and the dating of several of the documents makes it problematic to suppose they faithfully reflect the Judaism of Jesus' day. Furthermore, the logic of Schweitzer's case is strained. In one breath he claims that a rather univocal understanding of eschatology prevailed in Jesus' time, and that Jesus accepted this understanding in his preaching. But in another breath he speaks of competing views of the kingdom in the first century, and ascribes particular creativity to Jesus in respect of kingdom diction. Even on the dubious supposition that there was such a thing as a commonly held eschatological expectation in Jesus' time, Glasson shows from Schweitzer's own observations that the New Testament itself suggests that Jesus did not accept such a picture of the end without qualification. For these reasons, Glasson concludes, "apocalyptic" might well be dropped as a description of Jesus' teaching; it is probably more misleading than instructive. Glasson contrasts Schweitzer's view of the kingdom with what he takes to be the traditional view, that the kingdom is the era of redemption manifest in the Church. Exegetical support for such a definition is lacking, and for that reason the positive aspect of Glasson's case has not received wide support, despite his telling attack on Schweitzer's position. Moreover, while any such thing as *the* apocalyptic world-view of the first century is probably a scholarly phantom, it would seem imprudent not to acknowledge that the range of apocalyptic literature, along with the Qumran scrolls, the earliest Targums and other intertestamental works, present a common expectation, variously expressed, that God was to act on behalf of his people in the foreseeable future. To dissociate Jesus from this eschatological faith would be difficult to justify unless there were evidence that he explicitly rejected it himself.

My own contribution to the present volume represents a similar unease in regard to the adequacy of an apocalyptic understanding of the kingdom in the sayings of Jesus. The Targumic evidence is considered (1) because the Targums are written in Aramaic, the language of Jesus, (2) because there are clear indications that their kingdom theology may represent first century thinking, and (3) because their reference to the kingdom as "of God" or "of the LORD" corresponds exactly to Jesus' normal usage. In all three aspects, the Targums seem a more fruitful source than rabbinic literature in general for the understanding of the kingdom which Jesus and his hearers shared. In the Targum to the Prophets, where the largest number of kingdom references is to be found, "the kingdom" is mentioned in order to render passages which, in the Hebrew original, spoke of God intervening actively on behalf of his people. The emphasis is on the dynamic, personal presence of God – not on the nature of God in itself, but on his saving, usually future, activity (cf. Chilton, 1978).

The enquiry into the Targumic understanding of the kingdom as God's personal revelation was not, in the first instance, conducted in the interests of exegeting the Jewish documents. In a thesis entitled *God in Strength: Jesus' Announcement of the Kingdom* (1976, published in 1979), I analysed those dominical sayings in which the kingdom is publicly proclaimed. The programme, as summarized in the extract from the conclusion here reproduced, was to identify and eliminate from a given saying those elements which were introduced by the evangelist or his predecessors. Such additions were seen to be relatively minor, and were usually included for the purpose of interpreting the saying to readers who no longer had a first-hand familiarity with the Palestinian Jewish categories in which Jesus expressed himself. Once such material is eliminated from a saying, one may treat the residue as the purest ore available from which to distil the theology of Jesus himself. As this foundational evidence was compared to the various interpretations of the kingdom available in literature of or around the NT period, its consistent coherence with the Targumic kingdom theology – especially that of the Isaiah Targum – was striking. The kingdom was not a régime, whether present or future, at all, neither the moral association of Ritschl nor the apocalyptic utopia of Schweitzer. Rather, Jesus was impelled to preach by his certainty that God would reveal himself powerfully; the kingdom announcement affirmed vividly but simply that God was acting and would act in strength on behalf of his people. The simplicity of the idea was disturbing, because it implied that the great debate concerning the time of the kingdom has somewhat missed the point, as Weiss feared it would. One could no more fix the kingdom temporally than one could spatially, for it was in the first place God's disclosure of himself and only in the second place our response to the revelation.

Although we share an antipathy to the manner in which "apocalyptic" has been used in recent discussion, Glasson and I are in fact offering different corrections to the eschatological consensus. He has attacked the very wisdom of that consensus, contending that the kingdom is properly nothing to do with apocalyptic, but rather refers to the redemption given through Jesus (cf. also Glasson, 1980). I have suggested that the future-oriented, eschatological aspect of the kingdom is to be acknowledged, but that it stems from Jesus' view of God, and not from a particular expectation for the future. It is therefore unfortunate that in a recent survey of research W. G. Kümmel ([1982], 145) has declared that both our contributions were motivated by a desire to dismiss eschatology. It would have been more accurate to say that Glasson consciously and carefully denies that eschatology provides the framework of Jesus' preaching, whereas I have attempted to explain the source of Jesus' eschatology (cf. K. Koch, 1979, for a similar attempt).

When any questioning of the eschatological consensus is ascribed to tendentious motives, the consensus is being applied as a dogma. In fact, of course, eschatological understandings of the kingdom also have their uses in systematic theology; Ritschl was not alone in keeping an eye on the wider implications of his exegesis. The eschatological consensus consistently claims that Jesus inherited the future expectations of his time, and referred to the present activity of the kingdom in his consciousness of his own divinely given authority. That is, a christological meaning is commonly claimed for kingdom sayings which express a present aspect. Glasson and I have in different ways referred back to the concept of the kingdom itself in order to explain such sayings, by claiming Jesus held that God's redemption (Glasson) or God's saving activity (Chilton) were presently available.

A possibly dogmatic interest behind the eschatological consensus is that it explains the kingdom in Jesus' preaching in terms of Christology; historically, the reverse procedure would seem to be more appropriate.

There are questions which remain to be dealt with in my own thesis: the actual date of the Isaiah Targum is discussed in a later monograph (Chilton, 1982). Secondly, I have treated only the public kingdom announcement of Jesus. Although the conclusion of *God in Strength* suggests that other dominical sayings share an understanding of the kingdom as God's self-revelation, the possibility cannot be excluded at this stage that a revised conception of the kingdom is to be found in Jesus' teaching to and controversy with his contemporaries; he may have refined his language when he came to instruct his disciples and confute his opponents. Finally, the substantive agreement between Perrin's literary findings as to Jesus' understanding of the kingdom and my own, more historical, reconstruction, raises the question: Is this coincidence a sign of the validity of both methods, or is it rather to be taken to suggest that both of us, as Ritschl and Schweitzer before us, have been influenced unduly by the cherished notions of our own day? That, in the end, is for others to decide; no exegete can escape the influence of ideas which do not derive from the text he studies, and he relies on the critical evaluation of his colleagues, along with self-criticism, in order to test the soundness of his interpretation.

In "Eschatological or Theocentric Ethics?" (1979), Hans Bald pursues the question of the relationship between Jesus' eschatology and his view of God. His treatment of the ethics of Jesus in relation to his kingdom preaching rewards the careful reading it requires. He reminds us that the student who enquires after the meaning of the kingdom, even if his enquiry is conducted in linguistic terms, is not merely seeking to define one phrase among the many Jesus used, but also to appreciate the very heart of Jesus' message. For this reason, no account of the kingdom is satisfactory which fails to explain how other aspects of his teaching are developed from, or are at least consistent with, his view of the kingdom. Jesus' ethical teaching is of first importance in this regard, because his emphasis on the love commandment, and all that implied, is one of the distinguishing features of his ministry. Unless his characteristic ethical message is reconcilable with the understanding we have of Jesus' kingdom message, we must suspect that we have failed to evaluate the kingdom in his preaching properly. Bald himself summarizes various scholarly hypotheses, especially the Schürmann–Vögtle debate; our concern is merely to draw attention to the basic issue he isolates. This was raised, as was so much else in connection with the kingdom, by Albert

Schweitzer, who described Jesus' moral teaching as an "interim ethic", that is, a teaching valid only in face of and until the eschatological consummation.

The work reviewed by Bald, together with his own suggestion, is occasioned by the observation that Jesus' ethics are in fact basically motivated by his view of God, not eschatology. God's love, not an apocalypse, is the foundation of human love as Jesus saw it. How are an eschatological understanding of the kingdom and this theological understanding of ethics to be reconciled? As Bald traces the answers to this question offered in recent research, the beginnings of a consensus appear to emerge. Repeatedly, investigators are seen to redefine what is meant by "eschatology". If, when we say the kingdom is eschatological, we mean that it is a vehemently worded call to a decision before God in the present (Bultmann), or Jesus' way of calling attention to his identity as the final messenger of God (Conzelmann, Schürmann), or an announcement of a decision already taken by God (Merklein), we can without undue difficulty argue it is consistent with the ethics of Jesus, conceived of as theological. Bald is an excellent example of a scholar who proceeds by examining the work of others, identifying the tendency of recent discussion, and pursuing the tendency further. In his own formulation, Jesus' preaching is "eschatological" in the sense that it is concerned with God's imminent coming to men; but basically Jesus' idea of God as expressed in his teaching as a whole is not reducible to eschatology. This succinct summary of recent discussion of Jesus' ethics with particular reference to the kingdom shows how drastically terms such as "eschatological" have been reinterpreted since Schweitzer. Indeed, one wonders just what sort of "end" is in view when Jesus' eschatology is referred to by some authors: the element of actual futurity is replaced by a rather general notion of transcendence. If we in fact intend to use early Jewish expectations of the judgement which God was expected to bring, as the framework – or, at least, a framework – of Jesus' thinking, then we must resist the temptation to explain the kingdom in terms of abstraction. There is a danger that when we use such terms as "theocentric" only God's present majesty, not his ultimate and imminent vindication of his people, will be understood.

Modern discussion of the kingdom in Jesus' preaching has involved exegesis, systematic reflection and polemical exchanges. Areas of serious disagreement remain, but advances have been made. Jesus' message of the kingdom referred fundamentally and distinctly to a transcendent reality, not to any human organization. The kingdom is not a movement or a régime, but the sovereign activity of God. More particularly, the kingdom is to be understood within an appreciation of eschatology: what Jesus' announced was nothing less than the ultimate intervention of God in human affairs, the tangible end of the world. The transcendence and future orientation of the kingdom are what most exegetes have in mind when they speak of the kingdom as "eschatological", and the course of discussion has only confirmed the use of this term to characterize the kingdom. On the other hand, nearly a century of study and debate has taught us not to impute an apocalyptic calendar to Jesus' thinking. From the points of view of research into contemporary Jewish usage, of historical exegesis and of literary interpretation, the sayings of Jesus do not seem patient of a consistently apocalyptic understanding. Indeed, certain sayings are possessed of a present emphasis, as is recognized within the post-war eschatological consensus. In a sense, this reinforces the transcendent aspect of the kingdom; it can no more be identified with an element in a timetable than it can be with collective human efforts on its behalf.

A fundamental question which will, no doubt, engage future discussions concerns how Jesus could have spoken of an altogether transcendent kingdom in everyday terms. The eschatological consensus has it that Jesus, as it were despite his expectation of a purely future kingdom, came to see its operation already active in his own ministry. In the end, however, this amounts to a christological account of the kingdom, and the parables of the mustard seed and the leaven, for example, can hardly have been understood by Jesus' first hearers in exclusively christological terms. We need to bear in mind that the kingdom, not the messiah, was the burden of Jesus' preaching and (first of all) that of his disciples. Radical immanence, side by side with radical transcendence, appears to be basic to the kingdom of God, and not a subsidiary development of Jesus' messianic self-consciousness (whatever that may have been). The eschatological consensus requires further qualification in order to do justice to this observation. The contributions of Bald, Glasson, Perrin and myself are some of the attempts to move in this direction, and time will tell whether a fresh consensus will emerge. If it does, that would be the culmination of the movement Ritschl began: we will be better placed to perceive the vision of Jesus in the terms in which he framed it, rather than in those into which subsequent interpreters have sought to transfer it.

1

*The Kingdom of God Expels the Kingdom of Satan**

RUDOLF OTTO

We read in Matt. 12:25–9:

> 25. Every kingdom divided against itself is brought to desolation; and every city or house divided against itself shall not stand: 26. and if Satan casteth out Satan, he is divided against himself; how then shall his kingdom stand? 27. And if I by Beelzebub cast out demons, by whom do your sons cast them out? therefore shall they be your judges. [Accordingly it is not, as you say, by Beelzebub, but by God's Spirit that I drive them out.] 28. But if I by the Spirit of God cast out demons, then (*ara*) is the kingdom of God come upon you. 29. Or how can one enter into the house of the strong man, and spoil his goods, except he first bind the strong man? and then he will spoil his house.

Instead of verse 29 as above Luke says in 11:21f.:

> When the strong man fully armed guardeth his own court, his goods are in peace: 22. but when a stronger than he shall come upon him, and overcome him, he taketh from him his whole armour wherein he trusted, and divideth his spoils.

Luke's version manifestly preserves a more original form than Matthew's, and likewise allows that Old Testament passage to shine through more clearly which Jesus uses here, and into which he puts the idea of God's final struggle and victory over Satan.

1   Kingdom here struggles against and is victorious over, kingdom, the *chshathra varya* of the Lord over that of the chief and final foe. Material of very ancient Aryan-Iranian origin stands here in the midst of the gospel, and is palpably rugged and real. Here the kingdom is power victorious, coercive power. It is also a realm of power,

---

* First published in *The Kingdom of God and the Son of Man* by R. Otto (1938) 97–107.

which replaces another realm of power – the kingdom, the house, the *polis* ("city") of Satan. It advances against the latter; victorious and growing, it pushes forward its boundaries against it in Christ's activity as exorcist. It expands its realm; its beginnings were small, but it grows ever larger.

The impressive Iranian idea of a divine warfare is also operative in the Book of Enoch. It appears more clearly in other passages of late Jewish apocalyptic, e.g. in *The Assumption of Moses,* 10:1, 2. Here, at the close of the prophecy of the final period, we read:

"Tunc apparebit regnum illius (Dei) in omni creatura illius, Et tunc Zabulus (Diabolus) finem habebit et tristitia cum eo abducetur." (Then his [God's] rule will be manifest through all his creation, and then Zabulus [the devil] will be no more and sorrow will be removed along with him.)

That is the plain Iranian message of the victory of the *chshathra* of the Lord over God's enemy, the conquest of the evil one in the great divine victory at the End. The victory takes place here through God's leader of the hosts, the archangel Michael.[1]

We find Iranian ideas of an eschatological warfare expressed in greater bulk and in greater detail in materials embedded in different passages of our Christian apocalypse, the Revelation of John (They were certainly not newly invented, but found current by the Apocalyptist, who wove them into his special prophecy and adapted them to his particular aims.) In Rev. 12:7 the seer views the end of things, the inbreaking of the final time. "A great fiery dragon" appears,

And there was war in heaven [whither the dragon had been compelled to ascend]: Michael and his angels going forth to war with the dragon; and the dragon warred and his angels; and they prevailed not, neither was their place found any more in heaven. And the great dragon was cast down, the old serpent . . . he was cast down to the earth, and his angels were cast down with him.

Thus a great and decisive victory was gained at the outset, and the angels were already singing:

Now is come the salvation, and the power, and the kingdom of our God, and the authority (*exousia*) of his Christ.

But they closed with the words:

Woe for the earth and for the sea: because the devil is gone down unto you, having great wrath, knowing that he hath but a short time.

For although decisively defeated, the dragon now continued his attacks upon the earth:

and went away to make war with the rest of her seed which keep the commandments of God.

That is Iranian eschatology, applied and conformed to the supposed final fortunes of the Christian Church (at the same time, it fused with elements of Chaldean mythology, with which the Iranian tradition had long combined).

The fiery dragon is not, as Bousset thinks, an aquatic animal, for nothing can be fiery in the water. Rather it is the literal translation of *azhi dahaka* (Sanskrit: *ahi dahaka*), which means a fiery, burning dragon.[2] *Azhi dahaka*, like the aboriginal monster against which Trita fought, had three heads (and seven tails). Acting under Chaldean influence, John changed it into seven heads. The Iranian tradition described the arch enemy as pressing into heaven. "The Lord hurls down the evil spirit, who goes forth from heaven" (Söderblom, 267), and *azhi dahaka* "is cast down to the earth, to commit sin." Here he rages against man and beast. In like manner with John, the fiery dragon comes to earth and rages in great wrath and persecutes the righteous. Also the remarkable "third part" in Rev. 8:7, 9, 11, 12; 12:4:

> The third part of the earth was burnt up, and the third part of the trees . . . there died the third part of the creatures which were in the sea . . . the third part of the waters became wormwood . . . the third part of the sun was smitten, and of the stars . . . and the day,

comes from the same source, for *azhi dahaka* swallows a third of mankind, of the beasts, and of the other beings created by the Lord. His aim is the destruction of the world and the annihilation of the creatures (Söderblom, 268f.). According to a later tradition he swallows Ahriman, and so with the devil himself in his body he becomes "l'unique adversaire" (Söderblom, 267). The warriors against him (as the combatants on behalf of the *saoshyant*, the coming judge, the saviour, judge, and founder of the new world) are Keresaspa or Fretun (= Thraetaona athwya = Trita aptya), beings originating from the oldest Aryan myths. In the Johannine Apocalypse the *stratēgos* ("general") of God, the valiant angelic hero Michael, represents a further development.

2 With equal clarity we can trace the same Iranian echoes in the Beelzebub scene of the Gospels.

In speaking about the strong man and the stronger one who comes upon the strong man, overcomes him, and takes from him his goods or his spoil, Jesus refers primarily to a passage from Isaiah 49:24ff.

Shall the prey be taken from the mighty, or the spoil slip away from the powerful? ... With him that contends against thee [Israel] will I, Yahweh, contend, and my children will I save, that all flesh may know that I, Yahweh, am thy Saviour and thy Redeemer, I, the Mighty One of Jacob.

Two strong men (*gibbor*) are spoken of in Isaiah. They contend against one another. But Yahweh, the stronger, smites the strong one, i.e. the adversary, and gives deliverance. Isaiah meant the earthly oppressors of Israel in this world; but for Jesus this scene of strife takes on the deeper meaning of the divine struggle against God's enemy himself.[3]

3   The meaning and the logic of his answer to the accusation of being in league with Beelzebub is given most clearly in Luke's record, which follows an older form of the saying than do Matthew and Mark.[4] Jesus says: Were I to exorcize by Beelzebub, Satan would be arrayed against himself, which cannot be. Therefore concede that I exorcize by the finger of God. But if this is so, then what I teach holds good, viz. that the kingdom of God has already dawned, i.e. God's rule over Satan has already come to pass and Satan himself is already deprived of his power, i.e. his armour, since otherwise one could not take away from him his spoil, the demon-possessed. As long as the strong one sits in full armour and is not deprived of his armour, and thus equipped watches his household, no exorcist, not even I, can take from him what he possesses. But just because the kingdom has already dawned, because God has already achieved his victory and stripped Satan of his armour (we might continue: because Satan has already fallen from heaven, but still rages with the remnants of his power here on earth), it is possible by exorcism to take from him his spoil, i.e. those made captive by him, and taken into his possession. The stronger one (i.e. God himself), who had stripped him of his armour, now proceeds to take from him his spoil through the working of the exorcist Jesus, who was sent by God and is working with his [God's] power.[5]

4   We shall now give attention to a circumstance that is usually passed lightly over. What really is the reason that Jesus adds the clause *ara ephthasen hē basileia* ("then the kingdom has come") together with the entire detailed demonstration that follows? He had been charged with exorcizing by Beelzebub. This accusation he had refuted by showing it to be absurd, since in such a case Satan would be contending against Satan. The accusation was thereby answered. But what is the purpose of the subsequent remarks? They have no further reference to the accusation. We say: It was occasioned by, but advan-

ced beyond, what preceded; it was intended to prove a thesis which Jesus had propounded long before and which had been as much doubted as his working by the finger of God. Only on this theory does the continuation become intelligible. The word *ara* introduces, like our "really" or "actually", an assertion which is brought to the forefront. It means: Accordingly what was asserted is correct. It presupposes the assertion as known and possibly disputed. In the present instance it means: Therefore what I teach and what I have taught, i.e. that the kingdom has come, is correct. It points to statements which Jesus must have uttered at an earlier time; to an assertion which was peculiar to him and which also had been doubted as paradoxical; to propositions such as the kingdom is in your midst; to other propositions which were implied in his parables of the kingdom of heaven; to a teaching which he had presented generally as his own peculiar teaching, and which he had certainly presented much more generally and frequently than our surviving gospel tradition leads us to suppose. In this tradition that teaching almost falls into the background. It was growing obscure, and doing so because, from the standpoint of the later Church, it was becoming paradoxical in a new way.

5   It is not Jesus who brings the kingdom – a conception which was completely foreign to Jesus himself; on the contrary, the kingdom brings him with it. Moreover, it was not he but rather God himself who achieved the first great divine victory over Satan. His own activity lies in, and is carried forward by, the tidal wave of the divine victory. The victory and the actual beginning of the triumph of divine power, he not only deduces from his own activity, but knows of it because he has seen it. He has witnessed how Satan was cast out of heaven. This mysterious experience was the subject of a saying, which is a mere relic accidentally preserved from a context that was undoubtedly of larger extent. It reads:

I saw Satan fall from heaven like lightning.

It is almost a miracle that such a saying should be preserved at all, for it contradicts all the later Christology. But the very fact that this saying, and likewise the words of the Beelzebub incident, were no longer possible from the later standpoint, and so could not have been invented, proves that both sayings belong to the most solid and aboriginal of Jesus' words.

6   In the power of the divine victory over the armed strong man, Jesus himself now works "by the finger of God", or by "the Spirit of

God", i.e. with *dynamis, exousia, charis* ("grace"), *charisma* ("divine gift"). This *dynamis* of his is nothing other than the *dynamis* of the kingdom, the kingdom as *dynamis*. And this *charisma* and charismatic activity of his is nothing other and nothing less than the coming of the kingdom itself.

He does not bring the kingdom, but he himself, according to the most certain of his utterances, is in his actions the personal manifestation of the inbreaking divine power. "If *I* by the finger of God drive out the devils, then the kingdom has come to you" – can one fail to hear the tone of these words? What do they express? Some say an eschatological feeling of power. But is this vague expression satisfactory? The words do not witness to a general and undefined feeling, but rather to a highly defined, concrete, and unique consciousness of mission with reference to the kingdom of God. They witness to the consciousness of a unique attachment to and union with the kingdom that supports this person, and simply removes and tears him away from everything in the form of "law, prophets, and John" which was previously present as a mere preparation for the eschatological order, and which in comparison to that order must dwindle to a mere preparation, indeed at times to an actual contrast and opposition. They witness to the metaphysical background in which Christ believed his own person and activity were embedded. He was by no means a mere eschatological preacher, who originated certain thought complexes; rather his person and work were part of a comprehensive redemptive event, which broke in with him and which he called the coming and actual arrival of the kingdom of God. And that is the last and inmost meaning of this saying with its rich connotation.

7   The kingdom comes in and with him and his working, after it has first been realized in heaven by Satan's overthrow, in order that it might now become real "in earth as it is in heaven". And it comes chiefly not as claim and decision but as saving *dynamis*, as redeeming power, to set free a world lying in the clutches of Satan, threatened by the devil and by demons, tormented, possessed, demon-ridden; and to capture the spoil from the strong one, i.e. it comes chiefly as saving *dynamis,* as redeeming might. It is the realm of saving power which is ever expanding, ever advancing farther, in which the weary and heavy laden find rest for their souls. It makes claims, but that is not its new element; it demands decision and determination radically and fundamentally, but that is not its difference from the law and prophets. For, as we have already said, that had long ago been done by prophetic religion in the primordial words:

Ye shall be holy, for I am holy (cf. Lev. 11:44f.; 19:2; 20:26),

and:

> Hear, O Israel: The Lord our God is one Lord. And thou shalt love the
> Lord thy God with all thine heart, with all thy soul, and with all thy might.
>
> Deut. 6:4f.

The radical nature and completeness of claim of these words, and their power to put one in the situation which calls for decision, cannot be surpassed or heightened by any consistent eschatology. They are words whose radical meaning even the Sermon on the Mount can only repeat, illustrate by examples, bring to the mind afresh, and press into the inner recesses of the heart and conscience, i.e. into the depth of the soul. It does not disclose that meaning for the first time. New, however, is the knowledge that saving power from above – unnoticed by and hid from dim eyes – is at work, and is quietly but irresistibly extending its realm of power in opposition to the realm of power of God's enemy.

8   Therefore it is also utterly false and contrary to the original meaning of the person of Christ to understand him as a rabbi who uttered maxims and gained disciples, who was only later elevated to the miraculous messianic sphere by the circle of these disciples, and who chanced to possess also a certain gift of healing which one hesitates to deny him completely, since other rabbis had the same gift. Wilhelm Schubert, not a theologian, showed deeper insight in *Das Weltbild Jesu* (published in the series Das Morgenland, vol. 13). His book is short, but distinguished by understanding of the situation and environment, by intuitive penetration, and by excellent characterization. Schubert goes to the length of supposing (32) that Jesus had long seen his unique and most important task in his exorcistic healings, expelling the dark tormenting powers. That seems to me to go too far and not to be demonstrable from our sources. But he is right inasfar as Jesus was a miracle worker not by chance but quite essentially and in closest connection with his entire mission. He healed and exorcized, and showed separate concrete elements of both exorcistic and miraculous healing; Schubert is right inasfar as Jesus sent his disciples throughout the country as similar persons to himself. Nevertheless his activity was not exercised in the manner of so many others who healed by miracle and exorcism at that time. Our Gospels still bear witness to the latter, but Jesus, as the Beelzebub passage shows, knew himself to be, in this miraculous healing activity of his, the instrument of the *dynamis* of the inbreaking kingdom; on this side

Jesus was altogether different from the others. Moreover it would be theoretically possible to assume that Jesus became aware that the kingdom was breaking in when his charismatic powers came to life and as they operated.

Looked at from a higher point of view, however, this means that Jesus' person and his consciousness of mission include something more than, something quite different from, his transforming of John's call to repentance into that for a "decision to fulfil the divine will in its totality". He knew himself to be a part and an organ of the eschatological order itself, which was pressing in to save. Thereby he was lifted above John and everyone earlier. He is the eschatological saviour. Only thus understood are all his deeds and words seen against their right background and in their true meaning. Directly or indirectly, they are all borne up by the idea of a penetrating and redemptive divine power. This idea had its immediate correlate in the new God whom he preached, not the God who consumed the sinner but who sought him; the Father God, who had come near to men out of his transcendence, who asked for a childlike mind and a childlike trust, who freed not only from fear of the devil but from all fear and anxiety, who filled the entire life with childlike freedom from care. Thus also the *akolouthia*, "the discipleship" which Jesus demanded, did not signify adherence of disciples to a new rabbi in the way that other rabbis had had disciples and followers, but adherence to the soteriological and eschatological saviour.[6] Finally, only upon the basis of this understanding is there any possibility of rationally discussing the question whether Jesus was himself conscious that his mission was messianic in character, or whether a society consisting of the disciples of a rabbi elevated him at a later date to the rank of Son of Man.

NOTES

1   We likewise note the words "et tristitia cum eo abducetur" ("and sorrow will be removed along with him"). That is the purpose intended when someone comes with the message: the kingdom is near. This message is good news for sad and troubled people; it is *besorah* and *euangelion*.

2   The fiery dragon is at the same time the ancient serpent. Both are used here in the myth of the sun woman, and are applied again but in a different sense in Rev. 20:2. In Rev. 20:2ff. Bousset himself referred them (indeed, he had no alternative), to *azhi dahaka* and his war against Fretun. But that the dragon in Rev. 20:2 is of like origin with the fiery dragon here is indubitable. And no name is more suitable than fiery dragon on the one side, for *azhi* means dragon and *dahaka* means fiery, and the ancient serpent on the other side, for this figure does in fact belong to the most primordial mythology. The dragon and its conqueror Fretun = Trita, are the most primordial of primordial figures.

3   Perhaps it had taken on this meaning in apocalyptic circles before Jesus. The self-evident way in which he applies the words almost warrants that supposition.

4   In Matthew and Mark the logic of the verses Luke 11:21f. has already become blunted, and that from a cause which we can still conjecture. See n. 5.

5   The peculiar obscurity which lies over the corresponding narratives in Matthew and also in Mark seems plainly connected with the fact that this story was no longer intelligible from the standpoint of the later community. For this community it was a matter of course from the dogmatic point of view that Christ himself had gained the real victory over Satan. This was not Jesus' view at all, and was not intended even in Luke. In Matthew and Mark, however, the words are so oddly veiled that one is almost compelled to gather from them that Jesus himself was the stronger one who had bound the strong one. It is plainly in connection with this tendency that in Mark the saying: "then is the kingdom of God come upon you" is actually omitted. From the standpoint of later Christology this saying really was scarcely tolerable. For it clearly presupposed that Christ did not himself bring the kingdom of God, but that his own appearance was actually only a result of the fact that the kingdom had already come, that the powers of this kingdom were working in him and through him, but in such a way that he himself was part and parcel of this entity of the inbreaking kingdom, which was superior even to him.

6   This has been recognized by W. Bauer. In his essay, *Jesus der Galiläer*, which we have frequently quoted, he says on p. 29: "Jesus had summoned men to let themselves be completely permeated by the consciousness of the nearness of the divine sovereignty, to yield to the conversion which alone leads to God, and to attach themselves to his person as the God-sent Preparer of the new era."

2

*Eschatological Expectation in the Proclamation of Jesus**

WERNER GEORG KÜMMEL

Rudolf Bultmann introduces the description of Jesus' proclamation at the beginning of his *Theology of the New Testament* with the following statements: "The dominant concept of Jesus' message is the *Reign of God* (*basileia tou Theou*). Jesus proclaims its immediately impending irruption, now already making itself felt. Reign of God is an eschatological concept. It means the régime of God which will destroy the present course of the world . . ."[1] This basically futuristic-eschatological understanding of Jesus' message, for which J. Weiss and A. Schweitzer had laid the groundwork, seems to Bultmann so self-evident that he adduces no proof of it and mentions no contrary opinions. And yet this view, according to which Jesus proclaimed the temporal nearness of the coming of the reign of God, has always met with serious opposition and in the last few years has again been energetically disputed.[2] On the one side are those who deny that Jesus ever spoke of a future coming of the reign of God[3] or attribute to Jesus only a temporally completely indefinite expectation of the eschatological coming of the Son of Man, which, however, is totally insignificant alongside the basic proclamation of the presence of the reign of God.[4] On the other side are those who categorically deny to Jesus any expectation of a *near* End or of an *imminent* reign of God[5] and seek to show that Jesus' proclamation of the nearness of the reign of God does not stand in any temporal context, but rather that Jesus ignores the question of time because the vertical dimension of the Spirit cannot be temporal.[6] This is not to say that there are not also numerous recent scholars who hold firmly to the assumption that Jesus counted on a future coming of the reign of God,[7] and many have held to a very precise form of this, namely the assumption that

* English translation first published in *The Future of our Religious Past*, ed. J. M. Robinson (1971) 29–48.

Jesus expected the appearance of the reign of God soon, in his own generation.[8] Yet it must be said that this strictly "eschatological" understanding of Jesus' preaching is at present being very seriously questioned.

Of course the question of the exact meaning of Jesus' preaching of the reign of God cannot be raised in all its details here; and neither can we here demonstrate again the fact that the presence *and* the futurity of the reign of God are both equally certainly attested as Jesus' view.[9] But in view of the many-sided denial of the futuristic and temporal sense of Jesus' proclamation of the coming of the reign of God it has become a very pressing question whether we really have no sufficient evidence that Jesus counted on a coming of God's reign and a concomitant end of this world in a temporally limited near future, and also whether it is true that the assumption of Jesus' expectation of an imminent End "has no sufficient support in the texts".[10] In other words, if it can be shown that Jesus preached a *temporally* near coming of the reign of God this would provide a firmer point of departure for the whole understanding of Jesus' preaching of the nearness of that reign. We shall consequently limit our discussion here to those words of Jesus that speak expressly of the *temporal nearness* of the eschatological event.[11]

This question could, of course, be quickly answered if the declarations of Mark 1:15 par. Matt. 4:17; Matt. 10:7 par. Luke 10:9, 11; and Mark 13:29 par. Matt. 24:33, Luke 21:31 unequivocally attested the near coming of the reign of God or the events of the End as the opinion of Jesus. But against this a twofold objection has been raised: (*a*) Mark 1:15 is a summary statement by the evangelist that does not go back to Jesus, and Matt. 10:7 as a doublet of this statement can similarly be a formulation of the primitive Church;[12] (*b*) in the case of *engizein, engys* the meaning "near" is as well attested as "present", and besides *engizein* describes spatial as well as temporal nearness, so *ēngiken* says nothing about the coming of the reign of God soon.[13] Now it cannot be denied that Mark 1:15 is a summarizing formulation of Jesus' preaching that at least partially contains community formulations[14] and hence cannot be used unqualifiedly as evidence of Jesus' own view. On the other hand, while Matt. 10:7 par. Luke 10:9 is admittedly "no independent logion",[15] yet the whole missionary address in Mark 6:8ff. and Luke 10:4ff. par. Matt. 10:7ff. is the end-result of a very complicated development based on extremely diverse materials;[16] hence a judgement about the age of the individual elements making up this complex of tradition can only be made in the individual case. And since there is no adequate reason to doubt the sending out of the disciples by Jesus[17] there is methodologically no justification for denying the authenticity of Matt. 10:7 unless it can be shown on other grounds that this saying is contrary to Jesus' own view.[18]

But does *ēngiken* have the meaning "has come near" and is it used in a temporal sense? W. R. Hutton tries to show that in most NT passages *engizein* must be translated by "arrive" and that consequently in Mark 1:15 par. the translation "has come" is appropriate.[19] Now in a few cases the translation "arrive" in the sense of "to *have* come near" is possible,[20] but the perfect *ēngiken* in *all* NT passages means unambiguously "has come near" (Matt. 26:45; Mark 14:42 par. Matt. 26:46; Luke 21:8, 20; Rom. 13:12; James 5:8; 1 Pet. 4:7);[21] so there is no reason not to translate Matt. 10:7 as "the reign of God has come near". And R. F. Berkey's evidence that *engizein* (like *phthanein*) is ambiguous and may designate "arrival" as well as "coming near"[22] overlooks the fact that *engizein* can have the sense of "arrive" only in special cases and always involves the addition of the goal to which one has come so close.

That the proclamation, "the reign of God has come near", has a *temporal* sense is shown unambiguously by the parable of the fig tree, Mark 13:28f. par. Since this parable is isolated in its context and hence must be explained by itself,[23] the subjects of "these things taking place" and "is near at the gates" are hard to determine. But the picture of the fig tree, whose branches herald the nearness of the coming summer, can hardly be intended to set side by side anything except certain anticipatory signs and the coming of the eschatological consummation. Now there is no reason whatever to interpret the reference to the connection between unspecified anticipatory signs and the End as "justification of the Delay" and hence to deny the authenticity of the parable;[24] and it is equally groundless to suggest that the parable originally formed the conclusion of the Jewish apocalypse which has been reworked in Mark 13.[25] For the very fragmentary nature of the text shows that an old piece of tradition is involved, one that is formulated on the basis of the presupposition that the final consummation is soon to come regardless of whether one refers "these things taking place" to yet future anticipatory signs or, much more probably, to present events which the hearers are to *think* of as anticipatory signs. So in any case this "is near at the gates" shows that Jesus' proclamation of the nearness of the coming of the reign of God can only have been meant in the temporal sense that God's unqualified rule is soon to be actualized.

This conclusion is strengthened by the parable of the unjust judge, Luke 18:2–8. The assumption that in this parable we are dealing with a product of the community[26] is hardly convincing. E. Linnemann is able to object against the originality of the parable proper (vv. 2–5) only that neither a general admonition to perseverance in prayer nor a particular admonition to persevering prayer for the coming of the reign of God is fitting on the lips of Jesus, and neither is a promise that such a persevering request will be fulfilled. But Jesus did promise that faithful prayer would be heard (Mark 11:24), and he urged prayer for the coming of the reign of God (Matt. 6:10); though neither the Lord's Prayer nor Luke 18:2–5 led to the notion that man could or should "bring the reign of God by persevering prayer". If, then, it can hardly be doubted that this parable comes from Jesus, the objections to the authenticity of the explanation (18:6ff.) are more important.[27] The primary objections to the explanation are that the applications of the parables are often secondary, that *eklektoi* ("elect") does not occur in any genuine saying of Jesus, and that the explanation transforms the parable's general admonition to continual prayer into a specific admonition to pray for the coming of the kingdom. But of course the broad assertion that the applications of the parables are often secondary does not prove anything, and if the term *eklektoi* does not occur in any genuine word of Jesus the concept of election does (Luke 12:32; Matt. 11:25f. par. Luke 10:21). Finally, the interpretation does not disturb the meaning of the parable in any way; the emphasis in the parable is on the judge, not the widow, and the explanation corresponds exactly in that it promises God's certain fulfilling of the request for eschatological redemption.[28] Hence there is good ground for holding that Luke 18:2–8a belongs to the Jesus-tradition. Then Jesus promises to the disciples who pray for the coming of God's reign that God will soon vindicate them.[29] It has been objected against this understanding of the text that *en tachei* can mean "suddenly, momentarily", and that since this is the meaning in most instances it must also be the meaning here, so that Luke 18:8a consequently says nothing about the interval before the parousia.[30] But even though *tachys* occasionally can have the meaning "without warning, suddenly" (e.g., in 1 Tim. 5:22), there is no passage in the New Testament in which *en tachei* occurs (Acts 12:7; 22:18; 25:4; Rom. 16:20; Rev. 1:1; 22:6) where any translation except "quickly", "soon" is called for. There is thus no reason to abandon this most common meaning in the case of Luke 18:6.[31] In summary, everything points towards the fact that Jesus, even according to Luke 18:2–8a, proclaimed an imminent coming of the final consummation.

But this assumption becomes completely certain only when we investigate the three much-discussed texts in which an interval before the coming of the final consummation is expressly mentioned (Mark 9:1; 13:30; Matt. 10:23). It is quite characteristic to find repeated admonitions about "centring the discussion on texts that seem to contain a specific indication of a date",[32] or even to find these texts suspect and rejected simply *because* they contain such specific indications,[33] or to hear it said that these are "awkward fragments of tradition" that even the earliest Christian communities did not know how to fit smoothly into the overall structure of Jesus' eschatological message.[34] Yet of these texts, too, the question can only properly be what they really say and whether or not there are weighty considerations against dominical provenance in the case of each individual text. Mark 13:30 presents the fewest problems: "Truly, I say to you, this generation will not pass away before all these things take place." It has often been shown that this was originally an isolated logion.[35] Furthermore, it is beyond dispute that "this generation" can only mean the contemporaries of Jesus.[36] So the only real question that remains is what "all these things" means. In view of the fact that the logion was originally an isolated saying, the evangelist's interpretation, that the words refer to the totality of the eschatological events until the parousia, is not necessarily correct. Hence it is repeatedly suggested that "all these things" should be understood to refer to the events up to the destruction of Jerusalem.[37] But there is no basis for this suggestion (Mark 13:4 speaks only of "these things" while Mark 13:30 speaks of "all these things"), and it can only be designated "*une échappatoire*".[38] And the suggestion that Jesus originally spoke only of his death within the coming generation and the evangelist assimilated the saying to 13:4[39] is totally without support in the text. The literal and most likely reference of "all these things" is to the totality of eschatological events, and "this statement of our Lord's . . . simply requires grace to be received".[40] For "in itself this verse contains nothing that is in contradiction to Jesus' message"[41] and unless one starts from the preconceived notion mentioned above that Jesus *could not* have given a date for the End or *could not* have been mistaken, everything points towards the authenticity of Mark 13:30 and indicates that it announces the coming of the consummation within the interval designated roughly as "this generation".[42] Nothing in the wording points away from this to a "word of consolation" created by a Christian prophet "on account of the delay of the parousia".[43]

The problem in Mark 9:1 is similar: "Truly I say to you, there are some standing here who will not taste death before they see the kingdom of God come with power." It is widely recognized that this saying is also an individual logion which the evangelist has referred to the parousia and consequently connected with 8:38.[44] Whether by this connection Mark understood it in its original sense, on the other hand, is strongly disputed. C. H. Dodd has interpreted the statement of the future seeing of the reign of God by those whose lives extend to that point in time to mean that men will recognize at some appropriate time before their death that the reign of God *has* already come.[45] J. A. Baird has renewed this interpretation[46] in a special form: the men spoken of are those who will not die before they have come to an inward recognition that the kingdom of God is in the process of coming in their lives or in the life of the Church. But that Mark 9:1 speaks of a future *public* manifestation of God's reign, not a future interior realization of it, has been rightly shown from many sides and need not be demonstrated again here.[47] C. H. Dodd has therefore subsequently explained the promise that many of those present would see God's reign in power in the future to be an indication by Jesus of his subsequent resurrection and the kingdom of God on earth in the community; similarly, others have suggested the efficacy of Jesus' death or the influence of the Spirit in the Church.[48] But the connection of "seeing" and "coming in power" points too obviously to a publicly visible and tangible manifestation of the reign of God to allow for evading the conclusion that this promise refers to the eschatological appearing of that reign.[49] But then Mark 9:1 indicates that Jesus expected the beginning of the reign of God, visible to the whole world, within the lifetime of his generation and hence that he viewed the coming of that reign unambiguously as an event of the near future.

It is commonly held, to be sure, that this promise, which was undoubtedly not fulfilled in this form, cannot be brought within the framework of the message of Jesus. Hence some affirm that the original sense of the saying on the lips of Jesus can no longer be discerned;[50] others would see in the distinction between "some", who would have this experience, and the larger number who would die first an indication that in this text we are dealing with a primitive Christian prophetic saying which is intended to give an answer to the pressing problem of the delay of the parousia.[51] And to the argument that the community would hardly have created difficulties for itself by a prediction which then failed of fulfilment[52] it is asserted, "He who spoke such a word of consolation to the community in the name of the Risen Lord was concerned about the *arrival* of the Kingdom; so it was not possible for him to reflect on difficulties that would arise because of its non-arrival."[53] If the saying had actually arisen as an answer to the problem created by the experience of the delay in the parousia the one who formulated it would have been unable, of course, to reflect about the possibility of the kingdom's failure to arrive; but what he would have had to do is to make the consolatory statement in a form that actually bore a consolatory character or increased the assurance that the parousia would occur soon (cf., e.g., 1 Thess. 5:1–3 or Rom. 13:11, 12a). But Mark 9:1 *could not* fulfil this purpose because the dating of the End contained in it called out for verification and thus would actually have created a difficulty which surely no one in such a case would have created for himself. And the formulation "some who stand here" is easily explained on the lips of Jesus but much too bound to a specific situation to be comprehensible on the lips of a Christian prophet who wished to resolve a pressing community problem.[54] So there is no justifiable objection to the view that Mark 9:1 goes back to Jesus and shows that he reckoned on a temporally near arrival of the reign of God.

The third word to be discussed, Matt. 10:23, is particularly disputed. This saying, peculiar to Matthew, is added to the section in Matt. 10:17–22, par. Mark 13:9–13, which treats the matter of the persecution of the disciples: "When they persecute you in one town, flee to the next; for truly, I say to you, you will not finish the cities of Israel before the Son of Man comes." Since a new and unassociated theme begins in Matt. 10:24 there was doubtless originally no connection between 10:23 and 10:24ff. On the other hand, 10:23 fits very well with 10:22: persecution goes right along with being hated. Yet 10:22 spoke of enduring hatred *eis telos* ("to the end"), while 10:23a urges flight from one town to the next. This hardly attests an *original* connection between 10:22 and 10:23a. Now to the commandment to flee (10:23a) a consolatory promise is added (10:23b), namely, that the disciples will not finish the cities of Israel until the Son of Man comes. In the context this can only be understood to mean that the disciples will always have another suitable city left to flee to before their flight comes to an end with the coming of the Son of Man. And this is probably the way the evangelist interpreted the saying. But this interpretation presupposes that *ou mē telesēte tas poleis tou Israēl* is to be translated "you will not come to the end of the cities of Israel".[55] But there is no evidence for this nearly universal translation.[56] In the entire NT *teleō* has either the sense of "bring to an end", "complete" (or, in a weaker sense, "carry out") or the special meaning "pay". In secular Greek besides these two meanings the further specialized sense "consecrate" is attested. On the other hand, the intransitive meaning "come to an end" occurs only very rarely in poetic texts, naturally without an accusative object.[57] Hence on linguistic grounds the only possible translation is "you will not bring to an end, finish, the cities of Israel".[58] But this carries with it the unavoidable conclusion that 10:23a did not always belong together with 10:23b and that the interpretation of 10:23b required by 10:23a, namely the reference to flight from one city to another, is not the original meaning of the saying in 10:23b.[59] It is also unsatisfactory to unravel the origin of the saying in the history of the tradition as a means of illuminating the original meaning of 10:23b,[60] so we are left only with the possibility of deciding the meaning of 10:23b without reference to either its present context or some hypothetical one. But when looked at in this way, "you will not finish the cities of Israel until . . ." can hardly mean anything except "you will not accomplish the mission to Israel until . . ."; in other words, the disciples will not complete their missionary task with respect to their own people before the coming of the Son of Man. Elsewhere in the synoptic tradition the "coming of the Son of Man" always designates the eschatological consummation (Mark 8:38 par. Matt. 16:27/Luke 9:26; Matt. 16:28; 25:31; Mark 13:26 par. Matt. 24:30/Luke 21:27; Matt. 24:44 par. Luke 12:40; Mark 14:62 par. Matt. 26:64; Luke 18:8b; cf. "will be the coming of the Son of Man", Matt. 24:27).[61] This meaning is consequently the most natural one in Matt. 10:23b: the Son of Man will appear before the disciples' missionary activity can be completed. If this exegesis is correct, in this word as in Mark 9:1 Jesus predicted a temporally limited period of brief duration before the coming of the Son of Man, and this promise, too, was not fulfilled. Some have sought to avoid this fact by referring the imminent coming of the Son of Man to the establishment of the Church through Jesus' death and resurrection,[62] or to the fall of Jerusalem,[63] or by denying that Jesus' original word intended this "coming" in a futuristic sense.[64] But none of these explanations may be deduced in any natural way from the wording of the saying; they can at best be rendered possible. So it must be considered exegetically certain that Matt. 10:23b speaks of the eschatological coming of the Son of Man before the completion of the disciples' mission in Israel.[65]

It is sometimes suggested that the saying, which must be thus explained, is impossible on the lips of Jesus: it represents imminent expectation; it equates the appearance of the Son of Man and the coming of the reign of God; it presupposes a situation of persecution for the disciples. Furthermore, it is improbable that Jesus confined his preaching to the cities of Israel or spelled out the details of his coming. So it is clear, the suggestion goes, that the saying is a word of consolation from the earliest community or a saying from a narrow-minded Jewish–Christian group that rejected the Gentile mission.[66] But these are remarkably weak and quite unconvincing objections. That Jesus *could* not have represented the teaching of imminent expectation is a *petitio principii* which cannot be used as a critical principle. That the identification of the inbreaking of the reign of God and the appearance of the Son of Man was first comprehensible where the same Jesus who proclaimed the reign of God was expected as Son of Man (E. Jüngel) is a conception defended most vigorously by P. Vielhauer.[67] But if not only Mark 9:1 (see above) but also Mark 8:38[68] go back to Jesus the association of these two sayings shows that Jesus spoke equally of the reign of God and of the future coming of the Son of Man, regardless of whether one believes that Jesus distinguished between himself and the coming Son of Man[69] or designated himself as the coming Son of Man.[70] That Jesus did not confine his proclamation to the region of the cities of Israel (H. E. Tödt) is simply not true if Matt. 10:5b, 6 genuinely reflects Jesus' view, as all the evidence suggests.[71] Finally, the view that Matt. 10:23b is consolatory in nature has as little support in the language of the text as the judgement that the sentence implies a rejection of the Gentile mission, which seems rather to lie completely outside the purview of the text. So everything points towards the authenticity of Matt. 10:23, which in turn shows that Jesus awaited the eschatological coming of the Son of Man while the disciples were still occupied with the proclamation of the coming reign of God to the Jews.[72] Naturally this saying gives no precise temporal information about the date of the coming of the reign of God, while the reference to not being finished with the cities of Israel can hardly be understood as anything but an indication that the coming of the Son of Man will occur unexpectedly soon. So this word, too, shows that Jesus expected the reign of God, and with it the Son of Man, to come in the near future.

We have now fulfilled our intention of examining those words of Jesus which speak expressly of the *temporal* nearness of the reign of God or the eschatological event. This examination has shown that it is incorrect to assert that Jesus' expectation of the consummation in the near future "has no sufficient basis in the texts".[73] On the contrary, an unbiased critical examination of the relevant texts shows unequivocally that Jesus counted on the nearness of the future reign of God, a future confined to his own generation.[74] It is also beyond dispute, however repeatedly the fact may be set aside or disputed as a "foolish question",[75] that Jesus was mistaken in this expectation.[76] Of more importance, however, is the fact which this examination establishes once more: Jesus' proclamation of the near reign of God actually implies a *temporally* near event; hence the many-sided attack on this concrete temporal meaning of Jesus' proclamation[77] is untenable on the basis of the data in the text. In the statements cited at the beginning of this article R. Bultmann has quite correctly interpreted Jesus' proclamation of the near reign of God. From this two conclusions follow. For one thing, it is unnecessary to seek the reasons for the emergence in the primitive Church of an expectation of the kingdom oriented towards the near future, since this goes back to Jesus himself.[78] And further, the connection, doubtless characteristic for Paul, between this concrete futuristic expectation and eschatological fulfilment in the present has its roots in the proclamation of Jesus,[79] however much the Easter faith of the earliest community may have given a new direction to this basic element in Jesus' thought. This is not the place to elaborate on this.[80] But at any rate it has become clear that the proper understanding of the unity and diversity of the various forms of proclamation in the New Testament is essentially dependent upon an awareness of the concrete temporal sense of Jesus' eschatological proclamation.

NOTES

1 R. Bultmann (1951) 4.

2 For a survey of the history of research, cf. G. Lundström (1963); N. Perrin (1963); also the short summaries in W. G. Kümmel (1957) and B. Rigaux "La seconde venue de Jésus", *La venue du Messie* (1962), 173ff.

3 See C. H. Dodd, E. Stauffer, and J. A. T. Robinson, in W. G. Kümmel, *Journal of Religion* 43 (1963) 304f. and E. Jüngel, *Paulas und Jesus* (1962) 168f.

4 E. Fuchs, *Studies of the Historical Jesus* (1964) 259f.; G. Neville, *The Advent Hope* (1961) 59f.; J. A. Baird, *The Justice of God in the Teaching of Jesus* (1963) 100.

5 Fuchs (n. 4, 122, 182); Jüngel (1962) 154, 180; Neville (n. 4), 42f.; J. A. Baird (n. 4), 123, 142ff.; E. Linnemann (1966) 38, 132–6; J. W. Doeve, "Parusieverzögerung", *Nederlands Theologisch Tijdschrift* 17 (1962/3) 32ff. According to Perrin (1963) 198f., Jesus said nothing about the precise moment when the tension between the eschatological present and the future is to be resolved, and according to Sherman E. Johnson, *Jesus in His Own Times* (1957) 129, we cannot say whether or not Jesus believed the end of the world to be near.

6 Fuchs (n. 4) 123: ("The *proton pseudos* of our present research situation might well consist of the fact that from the outset we accommodate the *nature* of the Basileia within a secondary temporal context of phenomena"); also his "On the Task of a Christian Theology" *JTC* 6 (1969) 82f.; Jüngel (1962) n. 3, 139ff., 154, 174, 180: ("The future as the near future follows *directly* upon the present; it knows no intervening period"); Baird (n. 4) 125, 148ff.: ("The nearness of the spiritual dimension is primarily a spatial, dimensional nearness, and any sense of temporal immediacy derives from the eternally present nature of God"); H. Conzelmann (1968) 36 ("As long as I keep asking about the exact time I have completely failed to grasp the nature of the demand; Jesus is not concerned with time"); Linnemann (1966) 39: ("In the teaching of Jesus ... the irruption of the Reign of God is ... not that temporal borderline which by its imminent nearness qualifies or stamps a special character on the present. The irruption of God's Reign is itself 'enabling time' [*Zeit zu*]"); Perrin (1963) 185; ("We may not interpret the eschatological teaching of Jesus in terms of a linear concept of time"); E. Käsemann, *New Testament Questions of Today* (1969) 101: ("The situation was this: ... [Jesus'] own

45

preaching did not bear a fundamentally apocalyptic stamp but proclaimed the immediacy of the God who was near at hand"); and 112: ("Jesus is obviously speaking of the coming of the *basileia* ... with a reference not only or primarily to an end of the world which can in principle be dated within chronological time"); J. Gnilka, " 'Parusieverzögerung' und Naherwartung in den synoptischen Evangelien und in der Apostelgeschichte", *Catholica* 13 (1959) 277ff: ("Not prophecy in the temporal sense. Furthermore biblical man does not conceive of time as a linear entity").

7 R. H. Fuller (1954) 20ff.; J. Jeremias (1963) 51, 169–80; O. Cullmann, *Christ and Time* (ET 1950) 83ff.; R. Schnackenburg (1963) 77–86, 160–77; E. Grässer (1959) 3ff.; G. E. Ladd, "The Kingdom of God – Reign or Realm?", *JBL* 81 (1962) 230ff.; Perrin (1963) 81ff.; Lundström (1963) 232f.; P. Vielhauer (1957) 77; F. Hahn *The Titles of Jesus in Christology* (1969) 24; G. Bornkamm (1960) 90ff.; D. Bosch, *Die Heidenmission in der Zukunftsschau Jesu* (1959) 73f.

8 D. Selby, "Changing Ideas in New Testament Eschatology", *HTR* 50 (1957) 21ff.; O. Knoch (1962) 112ff.; G. R. Beasley-Murray, *A Commentary on Mark Thirteen* (1957) 9, 99ff.; H. P. Owen, "The Parousia of Christ in the Synoptic Gospels", *SJT* 12 (1959) 173ff.; M. S. Enslin, *The Prophet from Nazareth* (1961) 72, 87ff.; G. Gloege, *The Day of His Coming* (1963) 141f., 144f.; U. Wilckens, in *Revelation as History* (1968); Rigaux (n. 2) 212; Grässer (n. 7) p. 16.

9 See Kümmel (1957). Cf. further Cullmann (n. 7); Schnackenburg (1963) 114–17; Perrin (1963) 79ff., 159; Lundström (1963) 234; Bornkamm (1960); Bosch (n. 7); Knoch (1962).

10 Linnemann (1966) 132.

11 It is not my purpose to enter once more into a discussion of the literature criticized in Kümmel 1957.

12 Linnemann (1966) 132; Perrin (1963) 200f.; Fuchs (n. 4) 122.

13 W. R. Hutton (cf. p. 14) 89ff.; F. Rehkopf, *Die lukanische Sonderquelle* (1959) 44ff.; R. F. Berkey (1963) 177ff.; Jüngel (1962) 174f.; Baird (n. 4) 148f.

14 Perrin (1963) 200f.

15 Linnemann (1966) 132.

16 Cf. the bibliography in Grässer (n. 7) 18f.

17 W. G. Kümmel, *Kirchenbegriff und Geschichtsbewusstsein in der Urgemeinde und bei Jesus* (1943) 31; J. Jeremias, *Jesus' Promise to the Nations* (ET 1958) 27f.; B. Rigaux, "Die 'Zwölf' in Geschichte und Kerygma", *Der historische Jesus und der kerygmatische Christus* (1960) 475f.

18 That *both* words (Mark 1:15 and Matt. 10:7) were formulated in the primitive Church is an unproved assertion; and it is truly misleading to adduce in support of this assertion R. Otto (1938) 150–4, since he offers reasons for the *eclipse* of the fact that Jesus proclaimed the imminent appearing of the kingdom (so Linnemann [1966] 132). What Otto really tries to show is that the awareness of Jesus' strictly eschatological understanding of the reign of God as the future kingdom at the end of time did not die out – not that this conception was a secondary importation. Furthermore what Otto adduces in support of his thesis are generalizations devoid of exegetical basis. Fuchs (n. 4) 122, also gives no sufficient exegetical reason for his assertion that "the proclamation of the nearness of the Basileia more probably belongs to the Baptist and the early community [than to Jesus]".

19 See n. 13. (See also the addendum by M. A. Simpson, *ExpT* 64 [1952/3] 188.)

20 An examination of the passages adduced by W. R. Hutton in support of the translation "arrive" yields the following result: only in Luke 12:33; Acts 21:33; Heb. 7:19 is this meaning of *engizein* more probable than "draw near"; and even in these cases this translation is not necessary. Rehkopf (n. 13) has also succeeded in showing only that *ēngisen* in Luke 22:47 approaches the sense of *proserchesthai* ("to approach").

21 P. Staples, "The Kingdom of God Has Come", *ExpT* 71 (1959/60) 87f., has shown, against Hutton, that in Matt. 26:45; Luke 18:35 *engizein must* mean "draw near". Cf. also Kümmel (1957) 22ff. and F. Blass-A. Debrunner, *A Greek Grammar of the New Testament and Other Early Christian Literature*, ET R. W. Funk (1961) 176.

22 See n. 13.

23 Kümmel (1957) 20f.; Beasley-Murray (n. 8) 95ff.; Jeremias (1963) 119f.

24 Grässer (n. 7) 164f.; W. Grundmann, *Das Evangelium nach Markus* (1959²) 270, apparently ascribes this meaning only to the evangelist.

25 So Linnemann (1966) 135. It is by no means "a methodological mistake to combine Mark 13:28f. with Luke 12:54–6 and on that basis to interpret Luke 12:54–6 as referring to imminent expectation and to claim priority for Mark 13:28f.". For both texts ground their demand in the same way on the ordinary consequences of the observation of concrete natural events. So it is immaterial that in Luke 12:56 the *premonitory* character of the figure is not expressly pointed out, since the hearer will do this by himself in the application of it (so R. H. Fuller [1954] 46). The combination of Mark 13:28f. and Luke 12:54–6 is thus exegetically completely appropriate.

26 Linnemann (1966) 135, 186–9; and Fuchs (as n. 33).

27 The authenticity of the explanation is rejected not only by those mentioned in Kümmel (1957) 59 n. 126, but also by Grässer (n. 7) 36f.; Linnemann (1966) 187ff.; W. Grundmann, *Das Evangelium nach Lukas* (1961) 346; A. R. C. Leaney, *A Commentary on the Gospel According to St Luke* (1958) 235.

28 Cf. Jeremias (1963) 156. The originality of the explanation is rightly defended not only by Jeremias but also by C. Spicq, "La parabole de la veuve obstinée et du juge inerte, aux décisions impromptues", *RB* 68 (1961) 68ff.; and G. Delling, "Das Gleichnis vom gottlosen Richter", *ZNW* 53 (1962) 1ff. Verse 8b is, to be sure (against Spicq and Delling), to be viewed as a Lucan addition to this explanation, as is shown by the substitution of the Son of Man for God and the appearing of the concept of faith. (So also, rightly, Linnemann [1966] 189; Baird [n. 4] 145). We are dealing here with an addition even if Jeremias is right that v.8b is a pre-Lucan Son of Man saying; H. E. Tödt, on the other hand, considers v.8b a formulation by the evangelist (*Son of Man*, 1965).

29 The *crux interpretum*, "Will he delay long over them?" (v.7, end) is possibly to be understood like Sir. 35:19 and translated "even though he lets them wait for him". (So H. Riesenfeld, "Zu *makrothymein* [Luke 18.7]", *Neutestamentliche Aufsätze*, Festschrift für J. Schmid, 1963, 214ff.).

30 Spicq (n. 28) 81ff.; Jeremias (1963) 155; Delling (n. 28) 19f.; Grundmann (n. 27) 348; as a possibility: Grässer (n. 7) 38.

31 So also Linnemann (1966) 188f. This is the way the old versions understand it: *cito*

vet. lat., vg., *celeriter* a; *ba'gal* Pesh; d alone differs: *confestim*; cf. the edition of the *Itala* by A. Jülicher and W. Matzkow, 3 (1954) 202. If the translation mentioned in n. 29 above is correct it is a further confirmation of the temporal significance of *en tachei* ("quickly").

32 Schnackenburg (1963); Neville (n. 4) 60; Gnilka (n. 6) 31.

33 Jüngel (1962) 237f.; Baird (n. 4) 142; Doeve (n. 5) 32, n. 2; Fuchs (n. 4) [not in ET, but 70 in German, as nn. 26 and 66].

34 Schnackenburg (1963) 212.

35 See, e.g., Grässer (n. 7) 128f.

36 So, e.g., Schnackenburg (1963) 207f.; Rigaux (n. 2) 197; Beasley-Murray (n. 8) 99f.

37 Cf. those cited in Kümmel (1957) 60, n. 129, and Grässer (n. 7) 129, n. 4; hesitantly also Schnackenburg (1963) 208 and Grässer, *loc. cit.*,; C. E. B. Cranfield, *The Gospel According to Saint Mark* (1959) 409, thinks the most likely explanation is that "all these things" refers to the *premonitory signs* of the end, and H. P. Owen (n. 8) 176f., would refer it to the destruction of the Temple, but as an omen of the end within this generation.

38 Rigaux (n. 2) 215.

39 Neville (n. 4) 62f.

40 Beasley-Murray (n. 8) 99.

41 Grässer (n. 7) 130.

42 Beasley-Murray (n. 8) 99ff.; Grundmann (n. 24) 270f.; Bosch (n. 7) 145f.; Rigaux (n. 2) 197, 214f.

43 Grässer (n. 7) 131; Linnemann (1966) 132.

44 Cf., e.g., Grässer (n. 7), 131.

45 C. H. Dodd (1935) 42, 53f. (= Fontana Books [1961]35, 43).

46 Baird (n. 4) 142ff.

47 Cf. Kümmel (1957) 26f. and the literature cited there in n. 26; also Rigaux (n. 2) 184.

48 C. H. Dodd, *The Coming of Christ* (1951) 13f.; Neville (n. 4) 60f.; V. Taylor, *The Gospel According to St Mark* (1952) 386; A. Richardson, *An Introduction to the Theology of the New Testament* (1958) 63f.; J. A. T. Robinson, *Jesus and His Coming* (1957) 89; R. A. Cole, *The Gospel According to St Mark* (1961) 140; P. Carrington, *According to St Mark* (1960) 188ff.; cf. also the opinions cited in Bosch (n. 7) 144f. Cranfield (n. 37) 287f., sees Mark 9:1 as a prediction of the transfiguration 9:2ff.

49 Fuller (1954) 27f.; 118; Owen (n. 8) 181; Gloege (n. 8) 147; Perrin (1963) 138f.; Rigaux (n. 2) 192, 196f.; Bosch (n. 7) 144f.; Grässer (n. 7) 132.

50 Gnilka (n. 6) 289; W. Strawson, *Jesus and the Future Life* (1959) 74; Schnackenburg (1963) 207.

51 Cf. those cited in Kümmel (1957) 27, n. 28; further, H. A. Guy, *The Origin of the Gospel of Mark* (1954) 88ff.; Grässer (n. 7) 133f.; Linnemann (1966) 132; E. Percy, *Die Botschaft Jesu* (1953) 177; H. Conzelmann, *The Theology of St Luke* (1960) 104. W. Marxsen, *The Evangelist Mark*, 205 n. 193, does not wish to put the question of the dominical origin of the saying: Grundmann (n. 24) 177f., thinks that the mention of "some" is an addition spawned by the delay of the parousia,

but apparently he would trace back to the earliest community the original saying, which referred to all Christians. The question of authenticity is left open in S. E. Johnson, *A Commentary on the Gospel According to St Mark* (1960) 153.

52 Kümmel (1957) 27; Gloege (n. 8) 147; Perrin (1963) 138f.; Bosch (n. 7) 144.

53 Linnemann (1966) 132f.; similarly, Conzelmann (n. 51) 104; Grässer (n. 7) 134.

54 Guy (n. 51) apparently feels the force of the difficulty and consequently falls back again on the impossible escape route of interpreting *hestēkotōn* ("standing") in the sense of "stand firm", "be steadfast".

55 So Luther and the Zürich translation. The translation in the *Interpreter's Bible, ad loc.*, is especially clear, and so is the New English Bible: "(before you) have gone through all the towns of Israel".

56 Bauer's lexicon also gives this translation, but without any evidence (ET 818).

57 See H. G. Liddell, R. Scott, and H. S. Jones, *A Greek–English Lexicon* (1940⁹) 1772.

58 So Grässer (n. 7) 137; J. Dupont, " 'Vous n'aurez pas achevé les villes d'Israel avant que le Fils de l'Homme ne vienne' (Matt. 10:23)", *Nov T* 2 (1958) 231 vs. Vielhauer (n. 7) 59; Tödt (n. 28) 60, E. Feuillet, "Les origines et la signification de Mt 10, 23b", *CBQ* 23 (1961) 186; Linnemann (1966) 132–6. (The examples adduced by Feuillet ["a way", "life", "these words"] prove nothing, since in these cases *telein* means "terminate", not "come to the end of".) The old translations *non consummabitis* (so the whole Latin tradition; see Jülicher and Matzkow's edition of the *Itala*, 1 [1938] p. 60) and *tᵉšallᵉmūn* (syᵉ and Pesh) are correct but ambiguous. L. Albrecht's translation is also correct: "Before the coming of the Son of Man your work with respect to the cities of Israel will not yet be finished".

59 The original unity of Matt. 10:23 and hence the interpretation of 10:23b which refers it to the flight from city to city is defended by Schnackenburg (1963) 205; Vielhauer (1957) 59, n. 43; Tödt (n. 28) 60; Linnemann (1966) 133; Feuillet (n. 58) 186; H. Schürmann, "Zur Traditionsgeschichte von Mt 10, 23", *BZ* 3 (1959) 85; E. Bammel, "Matthäus 10, 23", *Studie Theol.* 14 (1960) 79ff. (He attempts to demonstrate the existence of a concept involving wandering from place to place and the termination of this wandering by an eschatological event, and hence to establish a Jewish *Vorlage* for the whole verse without the introductory *hotan* ["when"] clause; but the attempt is not notably successful.)

60 Schürmann (n. 59) 82ff. (in agreement with Feuillet [n. 58] 182ff.), tries to show that Matt. 10:23 was originally the conclusion of the Q section in Luke 12:8–12 and hence a consolatory word in time of persecution. But proof is lacking that the basis of Matt. 10:17–22 is Q and not Mark 13:9–13; and this hypothesis becomes completely untenable if Matt. 10:23 was not originally a unity. Dupont (n. 58) 228ff. thinks that Matt. 10:23b was originally the continuation of 10:5b, 6 and that Matthew placed it at the end of the mission charge. But this is completely incapable of proof.

61 I cannot enter here into a discussion with those who fundamentally reject this fact. Cf., e.g., A. Feuillet, "Le triomphe du Fils de l'Homme d'après la déclaration du Christ aux Sanhédrites", in *La venue du Messie* (1962) 159ff.

62 Neville (n. 4) 61 (the original reference was to the coming of the kingdom with power); R. V. G. Tasker, *The Gospel According to St Matthew* (1961) 108; V. Taylor, *The Life and Ministry of Jesus* (1955) 107f.

63 Robinson (n. 48) 80, 91f. (presumably the word was given "a chronological twist"

and thus assimilated to the hope of the parousia); Feuillet (n. 58) 192f. Feuillet lists on 190ff. other possible interpretations of the saying; older interpretations are given in P. Nepper-Christensen, *Das Matthäusevangelium ein judenchristliches Evangelium?* (1958) 185ff.

64 According to Baird (n. 4) 145, Matt. 10:23 originally had "a present, historic meaning", like that in Mark 9:1 (which he also interprets in a present sense). P. Bonnard, *L'Evangile selon Saint Matthieu* (1963) 149 eliminates any concrete date. Dupont (n. 58) 238ff., confines the prediction to the Galilean mission and refers "Son of Man" to the earthly Jesus. Feuillet (n. 58) 188, rightly says that in view of the solemnity of the language used this attempted explanation is "the most banal declaration imaginable". W. Grundmann, *Die Geschichte Jesu Christi* (1956) 245ff., and Schnackenburg (1963) 250ff., leave open the question of the original meaning of the saying.

65 Schweitzer's exegesis, according to which Jesus expected the coming of the Son of Man before the disciples' return from the Galilean mission, has been taken up again by M. Goguel "La caractère, à la fois actuel et futur, du salut dans la théologie Paulinienne", in *The Background of the New Testament and its Eschatology, in Honour of C. H. Dodd*, ed. W. D. Davies and D. Daube [1956] 323); but it is now generally recognized that this exegesis is untenable: cf. Kümmel (1957) 62ff.; and Feuillet (n. 58) 189f.

66 This or something quite similar is the view expressed by those named in Kümmel (1957) 56f. n. 137, and by Grässer (n. 7) 137f.; Linnemann (1966) 132–6; Vielhauer (1957) 58ff.; Tödt (n. 28) 60f.; E. Schweizer, *Lordship and Discipleship* (1960) 40ff.; Bammel (n. 59) 92; Fuchs; Jüngel (1962) 239f.; H. Braun, *Spätjüdisch-häretischer und frühchristlicher Radikalismus* II (1957) 102 n. 4; W. Schmithals, *Paul and James* (1965) 112f.; G. Strecker, *Der Weg der Gerechtigkeit* (1962) 41.

67 Vielhauer (1957) 71ff.; and "Jesus und der Menschensohn", *ZTK* 60 (1963) 135ff.

68 See Kümmel (1957) 44–7.

69 See Tödt (n. 28) 40–6; Hahn (n. 7) 38.

70 See Kümmel (n. 68) and his "Jesus Christus. Das Christusverständnis im Wandel der Zeiten", *Marburger Theol. Studien* 1 (1963) 7f. Vielhauer's objection that "in contemporary Jewish eschatology the reign of God and the Son of Man had nothing to do with each other" and that "the combining of them by Jesus is equally improbable on the basis of his presuppositions in terms of the history of religions" (*ZTK* 60 [1963] 136) may be met by noting that the objection is without force once one grants that Jesus spoke both of the reign of God becoming effective in the present in his activity (Matt. 12:28) and of himself as the Son of Man active upon earth (Mark 2:10; Matt. 8:20); for then Jesus was involved in any case in a conscious revision of the traditional Jewish eschatology.

71 See Kümmel (1957) 85; Jeremias (n. 17) 19–39.

72 So Jeremias (n. 17) 20; Owen (n. 8) 175f.; Bosch (n. 7) 157; G. R. Beasley-Murray, *Jesus and the Future* (1954) 185; apparently also Perrin (1963) 83 and Rigaux (n. 2) 194f.

73 Linnemann (1966) 132. Because of the limitations of space it is not possible to discuss here the texts further adduced by Miss Linnemann (Mark 14:25; Luke 12:54, 56), nor the "general admonitions to wakefulness" nor the so-called parables of growth; but an examination of them would not change our results in any

way, since these texts acquire significance as evidence of Jesus' expectations for the near future only in connection with the texts discussed above.

74 See n. 8.

75 Cf., e.g., Fuchs (n. 4) 165; Jüngel (1962) 237; Schnackenburg (1963) 213; Schür-mann (n. 59) 86 n. 17; Gnilka (n. 6) 289; Baird (n. 4) 142; Rigaux (n. 2) 190, 198 (Jesus did not teach that the End would come within his generation, so he was not mistaken in this – but he expected it!).

76 Rightly, Owen (n. 8) 176; Gloege (n. 8) 147: "It should be freely conceded that in this respect Jesus 'miscalculated'. But the more astonishing thing is that this error did not lessen his credibility in the community and that the non-arrival of the day of glory [more precisely: *his* delay] according to all the NT accounts was not in any way destructive of faith."

77 See nn. 3, 5 and 6.

78 See the reference to older attempts at explanation in Kümmel (n. 3). T. F. Glasson's conception is that the expectation of the parousia arose between the earliest community and Paul because of the transferral to Jesus of OT statements about the eschatological coming of Yahweh and that the expectation of this coming in the *near* future arose as a consequence of many influences, among them the setting up of Caligula's statue in the Temple at Jerusalem; this view, originally set forth in his *The Second Advent* (1947[2]) is repeated in the later edition, with the addition that the misunderstanding of several of Jesus' words about his triumph beyond the cross could have contributed to the emergence of the belief in the parousia, and with the further addition that the Christian expectation of the coming in the near future arose primarily out of the transferral to Christianity of the similar Jewish expectation (see the 3rd, 1963, edn, 176f., 208). On this, see my critique in *ThR*, n. F. 22 (1954) 144ff. Doeve (n. 5) would recognize an expectation of a *near* coming as at most *possible* in some circles of primitive Christendom (even 1 Thess. 4:15 creates no more than this impression!), but he does not discuss the emergence of these isolated conceptions. And J. G. Davies, "The Genesis of Belief in an Imminent Parousia", *JTS*, n.s. 14 (1963) 104ff., would deduce from 1 Thess. 4:15 that belief in the *nearness* of the parousia goes back to the revelation of a Christian prophet.

79 See n. 9.

80 See W. G. Kümmel, "Jesus und Paulus", *NTS* 10 (1963/4) 163ff.

3

*On Understanding the Kingdom of God**

ERICH GRÄSSER

I

In years past it was above all systematic theologians who made reference to "the kingdom of God" within their attempt to develop a practically-oriented theology. They sought by means of the phrase to make theological discourse and activity relevant both socially and politically.[1] Exegetes were hardly involved in the discussion, except to raise the warning that the NT proclamation of God's coming rule does not provide the basis of a political theology in the sense of a socially revolutionary movement.[2] The reasons for this are evident. The revolutionary attitude towards the world promoted by such movements and the involvement in the near end of the world required by the New Testament are not at first sight reconcilable: whoever awaits God's revolution will not wish to waste his time sewing new patches on old cloth.

Since that time the situation has changed somewhat. Exegetes still hold by their contention that the eschatological preaching of Jesus is not revolutionary, at least not in the political sense. But they see his proclamation as conditioned by its situation, formed within the horizons of the ancient world, so that – having regard to the historical condition of today's world – one might move beyond this preaching.[3] This hermeneutical programme demands the discovery of "progressive theological intentions" in primitive Christian kerygma and their application to questions of theology, the Church, society and ideology,[4] and it could be welcomed as a necessary hermeneutical undertaking for the present, analogous to the programme of demythologizing which was fashionable in the 1950s. At least, it could be if it confined itself to understanding within the horizon of how we think today what was intended, what was meant by the ancient formulation. But the political hermeneutic of the Gospel goes further. It

* First published in *ZNW* 65 (1974) 3–26. Translated by C. Marsh.

considers that the task of interpreting for today is only complete if one does not confine oneself to discovering the intended meaning, but then proceeds "beyond the message of Jesus in a creative way".[5]

This demand is not radically new, given the diversity of theologies in the New Testament itself, which do not simply repeat the message of Jesus. And those currently working in the field of hermeneutics know very well that in order to say the same thing in an altered historical situation, one must say it in a new way.[6] Nevertheless, a pressing question arises in this creative process of going beyond the witness to Jesus, the message about Christ: Who or what is to regulate this creative hermeneutic so as to be the *norma normans* (the norm that norms) of exegesis?

Agreement on this matter is problematic at the moment, since only brief exegetical experiments, not detailed presentations, exist.[7] Yet it would seem that the hermeneutical agenda is being determined by current critical awareness and by what is seen to be anthropologically and sociologically necessary in the light of that awareness.[8] To speak more precisely: "the future planned and produced by men for men", or "the political and human ideals" drawn up by men, must of necessity provide the basic material into which "the characteristic feature of the eschatological preaching of Jesus and the primitive communities is to be translated and elaborated upon, in order to produce a strategy for transforming the present".[9]

Whether a more appropriate understanding of the kingdom of God can be drawn up in this way than is found in the theologies of Bultmann, Conzelmann, Jeremias and Kümmel remains to be seen, especially when S. Schulz – in my opinion too hastily – decides on theological grounds against "all conceptions of the future which simply have to do with after-life and another world".[10] None the less, this hermeneutical assessment is not to be rejected from the outset as theologically untenable. Schulz abides by the belief that it is the kerygma "which changes a person radically" and which "empowers and obliges" us (note the order of words) "to protest not only against oppression, manipulation and inhumanity, but also to strive methodically and progressively, within the confines of our present situation, for more justice, more freedom and more peace, not in the world to come, but in our world with its technical, industrial, economic and political apparatus of power. Above all: it is not a matter of raising one's voice to all and sundry, but of a consistent strategy designed in a world oppressed by technology to produce timely changes in the interests of human aspirations."[11] The primacy of grace over law, the very character of the kingdom as the rule of grace, is thereby maintained. And when it is said, "The message of the kingdom of God ... *implies* (my italics) changes in inhuman social, political and economic conditions",[12] the danger of identifying the human and divine realms is guarded against.

Matters become difficult, however, if the kingdom of God, whose realization requires a fresh collective and practical effort, is seen as implying only a socio-political programme. The question cannot then be avoided whether the overriding aspect of the beyond, as well as the basis of Jesus' kingdom preaching – the revelation of God's free grace – have not been hopelessly corrupted. Whether this is occasioned by a new legalistic zeal, a reappearance of the idea of evolution so dear to Protestant culture, or by socialist interpretations of the kingdom of God, is of no consequence.[13] The creative new hermeneutic permits of at least a tendency in this direction. It is therefore advisable to discuss its potential and its limitations, in order that the present debate about method should not be complicated unnecessarily.

II

Our consideration is based on an exegetical essay by Theodor Lorenzmeier,[14] which seems to be an example of how the door to misconceptions damaging to theology and Church can be left open by a less than careful exegesis and the unsupported application of a method. I have chosen to deal with this essay mainly because it seems to me symptomatic of a catastrophic rift, evident elsewhere as well, between exegetical insight and systematic reflection.

Lorenzmeier takes an important saying from the sayings source (Matt. 12:28; Luke 11:20) as the basis of his investigation. He discusses recent exegetical work on the authenticity of the saying, the exorcism and Jesus' understanding of himself, and whether the kingdom is seen as actually present in the saying. He concludes with four theses on how the kingdom of God is to be understood.

What is at first striking is the degree of certainty with which these concluding theses are presented. Such certainty is in stark contrast to the uncertainty of the exegesis, referred to frequently in the analytical section of the essay (290; 292; 296; 300; 301; 302). It is thus the problem of Lorenzmeier's essay that the conclusions do not really represent the result of its exegesis. The question must therefore be asked whether the exegetical premises can support the systematic conclusions.

III

We turn first to the problem of authenticity.

That Lorenzmeier sees no need for a decision on the matter of originality in his traditio-historical analysis is understandable, for according to him both renderings of the saying, the Matthean and the Lucan, say the same thing: "the power of God makes itself known through the activity of Jesus" (291). And one may excuse a busy parish clergyman for not taking into account all of the more recent literature on Q, although that must be a disadvantage in considering the issues involved.[15] Incomprehensible, however, is the nonchalant ease with which the question of authenticity (Is this a saying of the earthly Jesus?) is passed over so lightly, although the exorcism to which the saying refers as its context is held to be among the incontestably historical data in the life of Jesus (291).[16]

The historical scepticism with which the entire stock of recorded sayings of Jesus is regarded was at no time truly justified. And the matter is no different today, especially if a very general criterion – namely, the "complexity of the synoptic tradition" (289) – lies at the root of this scepticism. Lorenzmeier rightly notes (290 n. 4)[17] that the more discriminatory criterion of authenticity used by Käsemann and others proves insufficient, but certainly his general criterion will not suffice as a replacement. The problem lies in the dependence of such an approach upon a historical–critical method which lacks the criteria and categories to come to terms with the gospel tradition in its true character. In other words, the tradition is not being treated as kerygmatic historical tradition.[18]

The search continues for an impartial method of criticism which could achieve this, one which would above all help us to reconsider the modern understanding of history and reality which we have taken up as a matter of course.[19] But in any case, no exegete should neglect the need to test from time to time the effectiveness of the criteria of authenticity proposed up till now. In the case of Matt. 12:28 par. Luke 11:20, that would have meant examining the saying within the whole context of Jesus' preaching of the kingdom. It would thereby have been shown that his preaching differs from contemporaneous religious views (cf. Judaism, Qumran, the Baptist, and also the later primitive community). This difference is still best explained when seen as deriving from Jesus himself.[20] Two characteristic features are immediately apparent in our saying. First, the kingdom of God is clearly the power of God which reveals itself in acts; the rule of God is the eschatological (i.e. definitive and decisive) act of God which he effects for the benefit of his people and through which he is made known as king.[21] Second, there is the use of the verb "to come" in connection with the kingdom of God, a feature which is without parallel, yet characteristic of the proclamation of Jesus.[22] "Further, the connection of the presence (or imminence) of the kingdom with the present experience of a man is a motif unparalleled in Judaism."[23] Only when this and more[24] is taken into account should one pass comment upon the question of inauthenticity. For that, not the authenticity, is what has to be proved, and that is generally true for the synoptic tradition.

IV

The decisive element in Jesus' ministry of exorcism is, according to Lorenzmeier, that: "confronted with the power of God, the demonic powers must yield" (291). But something is neglected in that statement, which affects both this judgement and his evaluation of the other crucial passages (cf. Mark 3:27; Luke 11:21; Mark 1:25; 5:8; Luke 4:36; Acts 10:36f., where the whole of Jesus' activity is summarized in the words, "He went about doing good and healing all that were oppressed by the devil, for God was with him" [v. 38]).[25] He neglects to describe the structure of the kingdom announced by Jesus within its overall context as the decisive struggle between God's rule and Satan's,[26] and this tells against his concluding systematic arguments (see below).

Instead of interpreting the exorcisms as evident manifestations of the kingdom of God on the basis of this saying (and they can be nothing else!) the emphasis upon the culturally relative nature of Jesus' ideas is monotonously repeated. We hear also the claim (and it is only a claim) that there exists no qualitative difference between Jesus and other Jewish exorcists, and that as an exorcist he is "no unique phenomenon" (293), as if the very fact that he brought the kingdom into play with his exorcisms did not make him precisely that! A concession is frankly made, however, in the remarks on Jesus' self-understanding. The fact that the demons yield and that the kingdom of God is evident brings to expression something without parallel, something inexpressible in any concept or title, namely "the sovereignty" of Jesus (297).[27] That this has to be demonstrated as a unique phenomenon is nowhere maintained.[28] The insistence upon this question (Is Jesus a unique phenomenon?) or its negative expression (as a phenomenon Jesus is nothing special) betrays the "all too basically subjectivistic habit of thinking and speaking", rightly criticized by Karl Barth, which sees Jesus in such acts primarily as confined to ancient "conceptions",[29] and constantly conjures up a "mythical picture of the world", a picture which – by the way – generally cannot explain these "conceptions".[30] History naturally concerns itself with the conceptions of the past, but theological exegesis must first of all discover the actual circumstances which occasioned the exorcist's power struggle *for* the suffering man and *against* the threat of the abyss. This power struggle is in my opinion completely undervalued if one explains it on the basis of a "popular dualism" which influenced Jesus (291).[31] Roger Garaudy has offered a more penetrating exegesis in this regard, "Christ never appears as a magician, a thaumaturge, who acts from the outside in order to bring about a change in a person, in the way that one would manufacture a product. Everything takes place through the consciousness and will of the person involved. Jesus does not say, 'I have saved you', as one would to a drowning man one had just rescued. Rather he says, 'Your faith has saved you'."[32]

Karl Barth called attention in a remarkable way to the actual circumstances which caused Jesus to act, although he paid too little attention to form criticism and redaction criticism in the course of his strongly theological interpretation. Under his analysis, it becomes evident that the question whether this is a commonplace or an unusual case in the history of religion is too narrow:

The truth was that Jesus did in fact experience reality within the context of Judaism and its presuppositions, which were not only subjective but also objective, not only anthropological, but also theological and therefore cosmological. For this reason he saw as any other Jew, but in a way which was incomparably more exact than any other's, what really was there to be seen. He experienced, in a way which was incomparably more precise than any other's, what was really there to be experienced: the tangible abyss of darkness, not merely supposed, imagined, invented or projected into the sphere of being, but actual, the presence and action of nothingness, of the evil in the background and foreground of human existence. He saw and experienced man *as he was*, invisibly, but also visibly, and in any case really, claimed and imprisoned by this actuality, terrified of his human surroundings and therefore chained, constantly breaking his chains and really suffering in the freedom won in this way, "possessed" by nothingness in one or other of its different forms, inescapably delivered up to it, corrupted even in the forefront of his being by the corrupted background of the human situation. All this was at issue in the exorcisms of Jesus, and for this reason they were important in the tradition not only as narratives which could be told for their own sake, but as representing the direction of his whole ministry. As only his raisings from the dead, they reveal the total and absolutely victorious clash of the kingdom of God with nothingness, with the whole world of chaos rejected by God, with the opposing realm of darkness. Far beyond the sin and guilt of man, but also far beyond his need and sadness, even beyond death itself, the activity of Jesus struck at the heart of that power which was introduced into the cosmos by the sin and guilt of man and works itself out in his need and sadness, enslaving all creatures. He struck at the poisonous source whose effluents permeate the whole cosmos and characterize its form as that of "this present evil aeon" (Gal. 1:4).[33]

Barth called the meaning and the force of Jesus' ministry "the free grace of God".[34] On this basis he observed faith most accurately as the utterly free "anthropological counterpart" of grace:

> Whoever can have dealings with God as one who is elected in Jesus and called by Jesus is free in the New Testament sense. He is free not only in the negative sense of freedom as independence, but in its positive definition: he is an able and powerful man, a man of unconditional and unlimited capacity within the terms of reference and limits of his relationship with God. He can think rightly and desire rightly, wait rightly and hasten rightly, obey rightly and defy rightly, begin rightly and end rightly, be with and for men rightly and by himself rightly. He can do all these things and do them rightly – not as arbitrary or dilettante bunglers, but properly and diligently – because in faith he is God's free partner. His freedom is not chosen or sneaked or stolen or robbed, but acquired for him by God in the act of freeing him. The believer can do all, and do all rightly, because the faith which God's grace bestows on man is freedom.[35]

The priority of grace over any act of men is most strictly preserved by Barth. "They do not anticipate the miracle, but are anticipated by Jesus who performs the miracle, by the God active and revealed in Him."[36]

V

All this finds some expression in the fourth thesis of Lorenzmeier's concluding chapter, "On understanding the Kingdom of God".[37] But this thesis stands in some tension with the other three, which, in my opinion, do not really explain the concept of the kingdom of God as it could have been explained on the basis of the preceding theological exegesis (had that actually been carried out).
The theses read:

1   Ancient demonology is a spent force so far as modern man is concerned. At least, this should be the case in an age of natural science. What is not brought to an end, however, is the phenomenon of man under the control of all sorts of anti-human forces. Everything which spoils man's life, and his life with others, is at issue here: aggression levelled destructively against one's fellow-man, against other races and peoples, or against oneself; diseases which wear man

down and wreck him both in body and soul; totalitarian ideologies by which men are spiritually tyrannized and enslaved; social systems in which men are degraded and exploited – and whatever else might be listed in this line. Wherever anti-human powers are deprived of their power or, expressed in more concrete terms, in every case where man is freed from destructive aggression, from excruciating illness, from enslaving ideologies or social wretchedness, there the kingdom of God is involved. That is where the kingdom of God takes place. God is within these events.

2   The kingdom of God does not come "vertically from above", that is: not directly. It requires someone who is determined to be God's fellow-worker. It comes about through people who deprive destructive aggression of power, people who bear the burden of their fellowmen in their misery, people who bring about release from totalitarian ideologies, people who render social systems more humane. Wherever the kingdom of God is brought to bear and the world is thus released from the demonic, there Christ is present.

3   The kingdom of God, which came to man in the past through Jesus, is an event which constantly seeks re-enactment. The hope of Christian faith is precisely this: that the kingdom of God as a permanent and never-ending process of events might constantly cast out anti-human forces. This hope is based upon the fact – expressed in mythical terms – that the power of demons is broken at its very roots. For God's benevolence, which found expression in Jesus of Nazareth, has proved itself more powerful. What the event of the kingdom of God puts in prospect is neither an apocalyptic drama nor the utopia of a perfect and restored world, a world without need, pain and death. What is in prospect is no more, and no less, than that the kingdom of God is constantly operative and drives away the demons.

4   Christian existence is that existence which is fully aware that it stands under God's rule. Such existence is also aware that it is, as every form of human existence, always threatened by demons (to use mythical terms once more). But it places its confidence in the fact that the kingdom of God, which it has experienced as a liberating force, will in future afford protection, so that the demons will again yield. Such existence is fully aware of its own inadequacy, and of its own failings, and yet it feels itself challenged – and experiences itself as enabled – to co-operate in the advent of God's rule, shown by Jesus to be the benevolence of God, within the realm of human social life.

59

The formulations chosen in these theses give the impression that the kingdom of God which is to be realized here and now is dependent upon human initiative. Such a contention only distinguishes itself from socialist interpretations offering secularized concepts of the kingdom of God (deriving from a variety of sources) in that it holds that "God is within" (303) the process described. It would require a careful distinction between God's activity and man's to escape the suspicion of a false legalism.

In the first thesis, the idea is expressed that Jesus' struggle against the demons is a struggle against the nothingness which plainly threatens man. But the thesis concludes with a passage which is at the very least open to misinterpretation in just the sense cited above. "Wherever anti-human powers are deprived of their power or, expressed in more concrete terms, in every case where man is freed from destructive aggression, from excruciating illness, from enslaving ideologies or social wretchedness, there the kingdom of God is involved. That is where the kingdom of God takes place" (303). Without the reference to God, that is precisely the belief of early socialism.[38] Yet perhaps the first thesis is merely clumsily expressed, and critics who demand a different wording should be reproached for cavilling. We would nonetheless reformulate the thesis thus (and claim that the difference is essential): Where God's kingdom is involved, where it comes about and indeed where it comes about through grace ("free grace, grace which is plainly powerful against the power which constrains all creatures"), which meets us and guarantees freedom,[39] there the kingdom of God is experienced. It is experienced, "not as the assault of a power-hungry oppressor, but as the liberating immediacy of a God concerned with man".[40] Here is where anti-human powers are rendered powerless and the new righteousness makes its presence felt as the conqueror of destructive aggression, of excruciating illness, of enslaving ideology, of social wretchedness. It does this as faith working through love (Gal. 5:6). For whenever Jesus speaks of the kingdom directed towards man, he refers man, without doubt, towards his fellow-man. "God's concern for man can only become an immediate event when man is concerned with his fellow-man."[41] But what becomes an event does not bring God's kingdom into play because we bring it about. Rather, Jesus brings on the kingdom because he proclaims it as God's effective action, and it is present among us as an experience or not, depending on whether we accept what we hear and stand by it or deny it and offer resistance.[42] Otherwise, the coming of God's kingdom preached by Jesus would be an occurrence which depended on our action for its realization.

And so we come to the second thesis which, like the first, is open to misinterpretation. Perhaps a change of emphasis would help here: where Christ is present, the demons have no chance, because the kingdom of God is coming about. A theological reference is apparent here (unfortunately all too coincidentally) and is basic for our under-standing of the kingdom of God. We can speak of it now only in christological terms. For both the cross and the resurrection have of necessity turned the *hapax* ("once") of the kingdom of God (to which Jesus gave expression in parabolic fashion in his teaching and con-duct) into the *ephapax* ("once for all") of the kingly rule of Christ.[43] This expresses the *extra nos* of salvation in that salvation remains even now *solus Christus*.[44] One part of the thesis, however, is quite wrong. I refer to the words: "The kingdom of God does not come 'vertically from above' that is: not directly. It requires (!) someone who is determined to be God's fellow-worker."[45] Quite apart from the fact that, in the saying in question, the kingdom does not need man but rather seeks men in their needy condition, the characteristic of God's rule as proclaimed by Jesus is precisely its directness: it comes without man's aid and changes the form of the world. The fact has often been demonstrated, so that illustrations are unnecessary here. Let it simply be said: man can in no way be considered as a fellow-worker in this connection.[46] Within Jesus' understanding, one would not say that the kingdom "happens through men", but that it comes, is near or appears. The notion that through moral action or socio-revolutionary activity men can assist in the realization of God's rule is presupposed and urged on us in Lorenzmeier's formulations, but it has no place in the preaching of Jesus.[47] Perhaps Lorenzmeier (and also H.-W. Bartsch) has the undeniably worldly aspect of the kingdom of God in mind: the kingdom of God is a secular kingdom insofar as it comes to men in this world, without their having in any sense to betray their concern for the world (see above). But if Lorenz-meier is here promoting man to a *co-operator Dei*, he thereby does away with the transcendental element which is so essential to the concept of the kingdom of God.[48]

VI

In the third thesis, the fact that the precise relationship between the present and the future aspects of the kingdom of God has been left undefined proves fatal for Lorenzmeier's contentions. Discussion of the exegetical controversy concerning the understanding of time in Jesus' preaching of the kingdom is foreclosed, in my opinion rashly, on the grounds that the uncertain results of biblical criticism lead nowhere in this case. In this way, where it concerns the understanding of God's kingdom only its presence as a dynamic event is mentioned. The future perspective is wholly omitted. The reader is left puzzling why this should be the case: because of the uncertain results of biblical criticism, or because the imminent expectation was a miscalculation? (Then demythologizing would indeed mean elimination and not interpretation!)[49] Or is it because the attempt to determine the relationship between the present and future aspects of the kingdom is too hastily given up? Lorenzmeier refuses to interpret "has come" in Luke 11:20 par. in the sense of "has drawn near" (299), although to do this would in no way be unreasonable, as J. Becker has recently shown.[50] Instead of offering an exegetical foundation for his opinion, he merely decrees "then the kingdom of God has already reached you" (298) as the straightforward translation, although it is still necessary to specify in what sense the existence of the kingdom of God is meant. The precise sense is indeed dependent upon the theological exegesis of the conditional clause, that is, upon the interpretation of the connection between the exorcism of demons and the figure of Jesus, and its significance for the kingdom of God.[51] For "existence" in the literal sense of the word would in fact render the sentence incomprehensible: where the kingdom of God is present, there is no longer a power struggle with Satan; he is a thing of the past (cf. *As. Mos.* 10:1, "and then his kingdom shall appear throughout all his creation, and then Satan shall be no more ..."). This is demonstration that the concluding statement at least, which is made to stand out by the emphasis on *ara* ("therefore"), is to be interpreted dialectically with respect to the present time.[52] In short: there has to be a reason for the choice of the word *phthanō* instead of the usual word. And our predecessors (J. Weiss, H. J. Holtzmann and others) might be right in claiming, on the basis of 1 Thess. 2:16, that we are here dealing with an unexpected coming.[53]

Be that as it may, the choice between "present" and "future", which the lexical evidence cannot make for us, is not the last word on this subject.[54] And to define the relationship between the present and future aspects of the kingdom is not a hopeless task,[55] as long as one recognizes that the purpose of emphasizing the radical nearness or presence of the kingdom is so to challenge men that the question of when the kingdom comes is put in the background.[56] I would like, for the time being at least, to reaffirm that the presence of the kingdom and the presence of its sign are to be distinguished,[57] and that Jesus speaks only of the latter. Yet I agree that the question proves ultimately to be purely academic, "as soon as we realize that the claim of the saying is that certain events in the ministry of Jesus are nothing less than an actual experience of the kingdom of God",[58] which on the basis of that experience cannot be taken to be a far-off event. This experience of the kingdom of God is indeed of a struggle between good and evil, God and Satan,[59] of a divine intervention for the sake of restoring a particular individual in his entire being, not a collective, a group or a people.[60] This individualizing tendency is a characteristic feature of the kingdom of God as preached by Jesus. That is recognized even by the Marxist Gardavsky who notes here a "blueprint" of a new life but sees that it is not in the first instance a matter of social change.[61] Everything ultimately comes to a head in the individual, irreplaceable in his uniqueness, before God (Karl Barth).

In my opinion this aspect receives far too little attention in Lorenzmeier's work. He places social salvation firmly in the foreground, but fails to affirm that its realization is not possible without the salvation of the individual. To this extent, his accusation that Bultmann and his followers neglected the question of society rebounds on him.[62] For the reality of the individual sinner before God is so clearly outlined in the proclamation of the New Testament and has been presented so clearly in the theology of Bultmann, that any "social teaching for our time" which purports to help this "vague" anthropology to a more sharply sociological focus simply misses the point.

In conclusion, a final proviso: even if the paraphrase of the kingdom of God as "an event which constantly seeks re-enactment" (303) is not without its difficulties, it can be accepted insofar as Jürgen Becker has demonstrated exegetically that the dynamic character of the kingdom is central to its understanding.[63] But it is incomprehensible that every eschatological aspect is removed from the event by Lorenzmeier: "The event of the kingdom of God puts in prospect neither an apocalyptic drama nor the utopia of a perfect and restored world, a world without need, pain and death. What is in prospect is no more, and no less, than that the kingdom of God is constantly operative and drives away the demons" (303). In other words, the perpetual improvement of what already exists, rather than the creation of something wholly new, is here being suggested. Many texts (e.g. Mark 2:21) say precisely the opposite. To ascribe such passages to the thought patterns of the ancient world in order to dismiss their message is to side-step, rather than face, the hermeneutical task.

Many attempts have been made to express the future aspect of the eschatological preaching of Jesus and render it comprehensible.[64] These attempts may be variously assessed. But one thing is certain: if there is no future which transcends the world and that death which is inextricably a part of it, then there is no Christian hope. There is certainly a strong emphasis upon the present, upon the "here and now" rather than the "only then", where a person is looked at as a whole in need of physical healing. But indeed: "The truth of the promise, the truth of what will be (and will be revealed) in the future, shines out already and distinguishes itself from all illusory hopes. Grace is so truly grace, and so truly free as grace, that it is capable even of this (so to speak doubly undeserved) overflow. The Evangelists attest the overflow of grace in the narratives of Jesus' miraculous deeds".[65] Do we want – or rather, are we able – simply to ignore this overflow of grace, as Barth called it? By whose authority do we want to let it be forgotten that faith speaks, after all, of the resurrection of the dead and the life of world to come? "But however that may be, and whatever may be the attitude of the world or Christians, if we are ready to keep to the only information we have (that is, the Gospels in the New Testament) about Jesus the Son of Man, we have to come to terms with the fact that what we are told about him is that he was the man who put his proclamation into practice in these acts (i.e. the exorcisms), thus characterizing it as the proclamation of the kingdom, or – and it comes to the same thing – of the superabounding free grace of God."[66]

NOTES

1 Cf. J. Moltmann, *Hope and Planning* (London: SCM, 1971) 101ff. H. Cox, *The Secular City* (London: SCM, 1965) 110ff.; also Pannenberg (1969).

2 Cf. W. Schmithals (1972); G. Klein (1970).

3 So S. Schulz (1972) 41; cf. also Schulz, "Strategie zeitgemässer Veränderungen", *Zeitwende* (1970) 226–36; *Q. Die Spruch quelle der Evangelisten* (1972) 487ff. H.-W. Bartsch follows a similar line to Schulz; see *Jesus. Prophet und Messias aus Galiläa* (1970). The kingdom of God proclaimed by Jesus is here understood "in its content and essence" as a change in social structure and as the demolition of "existing governing structures in society" (125, 107 and elsewhere).

4 S. Schulz, *Q* (n. 3) 487.

5 S. Schulz (1972) 41. Admittedly H.-W. Bartsch (n. 3) feels able to perceive a changed society as the "objective" in the eschatological texts (130). See below for criticism.

6 Cf. J. M. Robinson (1971) 20–70; E. Grässer, *Text und Situation* (1973) 128.

7 See n. 3; also S. Schulz, *Gott ist kein Sklavenhalter* (1972).

8 See M. Hengel, *Acts and the History of Earliest Christianity* (1979) 127–36.

9 S. Schulz, *Q* (n. 3) 487.

10 S. Schulz (1972) 42; *Q,* 487. It is naturally not a matter of conceptions of the future beyond death. It is rather a matter of the future character of "life", without which Christian hope would be empty. Cf. R. Bultmann (1952) 345ff.

11 S. Schulz, *Q* (n. 3) 487f.

12 Ibid. 488. I erroneously claimed that Schulz perceives the kingdom of God as

coming about through human activity. This was not his contention. He meant that man's conduct is determined by it, with humane goals in view. (I am grateful for his letter of 1st May 1973, which clarified this.)

13 Cf. C. Walter, *Typen des Reich-Gottes-Verständnisses* (1961). One of the century's influential Marxist interpretations derives from the pen of E. Bloch in his works, *Das Prinzip Hoffnung* (3 vols 1954–9), and *Atheism in Christianity* (1972). See further A. Jäger, *Reich ohne Gott* (1969); and C. H. Ratschow: *Atheismus im Christentum?* (1970).

14 T. Lorenzmeier, "Zum Logion Mt 12:28/Luke 11:20", *Neues Testament und Christliche Existenz*, Festschrift for H. Braun (1973) 289–304. All references quoted in the text are from this essay.

15 Lorenzmeier was unable to use Schulz's book on Q. But there are others: H. E. Tödt, D. Lührmann and P. Hoffmann. And there are grounds for the contention that Jesus himself could have been citing Exod. 8:15 in this saying, in order to allude to a new exodus (N. Perrin [1967] 66f.). At any rate there are redaction critical decisions which are important for the theological questions.

16 Lorenzmeier generally refers to the "unanimity" of recent historical-critical exegesis in a very arbitrary fashion. In the case of Matt. 12:28 par. Luke 11:20, where genuineness is accepted by most exegetes, such exegesis is in his estimation of little significance: authenticity is, after all "nothing more than an unproven contention, which in no way carries greater weight merely by frequent repetition on the part of NT scholars" (291 n. 8). As far as the question of the exorcism performed by Jesus goes, this same unanimity is of such significance "that any further time spent upon this question is time wasted" (291). Yet this unanimity is based on an analysis of the synoptic tradition, which allegedly can permit of no absolutely certain answer to questions of authenticity because of its "complexity". This may well be the case in respect of *wording*, but not in respect of meaning. There are enough passages which have to be regarded beyond any reasonable doubt as "authentic". The passage under discussion is one of these; see N. Perrin (1967) 64f; W. G. Kümmel (1957) 105ff; R. Bultmann (1968) 162.

17 The basic principle, in the words of Ernst Käsemann, runs as follows: "In only one case do we have more or less safe ground under our feet (i.e. for reconstructing authentic Jesus-material); when there are no grounds either for deriving a tradition from Judaism or for ascribing it to primitive Christianity, and especially when Jewish Christianity has mitigated or modified the received tradition, having found it too bold for its taste" (*Essays on NT Themes* [London: 1964] 15–47, 37). For criticism of this view cf. P. Stuhlmacher, "Kritische Marginalien zum gegenwärtigen Stand der Frage nach Jesus", Festschrift M. Doerne (1970) 345f; F. Neugebauer, *Jesus der Menschensohn* (1972) 11f.

18 Cf. P. Stuhlmacher, "Kritische Marginalien" 344, 359ff., and other essays.

19 Cf. F. Hahn, "Probleme historischer Kritik", *ZNW* 63 (1972) 1–17; also several essays by P. Stuhlmacher; M. Hengel (n. 8); H. Schlier, *The Relevance of the NT* (1968) 39–75.

20 P. Vielhauer (1957). Cf. N. Perrin (1967) *passim*; W. G. Kümmel, *Theology of the NT* (1974) 32ff; J. Becker, *Johannes der Täufer und Jesus von Nazareth* (1972).

21 Cf. N. Perrin (1967) 55: "It is not a place or community ruled by God; it is not even the abstract idea of reign or kingship of God. It is quite concretely the activity of

God as king" (55). Perrin points out, in my opinion correctly, that the concept of kingdom of God found expression in a number of forms in ancient Judaism. In view of this fact "and the endless variety of phenomena expected to be a feature of its manifestation, there could be no particular form or content necessarily implied by a proclamation such as 'the kingdom of God is at hand'; each hearer would supply his own, and it would be up to the proclaimer to make clear in what terms he conceived of the eschatological activity of God as king, which, as we shall see, is what Jesus did" (57). Cf. also G. Klein (1970) 25ff; H. Conzelmann (1969) 106ff.

22 The fact has often been demonstrated, and quite convincingly by G. Klein (1970), who also spells out its consequences. An important consequence of the application of terminology of the coming aeon in connection with the kingdom of God is that far-fetched speculations about the end of the world can be done away with; "instead of this, man is made ready for the demand which the creator makes, to set up his rule, a demand before which every religious curiosity founders" (27). A further important consequence is that the kingdom of God can in no way be thought of as a function of human activity. "On the contrary; human activity is wholly excluded. The kingdom of God appears 'by itself', like the fruit from the ground (Mark 4:28); man cannot do a thing to bring it about. His sole responsibility is to adopt an attitude towards it and to receive it, in the same way as a child (the most human embodiment of being human, one might say) does not live through its own activity, but through the gift of life which it has received (Mark 10:15)" (29). Moreover, the birth of apocalyptic bears witness to the fact that human history is powerless to bring about salvation. Only a transcendent intervention of God into history can bring salvation about. Cf. the excellent essay by H. Gese, "Anfang und Ende der Apokalyptik, dargestellt am Sacharjabuch", *ZTK* 70 (1973) 20–49 (now reprinted in *Vom Sinai zum Zion* [Munich: 1974] 202–30).

23 N. Perrin (1967) 64.

24 See, for example, J. Becker: *Das Heil Gottes* (1964) 199ff; G. E. Ladd (1966) 135ff.; R. F. Berkey (1963).

25 Cf. K. Barth, *Church Dogmatics* (*CD*) IV/2, 230f.: "Now, on the basis of this total war and victory can come the plundering of the house of the strong man, the dividing of the spoils, the forgiving of man's sins, the comforting of the sad and the healing of the sick. The peculiar feature in these passages is the absolute radicalism of the attack of Jesus, which reflects the wrath of God himself."

26 Cf. J. M. Robinson (1957) 33ff.; J. Becher *Das Heil Gottes*, 197ff.; R. Pesch, *Jesu ureigene Taten*? (1970) 151ff.

27 In the light of this correct recognition, the stark separation of person and object which is made later (302) is incomprehensible. It is certainly correct that Jesus does not make himself the content of his preaching of the kingdom. Yet it is also correct, and this is confirmed by our saying (Matt. 12:28), that he (i.e. Jesus himself) stands in a personal and unique relationship to the kingdom. He proclaims the kingdom of God with authority. This apart, E. Jüngel rightly draws attention to the fact that the temporal expression of the nearness of the kingdom of God favoured by Jesus must at the same time be interpreted with relation to his person. "Jesus *believed* in the nearness of God. This was much more than a hope in something yet to come. To witness the approach of that which is to come means that it has ceased to be an object of hope. It is a matter of certainty. We may even say that Jesus was more certain of the nearness of God than he was of himself.

Without in any way becoming untrue to his world, he knew himself to be wholly determined by the rule of God. Governed and determined in a personal way, the temporal distinction between 'already' and 'not yet' is overcome, although not wholly annulled. It is only in this sense that we can understand such a text as Luke 11:20" (*Death, The Riddle and the Mystery* [1975] 101). The single Käsemann quote upon which Lorenzmeier bases his thesis of the stark separation of person says only – and wisely so – that Jesus did not define the relationship of his own person to the kingdom of God in a precise way (E. Käsemann, *Exegetische Versuche und Besinnungen* I [244]. E. Fuchs has taken up the theme of the relationship of Jesus' person to his mission in *Jesus. Wort und Tat* (1971).

28 Even so, a crowd, amazed at the exorcism, can say, "Never was anything like this seen in Israel" (Matt. 9:33), even though it witnessed similar happenings carried out by the pupils of the Pharisees (Matt. 12:27). "But that 'the kingdom of God has come upon you' (Matt. 12:28) was not previously to be seen. In Jesus' deeds it was, whether recognized or not" (K. Barth, *CD* IV/2, 219). A significant difference between the exorcisms carried out by Jesus and those performed by the miracle-workers found in the wider religious environment can be shown in any case. Cf. the article "Wunder" by A. Vögtle, in *LTK*, vol. 10, 1255–61; W. Trilling: *Fragen zur Geschichtlichkeit Jesu* (1969) 96–105.

29 K. Barth, *CD* IV/2, 230.

30 K. Barth (*CD* IV/2, 228f.) points out that "in the medical schools of antiquity there had already been those, like Hippocrates, who had refused to find any place for demons even in relation to sick mental states of every type ... Even within the widely accepted consensus of opinion as to the existence and activity of beings of this kind the New Testament has certain distinctive features. It speaks of 'demons' (no attempt is made to define them, and they are obviously regarded as incapable of definition) which (a) take possession of man, to estrange him from himself, to control him, and to disturb and destroy him both in body and soul, and (b) do this in a very definite context, in the service of a whole kingdom of disturbance and destruction, summed up in the form (which is not defined) of the devil, or Satan, or Beelzebub."

31 Cf. W. Lütgert's *Das Reich Gottes nach den synoptischen Evangelien* which as long ago as 1895 made a distinction between the formal character of the kingdom of God and the nature of its content: "The form of the kingdom of God is character-ized by the power with which it appears, with which it shows its superiority over demons; its content is characterized by the restoration of life and freedom which it brings" (61). Lorenzmeier emphasizes especially that Jesus makes this freedom "recognizable as a restorative activity of God, which restores even physical life (by which is meant the conquering of illness)" (62).

32 R. Garaudy, "Revolution als Akt des Glaubens", *Evangelisches Kommentar* 6 (1973) 339–43, 343.

33 K. Barth, *CD* IV/2, 230.

34 Ibid., 243.

35 Ibid., 242f.

36 Ibid., 243.

37 See below.

38 W. Weitling, *The Poor Sinner's Gospel* (1843, ET 1969), for example, saw the

realizing of the kingdom of God as taking place in the context of work and material goods.

39 K. Barth, *CD* IV/2, 244.

40 E. Jüngel, *Death* (1975) 99.

41 Ibid.

42 On the worldly aspect of the kingdom of God, which is a kingdom not of this world, see: W. Schmithals (n. 2); E. Jüngel, *Death* (1975) 100. W. Lütgert had noted as early as 1895 the necessity to distinguish but not separate the kingdom as God's gift from the kingdom as a task to be fulfilled. "Man awaits, receives, inherits, possesses, enjoys the kingdom; he enters the kingdom – but he does not bring it about. The one who brings it about is God. The kingdom is an objective dimension. In other words, it is founded on God's activity. Human activity is certainly a condition of the acceptance or loss of the kingdom. Yet the outcome is not founded upon this activity. It does not originate from human action. It originates solely and directly from the will and action of God. The kingdom is a result of the creative activity of God. God does not bring the kingdom about by developing what is already inherent in the world. Essential to the hope for the kingdom is that it expects the renewal of the world in a form arising not through immanent development but due to a creative demonstration of the power of God" (26). The exegesis of Bartsch (see n. 3) and the programme carried out by Schulz (ibid.) are both to be tested by this dialectic of the worldliness of the kingdom of the beyond. Thus far they seem to me to have dealt insufficiently with this problem. This explains why the sentences quoted seem to fail as exegesis. The problem has been current in hermeneutics since R. Bultmann, *History and Eschatology* (1957).

43 On the proclaimer of the kingdom of God becoming the proclaimed, see Schmithals (n. 2) 101ff. and Jüngel, *Death* (1975) 103ff. K. Barth already anticipates his dogmatic solution to this problem by placing his discussion of the presence of the kingdom of God in the miracles of Jesus under the heading "The Exaltation of the Son of Man" (*CD* IV/2, 1). Characteristic of K. Barth's interpretation is the following statement: The perfect *ēngiken hē basileia* on the lips of Jesus (Mark 1:15) says exactly the same thing as it did previously on the lips of John (Matt. 3:2), but it says it quite differently. "The kingdom is no longer just at the doors; it has broken in and crossed the threshold in the power of the works and deeds of Jesus and then (confirmed and manifested in his resurrection) in his sacrifice and victory at the cross. Strictly speaking, then, it is only now that *ēngiken* means that the kingdom, having become a factor in world history, is brought right home to the human race like a house built in front of one's window" (*CD* IV/4, 76). All this is founded upon what Barth has elsewhere (*CD* III/3, 418ff.) termed the "real dialectic" of heaven and earth.

44 E. Lohse, "Apokalyptik und Christologie", *ZNW* 62 (1971) 48–67, deals with the theological significance of the linking of eschatology and Christology in the NT. M. Honecker discusses the theologically pertinent question whether "peace among peoples, calling for political efforts to make peace, and solidarity in the social order, meaning a need for socialism and a worldwide development programme, can be derived directly from the confession of the kingship of Christ". Cf. "Weltliches Handeln unter der Herrschaft Christi", *ZTK* 69 (1972) 72–99. Is this something to which Lorenzmeier pays but lip-service in his theses?

45 H. Braun likewise launches into polemic against the idea of "vertically from above". This polemic, in Braun's case (1979) 128 as well as in Lorenzmeier's, is based on the alternative "divinity or humanity?" E. Jüngel rightly perceives this alternative as too restrictive. The important thing is not whether one says "from above" or "from ahead" or "out of the future" or "from alongside" when one is speaking of the action of God. "What is decisive when speaking of God's action is that one says 'of God' or 'from God'. God's action has its source in God himself. This was what 'directly from above' once used to mean. That God's action encounters us in and through other people does not in any way exclude the fact that although in this sense it is indirect, the action still has its source in God. To introduce an abrupt alternative here is to break off the work of theology precisely at that point where its real difficulties and subtleties are just beginning to appear" (*Death*, 99f).

46 The apostolic writings in the NT refer to *synergoi Theou* ("God's fellow workers") on only twelve occasions. Only one of these displays a clear link with the kingdom of God: in Col. 4:11 Paul's companions are called "fellow workers for the kingdom of God". But the phrase "kingdom of God" as a formal expression has lost its full original meaning so that the eschatological character of the concept is no longer in the foreground. Cf. E. Lohse, *Colossians*, (1971) 172.

47 On this question the book on Jesus by H.-W. Bartsch (n. 3) gives a discordant impression. On the one hand he emphasizes that the coming of God's kingdom is for Jesus "purely the work of God and thus as wonderful as the growth of a seed or the healing of a sick person or the raising of a dead man" (126). On the other hand he sees in the kingdom a social "utopia" (105 and elsewhere) to be brought into being by us in the form of "a fundamental change to the structure of this world", which supposedly is part of God's kingdom (104). And "theological consideration" must lead precisely to this "making do without special forms of organization; rather, within existing structures aiming to bring about through gradual, exemplary realization what Jesus proclaimed: the kingdom of God" (130). Faced with such an exegetical slalom, the cultured despisers of theologians can rightly pour scorn. Where the texts are quite clear as to their meaning, the desire for contemporary interpretation should not be allowed to cloud the issue. And the character of the kingdom of God as a gift is self-evident. Words such as Luke 12:32 and Luke 22:29 emphasize this. One can thus only "go in" (*eiserchesthai*) or "enter" (*eisporeuesthai* cf. Matt. 5:20; 7:21; 18:3 par.; 19:23f.; 23:12 and elsewhere), one can receive it as a child (Mark 10:15 par.), one can expect it (Mark 15:43 par.), but one cannot "gradually bring it about". On this see the article by B. Klappert, "King, Kingdom etc . . ." in *The New International Dictionary of NT Theology* vol. 2, ed. C. Brown (Exeter: 1976) 372–90, 385ff.

48 This is at best demonstrated in the beatitudes from the Sermon on the Mount. Here I can refer simply to the excellent interpretation of G. Eichholz (*Auslegung der Bergpredigt* [1970] 26–54). In the interpretation of the kingdom of God offered by Bartsch, Lorenzmeier and Schulz, once again the age-old problem of the relationship between dogmatics and ethics rears its head. This subject receives impressive treatment in the lectures on ethics given by K. Barth in 1928 which have recently been published (ET 1981); cf. the introductory section 18ff., 22ff. Are we not here once more falling into the trap of allowing ethics to become the sole and self-supporting theme of theological study?

49 At this point it should be stated that I see in the attempt to understand the kingdom of God discussed here – and Lorenzmeier is but one example of many similar attempts – no parallels to Bultmann's demythologizing. On the contrary, R. Bultmann insisted that the beyond inherent in the activity of God resists every attempt to objectify it in this world. Thus he could rightly say, "Radical demythologizing is parallel to the Pauline-Lutheran doctrine of justification by faith alone without the works of the Law. More precisely: demythologizing is its consistent application in the sphere of knowledge" (R. Bultmann, "Zum Problem der Entmythologisierung", *Kerygma and Myth* vol. i (1953) 191–212, 211). Any political theology which sees itself continuing R. Bultmann's existentialist interpretation is thus tested by whether it abides by Bultmann's criterion or whether it wishes indeed once again to objectify the activity of God in the world. Cf. D. Sölle, *Political Theology* (Philadelphia: 1974); and for a discussion of the Bultmann/Sölle debate, see H. Hübner, *Politische Theologie und existentiale Interpretation* (1973).

50 J. Becker, *Das Heil Gottes*, 201f.

51 Cf. the article by G. Fitzer, *phthanō TDNT* vol. 9, 88–92.

52 See the discussion in J. M. Robinson, *Kerygma und historischer Jesus* (1967²) 153, 206ff. (Cf. *The New Quest of the Historical Jesus* [1959] 77, 116).

53 Cf. W. Lütgert (n. 31) 59 n.1.

54 Cf. E. Jüngel, *Paulus und Jesus* (1967³) 185ff.

55 Cf. G. Bornkamm (1960) 90ff.; H. W. Kuhn, *Enderwartung und gegenwärtiges Heil* (1966) 189ff.; J. Becker, *Johannes der Täufer und Jesus von Nazareth* (see n. 20) 81ff.

56 Cf. H. Conzelmann (1968) 36.

57 Cf. E. Grässer (1959) 6ff., and *Die Naherwartung Jesu* (1973) 64; H. Conzelmann (1968) 35f.

58 N. Perrin (1967) 67.

59 Cf. N. Perrin, *op cit.*, 67; J. Becker, *Das Heil Gottes*, 197–214; J. M. Robinson (1957) 33ff.

60 With regard to the "distinctly individualizing tendency of Jesus" see H. Braun (1979) 48; M. Hengel (1971); G. Klein (1970) 29f., who correctly points out that the force which opposes the kingdom of God is the rule of sin, which "has built its nest in man in temporarily concrete form". The decision can thus only take place in man (Mark 1:15). And B. Klappert (in C. Brown [n. 47] 384) presents an incorrect alternative in writing that the actual goal of Jesus' proclamation of the kingdom of God does not consist of a call to man to repent and to make a decision, but rather of a proclamation of the worldwide appearance of God's rule. God's kingdom directs itself primarily towards the individual. "The bastions of resistance against God are found in the heart of the individual and it is these which disappear at conversion. It thus follows that Jesus engages in no discrimination of any sociologically definable groups of people. He expressly avoids giving theological boundaries a sociological dimension. The only meaningful boundary lies from henceforth between obedience and disobedience" (G. Klein, 1970) 65f.

61 V. Gardavsky, *God is not yet dead* (1973) 44.

62 T. Lorenzmeier, *Exegese und Hermeneutik* (1968) 188: "Despite the emphasis that theology is concerned with man and his reality, this reality remains distinctly

shadowy: the society and sociology of our time ... are ignored. It is characteristic that sociology is taken into consideration neither in the work of Bultmann nor of Braun and Ebeling. Nor indeed is its relevance for anthropology ... recognized and evaluated ..."

63 Cf. J. Becker, *Das Heil Gottes*, 197ff.

64 In my book *Die Naherwartung Jesu* (1973) I have dealt critically with the most important attempts made.

65 K. Barth, *CD* IV/2, 246f.

66 Ibid.

4

On the Jewish Background of the Synoptic Concept "The Kingdom of God" *

MICHAEL LATTKE

I *Introduction*

In his monograph on the New Testament and the future of the world (1970), Anton Vögtle – the teacher to whom this article is dedicated – dealt, among other things, with "the cosmological relevance of Jesus' eschatological expectation". He begins with the questions: "Was Jesus' expectation of an apocalyptic/eschatological character? How did Jesus conceive of the future coming of God's kingdom?"[1] Like many other scholars, Vögtle (144) sees the Jewish expression "kingdom of the heavens" (Hebrew *malkūt šāmayim* and Aramaic *malkuta disᵉmaya*), which forms the basis of and corresponds to the concepts *basileia tou Theou* and *basileia tōn ouranōn* in New Testament Greek,[2] "as the central and essential concept in Jesus' hope for and actualization of salvation".[3] "To come to sound historical conclusions", he goes on, "one cannot devote enough attention to the origin and actual living usage of the rabbinic abstract concept *malkūt schāmaiyim*, 'kingdom of God' " (144).

Let us linger for a moment over this abstract concept which he would have us apply to Jesus' preaching. It plays a minute role within the whole of Jewish literature. Billerbeck realized fifty years ago that the kingdom of heaven, or of God, by no means stood at the centre of the "rabbinic thought-world", and that "in comparison to its extraordinarily frequent usage by Jesus the expression 'kingdom of God' only occurs relatively infrequently in the expanse of rabbinic literature".[4] Although it is more infrequent in pre-rabbinic Judaism and in the Old Testament, one must, to avoid coming to false conclusions

* First published in *Gegenwart und kommender Reich*, ed. P. Fiedler and D. Zeller (1975) 9–25. Translated by M. Rutter.

in haste, bear in mind what G. Dalman, *The Words of Jesus* (1902) 2, said: "The concept *malkhut*, although found in the Old Testament, belongs to the abstract formations whose use late Hebrew enjoyed and extended." There are many instances of this tendency in the Targums, but how far it was established in the time of Jesus is an open question. This implies that, in investigating the Jewish background of the synoptic concept, "the kingdom of God", one cannot restrict oneself to occurrences of the word *malkūt*. One must also keep an eye on those texts which speak of God as "king" (*melek*), and as being king or becoming king (*mālak*). That this is not an arbitrary linguistic procedure is shown, not only by the rabbinic Targums and Midrashim (from which Billerbeck and Dalman provide examples), but also by two passages in the *War Scroll* from Qumran. In 1QM XII.16 Israel's eschatological rule is spoken of with the verb *lim^{e}lōk*, and in its doublet (XIX.8) the noun is used: "Israel for an eternal kingdom (*malkūt*)".

We may now return to Vögtle's conclusions as they concern our topic. He depends on Kuhn for some of his judgements,[5] which can serve as a starting point and possible working hypothesis for further investigation. Did *malkūt šāmayim* become a purely religious (that is, non-ethnic and non-national), eschatological concept in Judaism (144)? Are "expectations of the messiah and of the kingdom of God" really "totally heterogeneous" (144f.)? Is the kingdom of God "not a typical apocalyptic concept, such as 'the coming age', 'the new creation', 'the new heaven' and 'the new earth'" (145)?

That Jesus' concept of the kingdom of God was "strictly eschatological" (145) cannot be seriously contested, in view of the work of J. Weiss and Schweitzer. Further, it is clear that "from its very inception it was the name of an action, a dynamic, eschatological concept which meant as such the realization of God's rule" in accordance with the Old Testament affirmation that God rules (*mālak Yahwe*) (145).[6] In the first place it "is not a question of an analogy with or a transference of the secular usage of kingdom (*malkūt*) to refer to God's 'kingdom'" (145), and for that reason an investigation of "*basileus*" ('king') in the hellenistic world"[7] would not benefit our understanding of the Jewish idea of God's kingship. Nonetheless, it would be interesting to contrast the theological concept with the image of the hellenistic (god-)king, its historical development and limitation to a definite area. But overwhelming importance, in my opinion, attaches to two questions: why did the Old Testament title for Yahweh as "king" survive, and – above all – did God's proclaimed claim to kingship (over his people and over the world) involve, implicitly or explicitly, the renunciation of secular government, so that it could be seen as dangerous and seditious? The question is still pertinent to Judaism and the synoptic tradition, even if Yahweh's (or heavens') *malkūt* or God's *basileia* do not mean "an area governed by Yahweh, an empire" (145) but a "king's rule".[8] The last statement raises the question of "spatial components"[9] of the kingdom. Do the aspects of future time and transcendent dimension belong to the Jewish background of the New Testament kingdom concept, as Conzelmann maintains (RGG³ III, 641)? Even if the temporal aspect "dominates", he asserts, one should not neglect the "spatial". Perhaps this offers some justification for the translation "*kingdom* of God", a concept which was to become "one of the most ambiguous"[10] in the history of its usage. The numerous misinterpretations occasioned by this translation were by no means unimportant in leading to the now dominant translation, "rule of God", which reflects the rediscovery of eschatology and the influence of dialectical theology and existential interpretation. In following (quite rightly) this usage, we must keep an eye on the Hebrew and Greek equivalents if we are to avoid inadmissible generalizations. It is well known that the Greek translation of the Old Testament writings called the Septuagint renders "Yahweh", the designation for God that occurs more than 6,000 times, with the word *kyrios* ("lord"). This resulted in "Lord" (although in conjunction with other names) being used continually in the hellenistic and Roman periods both in the writings and additions that were originally written in Greek and in the Greek versions of Jewish literature which are held to have Hebrew or Aramaic originals. But we may not on this basis posit a general Jewish custom of addressing God as, and naming him, "Lord". That the danger of such generalizations is not a figment of the imagination for our enquiry is shown by Buber, who regards "the realization of the all-embracing kingdom of God" as "Israel's beginning and end".[11] No longer can the Old Testament and intertestamental periods be represented as the history of the kingdom of God until Jesus Christ, as E. König did in 1908. Equally, all pre-Christian eschatology from exilic times to the late hellenistic and Roman periods cannot be placed under the heading, "the kingdom of God", as was attempted by A. Freiherr von Gall in 1926.

As Dalman, more than anyone else, has shown in his investigations, there are "various contexts" (102) in which our term appears in the New Testament, and these correspond linguistically again and again to expressions, to some extent apocalyptic but for the most part rabbinic, which deal with the "(life of the) future age". Can one draw any conclusions from this fact about the "substantive relation" (134) between this "age" and "God's kingdom"? Hardly. And whether, on the other hand, one can maintain with Vielhauer ([1957] 77f.) and Vögtle (146) that Jesus "substituted" the concept of the kingdom of God for the apocalyptic age concept and thereby "exploded the time scheme of the doctrine of the two ages", depends not only on the antiquity of such apocalyptic speculation but also on the solution of other problems, namely the relationships of the kingdom of God to the messianic kingdom and to the Son of Man (Vielhauer). We will examine these questions and interconnections as they appear within Judaism.

II *The Time and the Sources*

Historical information and background about the history of Judaism will be mentioned within this study only insofar as they are significant for an appreciation of the texts. It must first be stressed that the New Testament itself, whose pre-history is our special concern, must be regarded as a source of information concerning the Jewish concept of the "royal rule of God".[12] In most NT passages dealing with the kingdom, the Christian reinterpretation, designed to highlight Jesus, has such a strong effect – on the language, structure and content – that only its frequent mention gives an indirect indication that the royal rule of God was rather firmly rooted in the conceptions of Jews both in Palestine and in the Diaspora. Although it was by no means homogeneous, Palestinian Judaism provides the background against which the Baptist and Jesus taught and from which they both came. The earliest synoptic tradition grew up there, was handed down there, and coalesced there. But hellenistic Judaism, in Syria, Asia Minor, perhaps Rome, and presumably even (to a certain extent) in bilingual Palestine as well, provides – at least in part – the intended audience to which the Gospels as a whole were directed in the years around 70 A.D. and in the subsequent decades. These introductory facts are significant insofar as they determine our choice of relevant sources. The close of the first century A.D. should be set as the upper time limit of our analysis, at the end of what we now call early Judaism, whose demise was assured by defeat in the war with Rome.[13] The *terminus a quo* should be regarded as Ezra at the beginning of the fourth century B.C., in the so-called late post-exilic period,[14] but it must be stressed that our texts barely go back any further than the second century B.C. The end of early Judaism corresponds to the period when the OT canon was finally determined.[15] Yet it could be suggested that writings of this triple canon – or rather, most of them – had always had a fundamental effect within Judaism from the very beginning. Here was the reservoir of revelation from which, then as now, the enquiring, thinking Jew learns about God, discovers himself, and lets his actions be regulated. Nevertheless, we are not concerned here with a historical investigation and account of passages, especially since it is clearly a question of extremely ancient traditions with long-forgotten settings in life. This is not the place to examine the problem of the origins and interpretation of Yahweh's kingship, important though it is for OT studies.[16] On the other hand, we can assume with some certainty that in the period until the OT canon was formed, those Jewish writings from the hellenistic or Roman period that are called "apocryphal" and "pseudepigraphal" – in contrast to canonical writings – were enthusiastically read (depending on the situation and faction concerned) as if they were part of revelation. The most splendid proof of this is in the writings of the people of Qumran. Thus we have noted the most important sources other than the Old Testament: (1) the writings and fragments of writings of the Essenes at Qumran, which are still being published;[17] (2) the Apocrypha and Pseudepigrapha of the Old Testament.[18] The historical and apologetic works of Flavius Josephus (born 37/8 in Jerusalem, died at the beginning of the second century) have nothing to offer for our enquiry. This is all the more regrettable, as Josephus gives a comprehensive description of Jewish parties in several places.[19] The works of Philo, the Greek-speaking Jewish philosopher from Alexandria (born *c.* 25 B.C., died sometime after 40 A.D.), are not much more instructive. His conception of the kingdom of God is thoroughly ethical: *basileia* is for him "a chapter from the doctrine of virtue. The true king is the wise man."[20] As is shown by Wis. 6:20 or 4 Macc. 2:23, some Jews before him had already begun to consider the concept ethically. Nevertheless, Philo's reinterpretations bear indirect witness to speculation in the Egyptian Diaspora about God's *basileia* (cf. *Spec. Leg.* I.207; IV.164; *Mut. Nom.* 135; *Som.* II.285; *Abr.* 261; *Rer. Div. Her.* 301; *Vit. Mos.* I.290). That gives us all the more reason to look in the sources we have mentioned for tendencies which carried on to the point that they are apparent in the New Testament, or were, on the other hand, discontinued. We should note that some of these sources also come from Egypt, e.g. the Wisdom of Solomon, 3 Maccabees (so-called), and the *Sibylline Oracles*.

Apart from the sources mentioned, are there any others? Yes and no. No, because the Talmud, Midrashim, Targums and Jewish prayers are products or collections which were not brought forth until after the NT period.[21] Yes, because in the tractates of the Mishnah, Tosefta, and of the Jerusalem and Babylonian Talmuds older Pharisaic and rabbinic traditions are preserved. It was long suspected that there were Targums (viz., Midrash-like translations of the Hebrew texts into Aramaic, the language of the people) in pre-Christian times, and now this has been proven by finds in caves four and eleven at Qumran.[22] The Jewish prayers expressing hope in the kingdom of God will be discussed in particular below. These remarks should suffice to encourage care and discretion in referring to the examples compiled by Billerbeck (1922), Dalman (1902) and Volz (1903);[23] these have given rise to attempts to systematize the material for the purpose of commenting on the preaching of the kingdom in the Synoptics. But the variety within early Judaism cannot be treated in the same way as the relatively homogeneous, orthodox rabbinic Judaism of the first five or six centuries of our era. Since not only the Aramaic-speaking[24] Jesus of Nazareth (and before him, most probably, John the Baptist) proclaimed the *malkūt šāmayim*, but also his followers, and finally the writers of the Synoptic Gospels, who spoke and wrote about God's kingdom (assimilating the original message and working out their own version of it), we should let the Jewish background sources speak for themselves. In this essay, it is not intended to exegete New Testament statements and comment upon them as an historian of religions might.[25] Rather, we are concerned primarily only at the level of language and concept with the Jew in Palestine and in the hellenistic Diaspora, and in this sense we will examine the Jewish background of the synoptic concept, the "royal rule of God".

III *The Texts of Various Jewish Factions*

Both in working through and describing the sources we should recognize the "plurality of direction within early Judaism"[26] which began to form as early as the early post-exilic period "in Palestine and in the Diaspora".[27] As there are no guide-lines to hand for classifying the texts concerning the kingdom of God, it seems both appropriate and sensible to classify the texts according to their origins in the various groupings within Judaism. Only then can their contexts and special concerns be preserved, at least initially. Attention should, of course, be given to the genres and thematic emphases of the literature, especially when one is concentrating on a particular problem. It is impossible to fit all the extant material into the small space available here. The representative selection which has been made attempts, in discussing the documents, to preserve chronological order, insofar as that is known from the by no means certain historical evidence we possess.

1 *The Kingdom of God in Apocalyptic Writing*[28]

(a) As in the subsequent sections, brief note will be taken of the writings in which the royal rule of God plays no part: *Martyrdom of Isaiah, Baruch* (Greek), *Enoch* (Slavonic), 4 Ezra, *Baruch* (Syriac).[29] The last two are related to one another, and were written in Palestine towards the end of the first century A.D.; the absence of kingdom references in them is especially important because they ascribe overwhelming significance to, among other things, the scheme of the two ages,[30] and the coming of the messianic king or judge,[31] otherwise called "(son of) man".[32] The messiah of Judah is also the object of hope in the *Testaments of the Twelve Patriarchs*,[33] and above all in the *Testament of Judah* (cf. also *T. Reuben* 6:12 and *T. Iss.* 5:7). The *Testaments* do speak in some places of the eschatological theophany (*T. Simeon* 6:5; *T. Levi* 8:10; *T. Naph.* 8:1ff.). But only *T. Dan.* 5:13 and *T. Benj.* 9:1; 10:7 make explicit reference to God's "royal rule". While this last passage (after the injunction of the law) does promise that the king of heaven (*basileus tōn ouranōn*) will be worshipped at the resurrection, *T. Dan* 5:10–13, with its obviously Christian revision, announces the holy eschatological war against Beliar. Excluding its later additions, this "apocalyptic poem" reads as follows:[34]

> And he himself (God) will make war against Beliar
> and will exact victorious revenge from his enemies.
> And he will take the prisoners from Beliar.
> And he will turn the disobedient hearts to the Lord.
> And he will grant eternal peace to those who call on him.
> And the saints will repose in Eden,
> and the just will rejoice over the new Jerusalem.
> And Jerusalem will no longer endure desolation,
> nor will Israel remain in captivity,
> for the Lord will be among them
> and the holy one of Israel will be king over them (*basileuōn*).[35]

This proclamation of the eschatological kingdom of God certainly refers to OT promises,[36] and in a thoroughly apocalyptic context. Nonetheless, one looks in vain for references to the Messiah or to the two ages. Whatever the "main theme"[37] of the original might have been, it was certainly not the motif of God's royal rule.

(b) Before we attempt to look at the rest of the apocalyptic corpus, a brief word is in order in respect of the Book of Daniel,[38] the literary model for all later apocalyptic writings. This pseudonymous work in two parts (chaps. 1–6 and 7–12) was written in the Maccabean period, around 165 B.C. It is saturated with wisdom motives and expresses the hope of "God's intervention in establishing his royal rule"[39] only in the first part (2:44f.; 3:33; 4:31; 6:26). In the important and central seventh chapter, there is mention of the *malkūt* of the "son of man" (7:13f.) and of the *malkūt* of the people of the "saints of the most high" (7:18, 22, 27). Dan. 2:4–7:28 is, as is well known, written in so-called "Imperial Aramaic", yet it is interesting that *malkūt* is in synonymous parallelism with *šaltan* (rule, authority, kingdom), which – as in Syriac – has a much more general meaning,[40] and that it always appears in short hymns (3:33; 4:31; 6:26) which praise the "king of heaven" (4:34). In the same context, i.e. 4:23, "heaven" is equivalent to God. The point of the passages in this chapter is the principle, so basic to the Old Testament and Jewish thought, that the most high is ruler over the *malkūt* of mankind (4:14, 22f., 29, 31). The author or compiler of this story cycle[41] intended God's own *malkūt* to be similarly understood as ruled exclusively by him. The wisdom aspect is evident in Nebuchadnezzar's restoration to his kingship, albeit in a modified form, because he recognizes God's rule (4:23f.). Chapter 2 and chapter 7 are parallel to a certain extent, in that the court legends of the first part are clearly connected with the genuinely apocalyptic vision in the second part. If we are right in saying that the stone (2:34ff.) in the vision of chapter 2 can be interpreted as God's own, eternal and indestructible royal rule (2:44f.),[42] and if this accurately sheds light on the eschatology of the Maccabean era, then it is all the more striking that in chapter 7, the "crossroads of the book of Daniel",[43] the *malkūt* is promised to the son of man and the saints of the most high. It is an open question whether this is a doublet, and whether the saints can be harmonized with the son of man. The eschatological crisis here is really the same, and as acute, as in chapter 2 (viz., the tyranny of the Seleucid monarch, Antiochus IV Epiphanes), and the *malkūt* is expressly described as being "bestowed" by God (7:13, 27). Nonetheless, the writer avoids saying precisely that "the final victory of *God's* government is imminently impending".[44] In other words, the royal rule of God and of the son of man (and of the holy people) are separate complexes which should be kept apart. This distinction, established in the early period, is most easily seen in the later Apocalypses (see above on 4 Ezra).

(c) The Jewish sections of the *Sibylline Oracles* come from different times (between the second century B.C. and the first century A.D.) and from several authors among Egypt's hellenistic Jewish population. They are primarily interested in propagandizing monotheism as against idolatry, the Torah as against moral degeneration, and the utopian dominance of the Jewish nation as against all other nations.[45] Certainly, it would be wrong to attempt to classify the whole of this collection as apocalyptic; it is often hard to understand, sometimes meaningless, and in any case it gives the impression of being an incomplete work. The third book in particular, however, contains "relatively early documents of an apocalyptic origin".[46] Some passages originate from the middle of the second century B.C., and speak of the eschatological adoration of the great God, the immortal king (III.616f., 716f., with reference also to the law of the most high God). In close textual and substantive connection there is an eschatological promise, which certainly does not relate to the messianic kingdom, as Riessler (1328) or Lanchester (in Charles, *Apocrypha and Pseudepigrapha* II, 372) maintain, but rather to the coming royal rule of God: "And then he will erect a kingdom for all ages, over all men, he, who once gave the holy law to the pious, to whom he promised to confer the whole earth, and the world and the gates of the blessed and all joys and an immortal spirit and a happy heart." The Temple will then become once more the centre of worship of God, while everlasting peace will cover the earth. "The prophets (!) of the great God will take away the sword; for they themselves are judges of mortals and just kings. There will also be just riches among men; for that is the judgement and the rule (the kingdom) of the great God." A few lines later there is an oracle about the apocalyptic signs by which the "end of all things on earth" can be recognized. Finally, everyone is again called to make sacrifice to the great king (III.767ff., 796ff., 807). A typically Jewish characteristic is the emphasis on the Torah and the Temple, but this eschatological portrait of God's rule is surprisingly unrestricted and denationalized. The accent on the prophets underlines the eschatological, but thoroughly earthly, peace which goes with God's *basileia*.

We get chronologically nearer to the New Testament with III.46–56, which cannot possibly date "from the early Maccabean period".[47] In its much more pessimistic verses we read:

> But if Rome also comes to rule over Egypt, then the most great kingdom of the immortal king will show itself to mankind. A holy ruler (king) will come and govern the whole world in eternity. And then relentless wrath upon the men of Italy; three will bring Rome to ruin by a terrible fate. All people will die in their own homes, when a stream of fire flows down from heaven. Woe to the poorest! When will that day come, and the judgement of the immortal God, the great king?

In a typically apocalyptic manner, the affliction of the end time is painted in fine detail. Although the syncretistic apocalyptist does yearn for God's kingdom through the literary form of the oracle, this does not mean that the concept is typically apocalyptic. Just as Gnosticism, Apocalyptic possesses an amazing power of assimilation, as is attested in no small measure by the many forms and wide diffusion of this religious phenomenon in the history of the late hellenistic period.

(*d*) Turning again to Qumran, we now come to that apocalyptic literature which comes "from the sphere of influence of the Qumran group".[48] In the more ancient passages of *Enoch* (Ethiopic), God is repeatedly praised as the eternal king, the "king who has ultimate dominion over the measureless time of the world".[49] There are noticeable connections with his role as creator, on which his power over the world and (this is where the emphasis lies) his judgement of the world are founded (9:4f.; 12:3; 25; 27:3; 81:3). The emphasis in the old "Apocalypse of Ten Weeks" is also on the twofold judgement (93 and 91:12–17). In general terms the same can be said of the Ethiopic *Enoch* as holds for 4 Ezra and the Syriac *Baruch*: where the religion of the Torah and apocalyptic eschatology have such a close connection, the idea of judgement is not only pre-eminent, but at the same time inexorable. The "Similitudes" (chapters 37–71) probably date from the first century B.C. (not the second century A.D., as has also been argued); they are of extraordinary religio-historical significance for the understanding of the Messiah, of the son of man, his nature and his tasks (judgement!), of his kingdom after the resurrection of the dead, etc. Here we can only say that, as is the case in Daniel 7 (see above), they do not deal with God's royal rule, and that is why one should not speak of "the eternal kingdom of God of the Jewish Messiah".[50] The idea that God, the almighty and eternal, is lord over all heavenly and earthly powers and forces occurs so commonly within Judaism that we could use the Similitudes of the Ethiopic *Enoch* to define the kingdom of God in the Synoptics only in the most general way.

The book of *Jubilees*, dating from around 100 B.C., should perhaps not be counted as belonging to apocalyptic literature in the strict sense.[51] But the passage at 50:9, describing the sabbath as the day of the holy royal rule, is interesting. Of course, the whole book does revolve around the sabbath and the law, even if eschatology plays an important role, both in the positive sense of salvation (1:15ff.; 4:23ff.; 25:20ff.; 30:21; 31:32; 36:1; 50:5) and in the negative sense of judgement (4:19ff.; 5:10ff.; 7:29; 9:15; 10:1ff.; 16:9; 21:4; 22:22; 24:29ff.). One would look in vain, whether in these individual passages or in the longer eschatological text of chapter 23, for any mention of God's *basileia* – with the exception of 1:28.

The Essene apocalyptist who wrote the so-called *Assumption of Moses* shortly before the end of the first century B.C. was concerned in chapters 7–10 with the "dawning of God's rule":[52]

> And then his kingdom will appear over all creatures; then there will be no Satan any more and no sorrow ... The heavenly one will rise from his seat of dominion and step forth from his heavenly dwelling in anger and indignation on account of his children. Then the earth will tremble ... and the sun give no more light ... and the sea will retreat ... For the most high God, the only eternal one, will arise, will come forward openly to punish the heathen and to annihilate all their idols. Then you will be happy, my Israel ... And God will exalt you and install you in the starry heavens. Then you will look down from above and see your enemies on earth and recognize them and rejoice and give thanks and declare your faith in your creator.

What stood for "kingdom" (Latin: *regnum*) in the Semitic (probably Hebrew) original,[53] can only be hazarded now: probably it was *malkūt*. The creator will therefore assume once more his world-wide rule at the end of days, not only in such a way as to destroy all other spiritual and political powers, but also by freeing his people, Israel. On the other hand, the omission of a Messiah and of a messianic kingdom evidences an anti-Zealot quietism; chapter 7 manifests an anti-Sadducean tendency. For these reasons, many scholars have supposed that the writer was a Pharisee,[54] but recently the old idea has won new acceptance that he was an Essene, an unknown Palestinian author using the pseudonym "Moses" who wished to procure boundless respect for the law. His work would therefore join the many Qumran writings which help invaluably "to shed light on the religious climate before Jesus' public ministry".[55] It is highly questionable, however, whether the "theocratic kingdom" in the writer's understanding (as Charles thinks, II, 412) is to be established by keeping the Torah: the royal rule of God is expected rather on the basis of its own, self-effecting appearance – an idea which is thoroughly apocalyptic.

2 *God's Royal Rule in the Qumran Scrolls*

The *Damascus Document* and the *Habakkuk Commentary*, which are so significant for the "Teacher of righteousness", are quite unimportant for our enquiry. The extensive canon of the sect only once mentions the dominion (*mamšāl*) of the God who gave the law (1QS IX.24), and in contrast to Belial's dominion (I.18, 23f.; II.19). The entire (albeit badly damaged) hymn scroll praises God as king only in one passage (1QH X.8), and this is but one prayer formula among many others, as is shown by 1Q*Genesis Apocryphon* II.4ff. The eschatological midrash to Exodus 15.17 in 4Q*florilegium* 1.3 is evidence that the Old Testament expression, "May Yahweh be king for ever and ever", was popular not only among the rabbis. So of all the writings from Qumran only the *War Scroll* really remains as a testimony to or reference to God's royal rule. Even here in 1QM it is not a dominant theme, as can be said of the Qumran finds as a whole. What is important is that even in the *War Scroll* the messianic expectation of Qumran[56] is not expressed at all. Of course the eschatological *malkūt* of the people of Israel is mentioned more than once, in XII.3, 16 and in its doublet XIX.8 (cf. 1QSb III.5; IV.26; V.21), cf. X.12 (the rule of the saints) and XVII.8 (Israel's dominion; in both cases the Hebrew reads *memšālā*). All these passages allude to Exod. 19:6, an OT text which was taken up elsewhere in Jewish literature; this is a matter for discussion in itself. Israel's rule or kingship will begin when the utopian, holy war against the dualistic opponents (Belial, the Kittim, the sons of darkness and falsehood) is fought victoriously. Then the "king of kings" (XIV. 16, as reconstructed from 4QMa), the "king of honour" (XII.8, cf. XIX.1) – that is, the God of Israel – will regain his *malkūt* (VI.6; XII.7) and "he will exercise his power through the holy ones of his people" (VI.6). Even in XII.7, the dominion of God (*'el*) and Israel's eternal dominion are in close textual (see above) and thematic connection. One could say in this context that the kingdom of Israel, restoring itself – without any messianic king – from the nucleus of the Qumran "union",[57] is, or will be, the kingdom of God. However, because of the lack of corroborating evidence for this pattern in the *War Scroll* among literary parallels, we are not able to apply it generally, either to the Qumran sect or to Judaism as a whole. That a nationalistic folk identity formed the third pillar, so to speak, on which early Judaism was based (along with the uniqueness of God, the "Lord", and the value of the law) constitutes a wide-ranging topic which is not our immediate concern in this discussion.

3 *God as King of Heaven and Earth in Hellenistic Judaism*

The apocalyptic literature in this category (Slavonic *Enoch* and parts of the *Sibylline Oracles*) has already been discussed. The *Letter of Aristeas*, with its political philosophy,[58] has no room for the concept of the *basileia tou Theou*. The diatribe (according to E. Norden) called 4 Maccabees, written in the first Christian century by a Greek Jew loyal to the law, reminds one of Philo in 2:21ff.: the wise man stoically following the law is king (cf. 7:10). Even here there is no trace of God's *basileia*.

(*a*) God as King in the Jewish Wisdom Literature.
The reason for which God's royal rule plays such a minute role in the more recent Wisdom literature lies partially in the fact that it is mentioned nowhere in the older biblical Wisdom material (Job, Proverbs, Ecclesiastes). Only in Ecclesiasticus[59] and in the "Pagan Narrative"[60] of 3 Esdras (or 1 Esdras in the Septuagint) do we come across the prayerful address of God as king which was so very popular in early Judaism. Even in the Wisdom of Solomon,[61] God's kingdom is not a central theme.

(*b*) "King" as a Prayerful Address in the rest of the Apocrypha.
Praise of God in hymns and supplications as the king of creation (Judith 9), the eternal and great king of heaven (Tobit 13) or as the king of the universe (in the Additions to Esther) actually occurs relatively infrequently, when judged against the extent of the whole corpus. Much more important than this scarcity is the fact that the word "king" is regularly just one designation for God among many others that occur in these very verbose prayers, as the two prayers in 3 Macc. 2:2ff. and 6:2f. illustrate. It must be stressed that all these prayers from the last two centuries B.C. have no eschatological colouring whatsoever. That applies also to the entire literature into which they have been integrated. God's universal governance in the past, present and future is based finally on his sole power as creator, but it is only really effective when obedience to the Mosaic and Jewish law is achieved. Torah and its various expositions keep the one people of the one Lord together and at the same time divide them into religious movements and sociological groupings. The subdivision of early Judaism according to other (e.g., "eschatological" or "apoc-alyptic") principles is secondary.

4 *The Royal Rule of God in Pharisaic and*
  Early Rabbinic Witnesses

(*a*) God's kingdom in Pharisaic Writings.
Even if, when compared to 1 Maccabees, the historical value of 2 Maccabees is not all that great as regards the events it depicts concerning Judas Maccabeus, "the book, perhaps dating from the early years of the Christian era, still has a historical value as regards its own period which should not be underrated".[62] In addition to its theme of "Loyalty to the law" which is "an attitude precisely remini-

scent of Pharisaism",[63] there are also other characteristics which not only betray signs of Pharisaic bias, but also exhibit "important connections with the New Testament"[64] that go beyond anything in the Old Testament. In this context, belief in the resurrection, as is expressed in the stirring climax of the narrative (the passage from 6:18 to 7:42), should be mentioned. The hope of the (bodily) resurrection for those who keep the law and fear God (6:23, 30; 7:2, 9, 11, 14, 23f., 28f.) appears to be closely related to the concept of "the creation out of nothing", and could even be regarded as grounded precisely in this concept. The writer (or "*epitomator*") ascribes the strength to allow oneself to be murdered, maimed and burnt to the conviction that such readiness has to do with the "king of the world" (*tou kosmoubasileus*, 7:9) when enacted in obedience to the law of Moses (*nomos*, more frequently *nomoi*), the "holy legislation established by God" (*nomothesia*, 6:23; 7:30). Chapter 7 could even be headed: "God, the king of the world, in the struggle against the godless, inhuman temporal king, Antiochus". The universal kingship of the God of Israel therefore includes his creation and his eschatological power to raise the dead, as well as his sovereignty as the lawgiver and the just judge (e.g. 12:6).

The second letter (1:10–2:18) in the first part of 2 Maccabees – probably "a fictional epistle"[65] – contains a priestly sacrificial prayer (1:24–9). This is an expression of the Jewish faith and hope in being freed and gathered together again, and it shows very well how the theological sovereign title *basileus* is only one name for God among many others. This is perfectly typical of Jewish discourse about and to God. The prayer is, moreover, quite representative in content of the theology of the whole of 2 Macc.:

> Lord, Lord God, creator of all things, dreadful and powerful and just and merciful, you who alone is king and gracious, you who alone bestows all gifts, the only just and almighty and eternal one, you who saves Israel from all evil, who chose and sanctified the fathers, accept the sacrifice for the whole of your people Israel and protect your inheritance and make it holy. Bring those of us who have been scattered together. Free those who are in servitude among strange peoples. Look mercifully on the despised and detested, and the strange peoples will recognize that you are our God. Punish those who oppress us and who raise themselves up in arrogance. Plant your people once more in your holy place, as Moses promised.

Even if it is controversial whether Pharisaic circles stand behind the *Psalms of Solomon*,[66] it is certain that these basically homogeneous hymns constitute an "outstanding source for the mood within Palestinian Judaism"[67] just before the birth of Jesus. Historical and eschatological concepts of judgement (for the godless, the Sadducees?)[68] and of salvation (for the pious, the Pharisees?) run right through the collection. As is well known, *Pss.* 17 and 18 are very important for our understanding of Jewish "Christology";[69] they concern the kingship and judicial functions of the eagerly awaited Davidic Messiah. While God, the judge and saviour, is called our "king" as early as 2:30, 32 and 5:18f., the same is true for the beginning and end of *Ps.* 17:

> Lord, you yourself are our king forever and ever:
> in you, God, our soul rejoices.
> What, then, is the length of a man's life on earth?
> Just so long is his hope in him.
> But we put our hope in God, our saviour:
> and the power of our God (lasts) forever with mercy, and
> the kingdom of our God (stands) forever
> over the peoples in judgement.
>
> May God make his mercy come over Israel;
> may he rescue us from the defilement of unholy enemies.
> The Lord himself is our king forever and ever.

The OT source (Exod. 15:18) of the hymn's affirmation of the eternal royal rule of God is absolutely clear. What is problematic here – and as far as I know it is altogether unique – is the literary connection with the Messiah/king, who is introduced in 17:4:

> You, Lord, have chosen David as king over Israel and you have sworn to him concerning his descendants for all time, that his kingdom should not cease before you.

Hopeful messianic prospects are offered again and again with obvious traces of utopianism alongside important allusions to the history of the period. How are the royal rule of God and the royal rule of the Messiah related? The author has solved this question quite elegantly, by subordinating (in 17:34) the Messiah – who should really govern the people of Israel – to the Lord (Yahweh): "The Lord himself is his king".

(*b*) The Present and Future of the *malkūt šāmayim* (Yahweh) according to Early Rabbinic Traditions.
The rabbinic material can be found collected in the helpful handbooks compiled by Billerbeck, Dalman and Moore.[70] These compilations do, however, pose enormous methodological and hermeneutical problems for any critical researcher who is particularly interested in the provenance of the early traditions. In all honesty, we must leave three questions open:

1   How well established was the trend toward abstract terminology in the first Christian century?
2   How strong in this period was the tendency to use the stereotyped language of later rabbinic literature (viz. "the yoke of God's rule")?
3   What status did the coming age/life of (or in) the coming age have in early rabbinic expectations for the future?

None of these three questions poses any problem as regards later developments, as is proven by the countless references in the sources. What we can say with certainty for the (earlier) period in question is that Palestinian Pharisees and scribes used to talk about God as king and of his royal rule. Further, it is clear that this kingdom had a twofold aspect. Both aspects – of the present and of the eschatological future – are grounded in and connected with the self-revelation of the one God and of the Torah which this revelation enjoins, and at most only secondarily with the concept of creation. The aspect which is related more to the present comes to expression when a Jew takes God's rule on himself and submits to the yoke of the royal rule of God "by professing monotheism and the Torah",[71] and this is to be identified with the recitation of the *š⁰ma* (Deut. 6:4–9; 11:13–21; Num. 15:37–41). There are some examples from the period around 100 A.D. both for treating the fundamental confession "of Israel to the *one* God and to his commandments"[72] as equivalent to the expression "taking the yoke of God's royal rule on oneself", and for this expression itself. A few rabbinic dicta and prayer texts seem to express the eschatological hope of the same period, or perhaps a few decades earlier, that – as promised (again) in Exod. 15:18 – Yahweh might enter upon his royal rule (soon) before the eyes of all. The Eighteen Benedictions, which are probably ancient,[73] express this hope in the eleventh petition: "Be king over us, you alone." The whole prayer must be read before one can say with K. G. Kuhn that, "although the petition about the royal rule does appear in the Eighteen Benedictions, it is not central, but is rather one point along with others within the whole framework of the eschatological drama",[74] as is portrayed in the second section (petitions 10–14). The climax of the eschatological section of the Eighteen Benedictions is the petition concerning the *malkūt* of the Messiah from the house of David, while the first section, with its orientation to the present (petitions 4–9), begins characteristically with the "petition for knowledge of the Torah and understanding of the Torah as God's gracious gift. For the Jew, knowledge of the law was the precondition for religious existence as such."[75]

Michael Lattke

NOTES

1 Vögtle, *Das Neue Testament und die Zukunft des Kosmos* (1970) 143.

2 Dalman (1902) 91.

3 Ibid., similarly, R. Schnackenburg, "Basileia" in *LTK* II 25.

4 Str-B I, 183.

5 K. G. Kuhn, *TDNT* I, 571–4.

6 Cf. K. Galling and H. Conzelmann (1961) 912.

7 On this point, cf. H. Kleinknecht in *TDNT* I, 562f., J. B. Bauer (ed.), *Encyclopedia of Biblical Theology* (1970) 455ff.

8 Dalman (1902) 94; similarly Str-B I, 172f.

9 H. Conzelmann (1961) 915.

10 K. Thieme, "Reich Gottes", in *LTK* VIII, 1110.

11 M. Buber (1967) 58 (German original 1932, but this from preface to 3rd edn 1956).

12 This is repeatedly stressed by J. Maier, *Geschichte jüdischen Religion* (1972) 39 etc.

13 J. Maier and J. Schreiner (ed.), *Literatur und Religion des Frühjudentums* (1973) 1ff.

14 So G. Fohrer, *History of Israelite Religion* (1972) 337ff.

15 Cf. Eissfeldt, *Introduction to the Old Testament*, 560–74.

16 Cf. Schnackenburg (1963) 11–40; also RGG3³ 1706–9 and 1712–14.

17 E. Lohse, *Die Texte aus Qumran, herbräisch und deusch* (1964); A. Dupont-Sommer, *Die essenischen Schriften vom Toten Meer* (1960); J. Maier and K. Schubert, *Die Qumran-Essener: Texte der Schriftrollen und Lebensbild der Gemeinde* (1973). Prof. K. Schubert of the Jewish Institute at Vienna University stated in a letter that he used the much-used phrase "the kingdom of God" to refer to "the general expectation in the sense of imminent eschatology".

18 Cf. the editions of the Apocrypha and Pseudepigrapha of Kautsch, Charles and Riessler. Since 1973 W. G. Kümmel has been editing *Jüdische Schriften aus hellenistisch-römischer Zeit* (*JSHRZ*). See Eissfeldt, *Introduction* (1965) 571ff.

19 Cf. the "General Index" in the ninth volume of Josephus' works in the Loeb Classical Library (London: 1965). One particular passage, *Bell.* II 118, deserves attention: where it says of Judas, the founder of the Zealots, that he "called it a disgrace that they (the Galileans) should continue paying taxes to the Romans and tolerate any mortal master after having God for their Lord". Cf. the text with notes in O. Michel and O. Bauernfeind, *Der jüdische Krieg (griechisch und deutsch* (1962) I, 204f., 430f. Prof. M. Hengel of Tübingen has informed me by letter that Josephus' reticence is understandable in terms of his overall tendency to suppress the eschatological hope of Judaism because of its political risk. In reports of the sects of Judas the Galilean (Zealots and Sicarii) there is clear and consistent reference to the "rule of God"; Jesus' teaching should be contrasted sharply with this political rule of God. More precise details can be found in M. Hengel, *Die Zeloten* (1961). See also *Josephus-Studien* Festschrift O. Michel (1974), 175–96.

20 K. L. Schmidt, "*basileia* (*tou Theou*) in hellenistic Judaism", in *TDNT* I, 576.

21 On the entire complex, cf. H. L. Strack, *Einleitung in Talmud und Midrasch* (1921⁵).

22   Cf. Eissfeldt, *Introduction*, 696–8; E. Sellin and G. Fohrer, *Einleitung in das AT* (1965¹⁰), 566f.; E. Würthwein, *The Text of the Old Testament* (1979) 75–9.

23   In 1934 edn of Volz, see 165–73; also W. Bousset and H. Gressmann, *Die Religion des Judentums im späthellenistischen Zeitalter* (1966⁴), especially 213ff.

24   So also A. Vögtle, "Jesus Christus nach den geschichtlichen Quellen", in *LTK* V, 922–32, 924.

25   In fact it would then be "wrong to scrutinize the breadth of apocryphal and rabbinic literature, the writings of Jewish Hellenism and of the particular parties, purely on the basis of the expression 'God's rule' ", as Schnackenburg (1963) 41 cautions.

26   J. Maier, *Geschichte*, 5.

27   G. Fohrer, *History of Israelite Religion* (1972) 307ff.

28   Cf. in addition to the literature already cited: H. H. Rowley, *The Relevance of Apocalyptic* (1944); J. Schreiner, *Alttestamentliche Apokalyptik* (1969); Koch, *The Rediscovery of Apocalyptic* (1972, German 1970); Schmithals, *The Apokalyptic Movement* (1975, German 1974).

29   As well as "almighty", which is often used as a designation for God, we should also note such passages as *2 Apoc. Bar.* 48:7; 54:13f.; 75:7f.; 83:7, which speak of the rule of the creator, law-giver and judge. In contrast, cf. 48:2 and 82:4 (the declining rule of the ages, or of the peoples).

30   4 Ezra 4:26f., 36; 6:7, 20, 55; 7:11–13, 31, 47, 50, 113; 8:1, 52; 9:13; 11:44; cf. also the apocalyptic signs in 5:1–13; 6:11–28 and 9:1–6; *2 Apoc. Bar.* 14:13; 15:17f.; 32:6; 44:11–15, 48:50; 51:3; 74:2; 83:8; cf. references to the end of times in 6:8; 13:3; 19:5; 21:8; 29:8; 30:3; 54:21; 70:2; 76:2, 5.

31   4 Ezra 7:26–9, 33–44, 70; 12:31–4; *2 Apoc. Bar.* 25–7; 29:3–30:5; 39:3–40:4; 70:2ff.; 72:2; 73.

32   4 Ezra 13:1ff., 23ff.; cf. also Dan. 7 and the similitudes of the Ethiopic *Enoch*.

33   J. Becker *JSHRZ* (n. 18) III.1 (translation and commentary).

34   J. Becker, *Untersuchungen zur Entstehungsgeschichte der Testamente der zwölf Patriarchen* (1970) 404.

35   For the Greek text with critical apparatus, cf. R. H. Charles, *The Greek Versions of the Testaments of the Twelve Patriarchs* (1908, reprint Darmstadt: 1966) 139.

36   Cf. the exposition in Schnackenburg (1963) 1–22, especially §3 regarding "the eschatological kingship of Yarweh", 14f.

37   J. Becker (*JSHRZ* [n. 18] III.1, 27) thinks the radicalized "commandment to love" is the "main theme"; Charles (II, 292f.) thinks – more correctly, in my view – it is "forgiveness".

38   A. Bentzen, *Daniel* (1952²); O. Plöger, *Das Buch Daniel* (1965); N. W. Porteus, *Daniel* (1965). Important observations on Daniel chaps. 2 and 7 are made by P. v. d. Osten-Sacken in *Die Apokalyptik in ihrem Verhältnis zu Prophetie und Weisheit* (1969).

39   Porteus, 16.

40   Cf. W. Gesenius–F. Buhl, *Hebräisches und aramäisches Handwörter* (1921¹⁷) 928.

41   A. Bentzen, 6.

42   So O. Plöger, 54; A. Bentzen, 6. N. W. Porteus, 48f., holds the writer is already thinking of chap. 7, and therefore of "Israel's kingdom".

43 N. W. Porteus, 95.

44 Against A. Bentzen, 6.

45 Cf. the similar conclusions of H. C. O. Lanchester in the Charles edition (II, 374f.); F. Blass in the Kautzsch edition (II, 179 and elsewhere); Eissfeldt, *Introduction*, 615; Schmithals, *Apocalyptic*, 191.

46 Schmithals, *Apocalyptic*, 191.

47 Against Rost, *Einleitung*, 85, and H. C. O. Lanchester in Charles II, 371. With Eissfeldt, *Introduction*, 616 and F. Blass in Kautzsch II, 183, a later insertion (at the end of the first century B.C.) is to be seen in verses 36–92; cf. also Volz (1903) 47.

48 This is the classification of, among others, Rost, *Einleitung*, 98ff.

49 Dalman opposes the translation "king of the world" proposed by G. Beer in Kautzsch II, 243 and elsewhere. Cf. (1902) 164.

50 Against Beer, *op. cit.*, 265 note t.

51 Cf. Schmithals, *Apokalyptic*, 200, n. 45.

52 Eissfeldt, *Introduction*, 623.

53 Cf. Rost, *Einleitung*, 110; Riessler, 1301; Eissfeldt, *Introduction*, 624.

54 C. Clemen in Kautzsch II, 314f.; Charles II, 407ff.

55 Rost, *Einleitung*, 112.

56 1QS IX.II; *Dam.* XII.23–XIII.1; XIV.19; XIX.10f.; XX.1; 1QSa II.12, 20; 4Qflor 10f.; 4QPatr 1–4 (connected with the rule, *mimšal*, of Israel).

57 "A common self-designation" of the people of Qumran in all the great manuscripts, cf. J. Maier (n. 17) 143, note b.

58 Cf. H. T. Andrews in Charles II, 89.

59 Sir. 51:1 (appendix), and the more recent gloss after 18:2; cf. V. Ryssel in Kautzsch I, 242ff., 318, 471.

60 On this special feature of Wisdom, cf. Eissfeldt, *Introduction*, 780f.; Rost, *Einleitung*, 72f.; H. Guthe in Kautzsch I, lff.

61 Wis. 3:8; 6:4; 10:10.

62 A. Kamphausen in Kautzsch I, 84.

63 Eissfeldt, *Introduction*, 581.

64 Rost, *Einleitung*, 61.

65 Ibid.

66 Eissfeldt, *Introduction*, 613 has grave doubts as to the Pharisaic origin.

67 R. Kittel in Kautzsch II, 128.

68 The identification, still accepted by R. Kittel, is today held in question, cf. Eissfeldt, *Introduction*, 612f.

69 Cf. H. Gunkel in Kautzsch II, 337.

70 G. F. Moore, *Judaism in the First Centuries of the Christian Era* (1927–30). K. G. Kuhn also makes reference to these compilations in *TDNT* I, 563, 573.

71 Str.B I, 173.

72 Cf. Excursus 9 in Str-B IV.1, 189–207.

73 Evidence of this is adduced in K. G. Kuhn, *Achtzehngebet und Vaterunser und der Reim* (1950) 10ff. Cf. also Excursus 10 in Str-B IV.1, 208–49.

74 K. G. Kuhn, *op. cit.*, 42, which should be compared to 25f.
75 *Op. cit.*, 14.

5

*Jesus and the Language of the Kingdom**

NORMAN PERRIN

The roots of the symbol kingdom of God lie in the ancient Near Eastern myth of the kingship of God. This "was taken over by the Israelites from the Canaanites, who had received it from the great kingdoms on the Euphrates and Tigris and Nile, where it had been developed as early as ancient Sumerian times."[1] In this myth the god had acted as king in creating the world, in the course of which he had overcome and slain the primeval monster. Further, the god continued to act as king by annually renewing the fertility of the earth, and he showed himself to be king of a particular people by sustaining them in their place in the world. This myth is common to all the peoples of the ancient Near East, and elements from one version of the myth were freely used in others. Essentially it is only the name of the god which changes as we move from people to people. In Babylonia Marduk is king; in Assyria, Asshur; in Ammon, Milcom; in Tyre, Melkart; in Israel, Yahweh.

A feature of this myth of the kingship of God was that it was celebrated annually in cultic ritual. In the ancient world life was seen as a constant struggle between good and evil powers, and the world as the arena of this struggle. So each winter threatened to become a permanent blight on the fertility of the earth; and each spring was a renewal of the primeval victory of the god over the monster, as each spring the god renews the fertility of the earth against the threat of his enemies and man's. It was this that was celebrated cultically in an annual New Year festival. In the cultic ritual of this festival the god became king as he re-enacted the primeval victory of creation; he acted as king as he renewed the fertility of the earth; his people experienced him as king as he entered once more into their lives.

* First published in *Jesus and the Language of the Kingdom* by Norman Perrin (1976) 16–32, 127–31, 197–9.

That ancient Israel learned to think of their god in this way, and to celebrate his kingship in this way, can be seen from the so-called enthronement psalms, Psalms 47, 93, 96, 97, 98, 99, with their constant refrain, "Yahweh has become king!", a cultic avowal often mistranslated, "The Lord reigns."[2]

Perrin's chapter 2A, "The Kingdom of God in Ancient Jewish Literature" (16–32), continues with quotations from the royal psalms and the earlier salvation–history traditions of the tribal confederacy (Deut. 26:5b–9). He sees these streams combined in Ps. 99:6–7, 136, and in the Pentateuch, and thus "the stage was set for the emergence of the symbol kingdom of God" (20) which evokes features of the salvation history. He quotes Ps. 145:10–14 and Exod. 15 to illustrate the meaning and use of kingdom (of God – though the phrase itself does not occur). God has brought his people to the Promised Land and to Mount Zion, to Jerusalem and the Temple. Perrin continues (22f.):

In all this God was acting as king, and it is to be expected that he will continue to act as king on behalf of his people: "The Lord shall reign for ever and ever."

In these early uses of the symbol we have a consistent myth, the myth of a God who created the world and was continually active in that world on behalf of his people, with the emphasis upon the continuing activity of God. The symbol functions by evoking the myth, and in turn the myth is effective because it interprets the historical experience of the Jewish people in the world. They knew themselves as the people who had successfully escaped from Egypt, who had settled in Canaan, who had built a temple to their God on Mount Zion. In their myth it was God who had done these things on their behalf, and by using the symbol in their songs of praise they evoke the myth and so celebrate their history as the people of God.

It is obvious that at this point I have begun to use the word myth in a particular way. Myth is a word that is notoriously difficult to define, but in the case of the myth of God acting as king I like Alan Watts' statement, as quoted by Philip Wheelwright: "Myth is to be defined as a complex of stories – some no doubt fact, and some fantasy – which, for various reasons, human beings regard as demonstrations of the inner meaning of the universe and of human life."[3] "A complex of stories – some no doubt fact, and some fantasy", that statement describes exactly the ancient Israelite people's understanding of their deliverance from Egypt, their conquest of Canaan, the bringing of the Ark to Mount Zion by David and the building of a temple there by Solomon. "A complex of stories ... which, for various reasons, human beings regard as demonstrations of the inner meaning of the

93

universe and of human life", that too describes exactly the Israelite understanding of life in the world as being under the direct control of the God who had acted as king on their behalf *and who would continue to do so*. The ancient Israelite people believed that their myth of the kingly activity of God demonstrated "the inner meaning of the universe" and gave them a true understanding of the nature of human life in the world. It is because they believed this that the symbol was so effective: it was effective precisely because it evoked the myth by means of which they had come to understand themselves as the people of God, the beneficiaries of his kingly activity in the world. The symbol is dependent upon the myth, and it is effective because of its power to evoke the myth. The myth in turn derives its power from its ability to make sense of the life of the Jewish people in the world.

With this understanding of things the historical destiny of the Jewish people in the world becomes an important factor in the functioning of the symbol and the effectiveness of the myth ...

> Perrin traces the history of Israel from Solomon on to show "the impact of these historical events upon the use of the symbol kingdom of God with its evocation of the myth of God active as king on behalf of his people in the world" (24). Prophets interpreted the events and so the myth maintained its force. Judgement and temporary reprieves were signs of God, still active on behalf of his people, and there was hope for a new act of God as king (Isa. 33:22; 52:7–11). When this hope is fulfilled, Zeph. 3:15 uses kingship language. But again "the events of history called into question the validity of the myth" (25), as the state again lost its independence under Persia and Syria and finally (63 B.C.) Rome. Perrin continues (26):

Under these circumstances the Jewish people continued to evoke the ancient myth, but now the formulations have a note of intensity about them, a note almost of despairing hope. In the *Assumption of Moses*, an apocalyptic work written shortly before the time of Jesus, we find the symbolic language of the kingdom of God used again to express the hopes of the people. The myth remains the same – that of God as king active on behalf of his people – and the symbol remains the same – it is God's kingdom that will appear – but the formulation has changed. On the one hand, the language has grown more metaphorical: "... Satan shall be no more, and sorrow shall depart with him...." "The Heavenly One will arise from his royal throne ... with indignation and wrath on account of his sons."

On the other hand, the hope itself is coming to take a form in which the expectation is for a dramatic change in the circumstances of the Jews over against the hated Gentiles. "The Most High will arise ... he will appear to punish the Gentiles ... Then thou, O Israel, shalt be happy ... God will exalt thee ... he will cause thee to approach the heaven of the stars ..."

This is the language of apocalyptic, as this is the apocalyptic hope, and there is some question as to what the apocalyptic writers actually expected. It has been pointed out, above all perhaps by Amos Wilder,[4] that apocalyptic imagery is a natural form of expression when one is in extreme circumstances, and Wilder himself has turned to it in poetry arising out of his combat experiences in the First World War. What one can say perhaps is that the extremity of the situation of the Jews under the Romans in Palestine after 63 B.C. escalated their use of language in the expression of the characteristic hope for the activity of God on their behalf, as it also created circumstances under which they were no longer sure what they hoped for – except that it was for a deliverance like those from Egypt and Babylon in the past, but this time a permanent deliverance from all the evils of history.

One particularly prominent form of this apocalyptic hope for a deliverance from history itself is that of the hope to begin a war against Rome in which God would intervene, and which God would bring to an end by destroying the Gentiles and their Jewish collaborators or sympathizers, and by creating a world transformed, a world in which "Satan and sin will be no more". Just how widespread and realistic this particular form of the apocalyptic hope was can be seen from the fact that the Jewish people rose in revolt against Rome in 66 A.D. and again in 132; both times they began a war against Rome in which they expected God to intervene, and which they expected God to bring to an end in victory for them as his people.

The people we have come to know through the Dead Sea Scrolls shared this hope. Indeed one of the Dead Sea Scrolls is a battle plan for this war against Rome, and all evil, the war in which God would intervene and which he would bring to victory on their behalf. This is the so-called War Scroll (1QM) and in it we find a use of the symbolic language of the kingdom of God. We read, "And to the God of Israel shall be the kingdom, and among his people will he display might", and, "Thou, O God, resplendent in the glory of thy kingdom ... [art] in our midst as a perpetual help" (1QM 6:6 and 12:7). In both instances the symbol kingdom of God is being used to express the hope, indeed the expectation, that God would act on behalf of his people by intervening in a war against Rome and the Roman legions. In this hope and expectation they began the war, but the war itself, contrary to their expectation, went the way of Rome and of the Roman legions.

One last use of the symbol in ancient Judaism remains to be

mentioned, the use in the Kaddish prayer, a prayer in regular use in the Jewish synagogues immediately before the time of Jesus, and for that matter still in use today. In an English translation of the ancient form, the prayer is as follows:

> Magnified and sanctified be his
>   great name in the world that he
>   has created according to his will.
> May he establish his kingdom in your
>   lifetime and in your days and in
>   the lifetime of all the house of
>   Israel, even speedily and at a
>   near time.

This is so close to a central petition of the prayer that Jesus taught his disciples,

> Hallowed be thy name
> Thy kingdom come

that the two must be related, and the most reasonable supposition is that the prayer of Jesus is a deliberate modification of the Kaddish prayer, a point to which I shall return below. But for the moment I wish to make the point that this is a use of the symbol in a prayer used regularly by the synagogue community *as a community*. The very fact that the symbol is being used in prayer by a whole group of people means that while it will always have evoked the myth of God active as king on behalf of his people, the form of the expectation expressed by the petition, "May he establish his kingdom", will have varied from individual to individual, and no doubt that for many Jews living in the period between Pompey's "settlement" of the East in 63 B.C. and the beginning of the Jewish revolt against Rome in 66 A.D. the prayer will have expressed the hope for the kind of dramatic irruption of God into human history that is the central theme of ancient Jewish (and Christian) apocalyptic. But it can never have been *limited* to the expression of that hope, for it is of the very nature of religious symbols that they are plurisignificant, that they can never be exhausted in any one apprehension of meaning; and this is, of course, true of most symbols.

Before we can make any final statement of the use of the symbol "kingdom of God" in ancient Jewish apocalyptic, therefore, we need to digress somewhat and discuss the nature and function of symbols altogether. We will do this in relationship to two modern discussions of symbols: Philip Wheelwright (1962), and Paul Ricoeur, *The Symbolism of Evil* (1969). This is a valid approach to the use of a particular symbol in ancient Jewish apocalyptic, and in the message of Jesus, for the nature and function of symbol are of the very stuff of language itself and do not change in essentials from language to language, or from age to age.

I will begin this digression on the nature and function of symbol with Philip Wheelwright's definition of a symbol: "A symbol, in general, is a relatively stable and repeatable element of perceptual experience, standing for some larger meaning or set of meanings which cannot be given, or not fully given, in perceptual experience itself" (92). A symbol therefore represents something else, and Wheelwright makes a most important distinction within symbols in terms of their relationship with that which they represent. A symbol can have a one-to-one relationship to that which it represents, such as the mathematical symbol *pi*, in which case it is, in Wheelwright's terms, a "steno-symbol", or it can have a set of meanings that can neither be exhausted nor adequately expressed by any one referent, in which case it is a "tensive symbol".

Paul Ricoeur makes a similar distinction. For Ricoeur a symbol is a sign, something which points beyond itself to something else. Not all signs are symbols, however, for sometimes a sign is transparent of meaning and is exhausted by its "first or literal intentionality". But in the case of a symbol the meaning is opaque and we have to erect a second intentionality upon the first, an intentionality which proceeds by analogy to ever deeper meanings. Concerned with the symbolism of evil, Ricoeur discusses "defilement". This is a sign in that it has a first, literal intentionality; it points beyond itself to "stain" or "unclean". But "defilement" is also a symbol because we can, by analogy, go further to a "certain situation of man in the sacred which is precisely that of being defiled, impure"(15). What for Wheelwright is a distinction between a "steno-symbol" and a "tensive symbol" is for Ricoeur a distinction between a "sign" and a "symbol".

We now return to the symbol "kingdom of God" in ancient Jewish apocalyptic, and I want to take up this aspect of the discussion by quoting a paragraph from my SBL Presidential Address, delivered in 1973.

Let me begin this aspect of my discussion by pointing out that in ancient Jewish apocalyptic in general – and for that matter in early Christian apocalyptic in general – the symbols used are, in Wheelwright's terms, "steno-symbols"; in Ricoeur's, "signs" rather than "symbols". Typically, the apocalyptic seer told the story of the history of his people in symbols where each symbol bore a one-to-one relationship with that which it depicted. This thing was Antiochus IV Epiphanes, that thing was Judas

Maccabee, the other thing was the coming of the Romans, and so on. But if this was the case, and it certainly was, then when the seer left the known facts of the past and present to express his expectation of the future his symbols remained "steno-symbols", and his expectation concerned singular concrete historical events. To take an actual example, if in chapters 11 and 12 of the Book of Daniel the "abomination that makes desolate" is a historical artifact – and it is – and if those who "make many understand" and the "little help" are historically identifiable individuals – and they are – then the "Michael" of Dan. 12:1 is also someone who will be historically identifiable, and the general resurrection of Dan. 12:2 is an event of the same historical order as the setting up of the altar to Zeus in the Jerusalem Temple. The series of events described in Daniel 11 and 12 are events within history: insofar as they are described in symbols, those symbols are "steno-symbols" (Wheelwright), or they are "signs" rather than "symbols" (Ricoeur). [5]

In the year since I made that statement a number of my friends and colleagues have challenged it, and in the light of their challenges I have rethought the matter as carefully as I could. It now seems to me that I have pressed too hard the distinction between a "steno-" and a "tensive" symbol in the case of apocalyptic symbols. It is still a most important distinction, and it is still true that most apocalyptic symbols are steno-symbols. But it is also true that the distinction is not hard and fast, and that in the case of such major symbols as the coming of Michael and the resurrection of the dead, or the establishment by God of his kingdom – or the coming of Jesus as Son of Man – then no hard and fast line could be drawn, and some seers no doubt saw the symbols as steno-symbols while others saw them as tensive.

What this means is that, for example, in the case of the symbols used to represent God's irruption into history, it was always possible to see the symbols as steno-symbols, and for Jews to identify the Messiah and seek signs of the coming of the one historical moment of God's final intervention on behalf of his people. Similarly for Christians it was always possible to see the symbol of Jesus coming "on the clouds of heaven" as Son of Man as a steno-symbol, and to seek to calculate the time and place of that coming. There is ample evidence that large numbers of both Jews and Christians did in fact do exactly those things, that, to use the words we are now using, large numbers of both Jews and Christians used and understood the symbols of God's eschatological activity on behalf of his people as steno-symbols. But the point I now concede – indeed the point I am now eager to embrace – is that this was not necessarily the case in any one instance. We have to investigate each case on its merits, recognizing that symbols of the order of those representing the eschatological activity of God can be either steno- or tensive symbols.

If we view the symbol kingdom of God in ancient Judaism in this light, then we can see that fundamentally it is a tensive symbol and that its meaning could never be exhausted, nor adequately expressed, by any one referent. However, in view of the identification of historical individuals as the Messiah, and in view of the undoubted expectation that God would intervene in the course of the war against Syria at the time of the Maccabees and that this would be the active beginning of the End – as well as in view of similar expectations in the case of the Jewish War and the Bar Cochba revolt – we would have to conclude that in ancient Jewish apocalyptic kingdom of God was predominantly understood as a steno-symbol. But then there is the Kaddish prayer to remind us that even during the heyday of ancient Jewish apocalyptic such an understanding was neither necessary nor universal.

As we approach the message of Jesus, then, there are three things to bear in mind. In the first place, "kingdom of God" is a symbol with deep roots in the Jewish consciousness of themselves as the people of God. Then, secondly, it functions within the context of the myth of God active in history on behalf of his people; indeed by the time of Jesus it had come to represent particularly the expectation of a final, eschatological act of God on behalf of his people. Thirdly, it could be understood and used either as a steno- or as a tensive symbol, to use a modern but nonetheless appropriate distinction. It is against this background that we must view the message of Jesus.

Perrin's chapter 3 traces "The Modern Interpretation of the Parables of Jesus" (89–193) from Jeremias through Fuchs, Linnemann, Jünger, Wilder, Funk, Via and Crossan to the SBL Parables Seminar, Amos Wilder occupies a key position (127–131). The excerpt begins at 128:

The work of A. Wilder's which concerns us here is his book, *Early Christian Rhetoric: The Language of the Gospel*. This book offers only a brief discussion of the parables (71–88), but it proved to be seminal because of the combination of insights and skills he brought to the interpretation of the parables. For the first time a scholar looked at the parables who, on the one hand, fully appreciated the results of the discussion among NT scholars, while, on the other hand, was able to bring insights from the worlds of literary creativity and of literary criticism.

Wilder enters the discussion at the level of literary criticism, concerned with the literary features of the parables, but moving backward from there to a historical concern as he attempts to understand

the creative vision of their author, Jesus, and moving forward from
there towards the interpreter as he attempts to understand the particular, distinctive impact of the literary form and language of the
parables. He begins by distinguishing various kinds of parables.
"Some of the parables are straight narratives about a given individual
case, ending with an application: The Good Samaritan, The Rich
Fool ... Here we have 'example stories', not symbolic narrative. The
point in these cases is that we should go and do likewise, or take
warning by a given example." But then there are also parables like
that of the lost sheep, where "the upshot is not that we should or
should not go and do likewise". Here we have rather "an extended
image – the shepherd's retrieval of the lost sheep and his joy – a
narrative image which reveals rather than exemplifies" (72).

This distinction between the parable as exemplary story and the
parable as revelatory image is an important one, and Wilder, having
made it, goes on to emphasize that "it is this revelatory character of
Jesus' parables which is to be stressed", quoting with approval Günther Bornkamm's dictum, "the parables are the preaching itself", and
claiming that Jesus used "extended images to unveil mysteries ...
above all to mediate reality and life" (ibid.). Moreover, he claims the
support of modern literary criticism in this, making a most important
distinction between a simile and a metaphor in the process. "This
understanding of Jesus' figures of speech is supported by our modern
discussion of the metaphor in literary criticism. A simile sets one
thing over against another: the less known is clarified by the better
known. But in the metaphor we have an image with a certain shock to
the imagination which directly conveys a vision of what is signified"
(ibid.). What the previous discussion had differentiated as similitude
and parable is here identified, not as simile, but as metaphor. The
similitude is a metaphor, and the parable is an extended metaphor.
The idea of a comparison which clarifies is abandoned in favour of
the metaphor which reveals. That metaphor can be simple or extended but it is always essentially a revelatory image. But Wilder
recognizes that even with this emphasis as central, there still is reason
to acknowledge that Jesus also taught "teaching parables and
polemic-parables, like those of the Prodigal Son or the Workers in the
Vineyard in which the revelatory-image is used to justify and defend
Jesus' mission ... The larger observation is that Jesus uses figures of
speech in an immense variety of ways" (72f.). But the idea of the
parable as revelatory image remains central.

Another literary aspect of the parables which concerns Wilder is
their realism. They are "human and realistic"; one may even speak of
their "secularity". In these parables a shepherd is an actual shepherd

and not "a flash-back to God as the Shepherd of Israel" (73). The realism and actuality of the parables are important because they command the attention of the listeners at the level of the actuality of their everyday existence. "[Jesus] is leading men to make a judgement and to come to a decision. The stories are so told as to compel men to see things as they are, by analogy indeed. Sluggish or dormant awareness and conscience are thus aroused. The parables make men give attention, come alive and face things. And they do this by evoking men's everyday experience" (75). Or, again, "The parables of Jesus, in addition to their revelatory character, are shaped more consistently towards a direct personal appeal or challenge, and their sobriety of style and sharpness of focus serve well the fatefulness of the issue in view" (77).

Against the background of these considerations Wilder turns to a discussion of the "parables of the kingdom"; the sower, seed growing of itself, mustard seed, from Mark 4:the leaven, hid treasure, pearl of great price, from Matthew 13 (82–6). These are to be counted as authentic parables of Jesus. "The characteristic design, the tight form of these utterances helped to guarantee them against change and supplementation. A coherent image-story is resistant to change ... The parables of Jesus have an organic unity and coherence" (82). But there is a further criterion for the authenticity of these parables, and it is a characteristic which they share with other forms of Jesus' speech. Jesus used various forms of speech; he "used trope and metaphor in the most varied way", but there is always the same element of "force" and "significance" in his imagery. In this connection Wilder makes a statement that is important, both in connection with understanding the natural force of the parables, and also in providing the link between the parables and the use by Jesus of the symbol, kingdom of God, in other forms of speech.

> In the parables we have action–images. But these are only one kind of metaphor, extended metaphor. Jesus' communication, just because it is fresh and dynamic, is necessarily plastic. Now we know that a true metaphor or symbol is more than a sign, it is a bearer of the reality to which it refers. The hearer not only learns about that reality, he participates in it. He is invaded by it. Here lies the power and fatefulness of art. Jesus' speech had the character not of instruction and ideas but of compelling imagination, of spell, of mythical shock and transformation (84).

"A true metaphor or symbol is more than a sign, it is a bearer of the reality to which it refers." These words are the essential clue to understanding both the symbolic language of the kingdom sayings and the metaphorical language of the parables on the lips of Jesus.

But there is a further point about this language which is important to Wilder, and that is its relationship to the vision of the poet using it. Such language is not used idly; the poet who turns to symbol and metaphor does so because of some vision of reality which demands expression, and which can only find expression in such evocative or mind-teasing language. So it is with the parables of Jesus, as Wilder understands them. They are not "homiletic illustration drawn from nature". The sower (Mark 4:3–8) "is not just an example of what happens every day offered as an encouragement", nor is the seed growing of itself (Mark 4:26–8) to be taken in such "a banal sense". Their real authority and power emerge when we see them "in Jesus' own situation", that is, in the situation of Jesus addressing his disciples, in the situation of Jesus seeking to impart to his disciples "his own vision by the power of metaphor" (84f.).

The secret of the power of the parables of the kingdom then, as Jesus addressed them to his listeners in their original historical situation, lies not only in their reality-bearing power as metaphor, but also in the fact that the reality they bear is that of Jesus' own faith. "It is Jesus' own certain faith that paints in the feature of the great harvest. The formal felicity and coherence of these parables reflect the intensity of his own vision" (85). But this is not only the secret of the power of the parables in the original situation of Jesus' using them as he addresses his hearers; it is also the secret of their power as we seek to interpret them in a later day and a different situation. "For us, too, to find the meaning of the parable we must identify ourselves with that inner secret of Jesus' faith and faithfulness" (85). In this context Wilder quotes Fuchs. "The distinctive feature in the teaching aspect of Jesus' proclamation is the analogical power with which tacitly he sets forth himself, his own obedience, as a measure for the attention of his disciples" (85).

The fact that Wilder can quote Fuchs in this context shows that he is close to him in his fundamental concern for Jesus, and for the highly personal aspects of the message of Jesus. But this should not be allowed to obscure the point that in fact Wilder and Fuchs are far apart at the very point at which they seem to be close: their interest in the highly personal aspects of the parables of Jesus. Fuchs is interested in Jesus as the supreme revelation of God to man, and hence as the one who actualized the possibility of faith in his own experience, and who verbalized the possibility of faith for his hearers in his parables. Wilder, on the other hand, is interested in Jesus as a poet who imparted to his hearers his own vision of reality in the metaphorical language of his parables. But both are raising the question as to whether there is or is not an essential relationship between the author and the text of the parables as the interpreter seeks to interpret that text in a subsequent and quite different situation. They would both maintain that there is such a relationship, though on different grounds.

It is, I hope, evident that I regard Amos Wilder as enormously important in the discussion of both kingdom of God and the parables in the message of Jesus. He is important because he taught us to see the significance of the literary factors in the kingdom proclamation and the parables, the one as symbol and the other as metaphor. I have attempted to develop the former insight myself; the latter was developed in the subsequent American discussion of the parables.

The final excerpt is from Perrin's conclusions (chapter 4), beginning at 197:

A major feature of the discussions above has been the deliberate attention given to literary factors. I was concerned to claim that kingdom of God is a *symbol*, rather than a *conception* in the message of Jesus, and that indeed considering it as a conception had in fact caused difficulties in the discussion. Once it was seen as a symbol such unanswerable questions as whether it was present or future, or both, in the message of Jesus could be seen to be false questions, and one could begin to ask the true questions. The questions that should be asked, in my view, are questions as to what kind of symbol kingdom of God is in the message of Jesus, and what does it evoke or represent.

In the exegesis I carried out, I argued the kingdom of God was a *tensive* symbol in the message of Jesus, that it was, to use Wheelwright's terms again, a symbol of cultural range, a symbol having meaning for people in cultural continuity with ancient Israel and its myth of God acting as king, a cultural continuity in which Jesus certainly stood. On the lips of Jesus the symbol evoked the ancient myth, and the claim of his message was that the reality mediated by the myth was to be experienced dramatically by his hearers. Thus a literary concern was important to an understanding of the message of Jesus at the historical level.

As we move from a historical understanding of the message of Jesus to the possibilities for interpreting that message in a subsequent day and age, then a consideration of literary factors remains essential. The interpretation of the coming of the kingdom of God in terms of the coming of the Son of Man in the New Testament involved an understanding of the symbol as a steno- rather than as a tensive symbol. The speculative theological use of the symbol by Augustine also involved literary features in that Augustine was reading the NT texts as allegories and kingdom of God had become for him a speculative cipher to which he could give any meaning demanded by his overall theological system. With the rise of the historical sciences the interpretation of kingdom of God in the message of Jesus became more self-conscious and Johannes Weiss carried through the first modern scientific (*wissenschaftlich*) interpretation. He thought of kingdom of God as a conception and decided that as a conception it had nothing to say to modern man, thereby opening up what I have called the "hermeneutical gulf" between the message of Jesus and modern, technological man.

After Weiss we considered only two further interpreters and we considered these from the literary standpoint of their interpretation of kingdom of God in the message of Jesus as a symbol evoking a myth. We considered Walter Rauschenbusch because he fully accepted the ancient myth and hence was able to return to a direct and natural use of the symbol. Using the symbol directly and naturally remains a hermeneutical option for those for whom the myth is still valid and meaningful. We considered Rudolf Bultmann because he is much the most important modern interpreter of Jesus' use of kingdom of God, and because he represents the hermeneutical option diametrically opposed to that represented by Rauschenbusch. For Bultmann the myth is dead and the symbolic language, archaic; he, therefore, sought a means of translating the myth as an "expression of life", and found it in the hermeneutics of "demythologizing". Bultmann's interpretation remains an option for those for whom the myth is dead and the symbolic language archaic, but there are problems, both with Bultmann's understanding of myth – which he sees as prescientific cosmology – and with his understanding of the symbolic language – which he sees as symbolizing a conception and in which the symbols are steno-symbols. The question, therefore, arises as to whether Bultmann's demythologizing is the *only* hermeneutical option open to those who can no longer accept the myth and use the symbol as naturally and directly as did Rauschenbusch.

The answer to this question is, No it is not. Other possibilities arise if kingdom of God is seen as a tensive symbol in the message of Jesus, and if the myth it evokes is seen as true myth, i.e., as a narrative means of demonstrating "the inner meaning of the universe and of human life", or as a means of verbalizing one's basic understanding of the historicity of human existence in the world in language meant to be taken seriously but not necessarily literally. In my SBL Presidential Address I expressed the hermeneutical option which challenges me personally as the responsibility to explore "the manifold ways in which the experience of God can become an existential reality to man" and to understand kingdom of God not as "a single identifiable event which every man experiences at the same time", but as something "which every man experiences in his own time".[6] Since I would be fully prepared to argue that "activity of God" and an "event which every man experiences" is ultimately mythological language to be taken seriously but not necessarily literally, in the last resort my option may not produce a result significantly different from "a Bultmannian understanding of the eschatology of Jesus". But I would claim that it had been arrived at by a more defensible hermeneutical method. Nor would I claim that the option which challenges me is the only possible option between those represented by Rauschenbusch and Bultmann. Others, more skilled than I in the understanding of symbol and myth, may arrive at other and more persuasive hermeneutical options. What I am concerned to claim is that a valid hermeneutics to be applied to Jesus' proclamation of the kingdom of God must take seriously and deal most carefully with the elements of symbol and myth in that proclamation. The nature of the language of the proclamation demands this.

NOTES

1 S. Mowinckel, *The Psalms in Israel's Worship* (1962) I, 114.

2 Ibid., 107. The English translations all have "The Lord reigns", or the equivalent. RSV: "The Lord reigns"; NEB: "The Lord is king"; Jerusalem Bible: "Yahweh is king".

3 Philip Wheelwright (1962) 130. A problem in this particular discussion is that we are dealing with two different kinds of myth. On the one hand, we have the myth of creation, the cosmogonic myth, mediated to Israel by its Canaanite neighbours, and forming the basis for the slightly different myth of the kingship of God. Then, on the other hand, we have the myth of the salvation history, the myth of God active as king in the history of the Israelite people. Because of the link with history in the case of the salvation history, some scholars tend to resist the use of the word myth in this connection. F. M. Cross, for example, prefers to speak of "epic", and the title of his book, *Canaanite Myth and Hebrew Epic*, expresses his understanding of the contrast between the cosmogonic myth and the epic of the redemptive history. (Cross prefers history-of-redemption to salvation history to represent the German *Heilsgeschichte*, e.g. 83). But the element of history involved in the salvation history does not make it any less a myth, in the sense of the Watts definition, which I accept as a valid definition of this kind of myth. The cosmogonic myth and the salvation history myth are different kinds of myths, but they are both myths, and they both function as myths in ancient Israel, especially as they are amalgamated. Moreover, the salvation history myth continues to function as myth right into the present, as we shall argue in the course of this study. For an introductory discussion of the element of history in biblical myths see Perrin, *The New Testament: An Introduction* (1974) 21–33.

4 See, for example, A. Wilder, "The Rhetoric of Ancient and Modern Apocalyptic",

Interpretation 25 (1971), 436–53, rep. in *Jesus' Parables and the War of Myths* (1982).

5 Perrin, "Eschatology and Hermeneutics," *JBL* 93 (1974) 11.

6 Ibid. 13.

6

*Schweitzer's Influence: Blessing or Bane?**

T. FRANCIS GLASSON

It was in 1906 that Albert Schweitzer's notable book *Von Reimarus zu Wrede* appeared. At first it made little impact; but the English translation *The Quest of the Historical Jesus* (1910) – referred to in the following pages as *Quest* – created a stir in the universities and it is now regarded as a kind of landmark. Schweitzer's interpretation of the life and teaching of Jesus had of course been put forward earlier in his sketch of the life of Jesus (1901) and the apocalyptic interpretation which he followed had been clearly set forth by Johannes Weiss in 1892. But whereas Weiss had concerned himself with the *teaching* of Jesus, Schweitzer showed that the whole ministry and course of events could only be understood with the help of the eschatological key. References are continually made to our great debt to these two scholars who opened a new era in the interpretation of the Gospels. Thus, to give one example, Barnabas Lindars in his *Apocalyptic Myth and the Death of Christ* (Manson Memorial Lecture for 1974) says of the connection between the apocalyptic frame of thought and the ethical teaching of Jesus: "Modern scholarship has largely accepted the results of Albert Schweitzer's classic study of this issue in *The Quest of the Historical Jesus*" (381). And on the next page Lindars inclines to the view that "Schweitzer was right in his fundamental position".

The purpose of this article is to examine what this alleged debt is and to see if the eschatological interpretation in question is soundly based.

I

The crucial question is the nature of the kingdom of God. In this connection it will be helpful to distinguish three interpretations:

* First published in *JTS* 28 (1977) 289–302.

1   The term was applied by the Rabbis to the messianic age. Strictly speaking they spoke of "the kingdom of heaven"; and they applied to it the words of Zech. 14:9: "The Lord shall be king over all the earth."[1] The kind of Messiah associated with this kingdom was to be a son of David, ruling at Jerusalem as a literal king whose kingdom belonged to this world. In Luke's Gospel the Jewish hope can be expressed as "looking for the consolation of Israel" (2:25), or "looking for the redemption of Jerusalem" (2:38), or "looking for the kingdom of God" (23:51).

2   Throughout the major part of Christian history it has been held that Jesus reinterpreted this nationalistic, material kingdom; and though the term "spiritual" is not altogether satisfactory, we may distinguish the nationalistic and political view (still held by Jews today) from the Christian by describing the latter as a spiritual kingdom. It is the era of redemption; it finds expression in the Church, and God has already "translated us into the kingdom of the Son of his love" (Col. 1:13). In the teaching of Jesus the term kingdom of God is also used for the eternal state.[2]

3   Weiss and Schweitzer said that neither of these interpretations corresponds to the teaching and the hopes of Jesus. Our lord followed the interpretation set forth in the apocalyptic literature, in which (so it is alleged) the kingdom does not belong to this world at all. Jesus looked for the imminent end of this world and its replacement by a new heaven and earth.[3] Thus the kingdom which Jesus proclaimed is not spiritual; nor does it conform to the nationalistic and materialistic hopes of the old messianic teaching; it is eschatological, apocalyptic.

The distinction which Schweitzer marks is perfectly clear-cut and intelligible. He dismisses the spiritual view as a modernism and thus has to choose between the other two. On the one hand we have a Messiah who is born on earth as a son of David, who reigns as a king in a kingdom belonging to this world. On the other hand we have the destruction of the present world, the resurrection and the judgement followed by a new heaven and earth; and the Messiah, or whatever name we give to this figure, descends in glory from the heavens as judge of mankind. It is the latter which Schweitzer describes as "the late Jewish view"; it is this which is to be found in the Gospels. In some passages of his writings he affirms that this late view of the Messiah and the kingdom had ousted the older "son of David" conception.[4]

In connecting this view of the kingdom with Jesus, Schweitzer does not take our Lord's teaching as his point of departure. He rests everything on the apocalyptic literature which (as he affirms) sets forth this conception. It is most important to observe this. The late Jewish view, he affirms, was so familiar to the hearers of Jesus that he had only to utter the phrase "the kingdom of God" and the whole eschatological drama would immediately leap to their minds. He does not derive this late Jewish view from a study of the Gospels; *he brings it to the Gospels.* This and that saying of Jesus can only be interpreted in one way, the way which harmonizes with the late Jewish view.

Schweitzer indicates four particular writings which set forth this eschatology, and a number of times calls attention to the *Psalms of Solomon, Enoch, 2 Baruch*, and *4 Ezra*.[5]

The first of these is a work usually dated about the middle of the first century B.C. It is not an apocalypse but a collection of psalms; however, certain passages throw light upon current expectations. The following is from *Ps.* 17:

> Behold, O Lord, and raise up unto them their king, the son of David,
> At the time in which thou seest, O God, that he may reign over Israel
>   thy servant.
> And gird him with strength, that he may shatter unrighteous rulers,
> And that he may purge Jerusalem from nations that trample her
>   down to destruction.
> Wisely, righteously, he shall thrust our sinners as a potter's vessel.
> With a rod of iron he shall break in pieces all their substance,
> He shall destroy the godless nations with the word of his mouth.[6]

Here we clearly have the traditional figure of the Messiah, the son of David; allusions to Ps. 2 and Isa. 11 may be traced. It has always been a mystery to me that Schweitzer repeatedly calls attention to the *Psalms of Solomon* as giving the apocalyptic view which had replaced the traditional one; they do nothing of the kind.

When we look at the three remaining items we cannot help observing that the apocalypses of *Baruch* and Ezra are in their present form usually dated about A.D. 100; they can hardly be appealed to with confidence as presenting views extant in the lifetime of Jesus. Both writings are overshadowed by the tragic fate of Jerusalem in A.D. 70. However, since it is argued that their messianic hopes are in line with the late Jewish view which dominated the thinking of Jesus and his contemporaries, let us see what can be gathered concerning these expectations. Both of them depict the Messiah as a king who reigns for a limited period on the earth; in 4 Ezra the period is given as 400 years (7:28–33) and at its close come the judgement, resurrection, and the new creation. A number of visions are included in this apocalypse, and in one of these a man is seen arising from the sea and flying with the clouds of heaven (13). This is not a descent from heaven but an ascent from the sea; the picture should be taken as indicating in a symbolic way the emergence of the Messiah from concealment, as the writer himself explains (13:52). The pre-existence of the Messiah appears to be mentioned in a few places, a notable feature of this work. But at the moment we are emphasizing the fact that his reign is an earthly one in accordance with traditional teaching and lasts for 400 years. If the beliefs of Jesus were in harmony with this work he could not have believed that the end of the world was near; it was at least 400 years away!

2 Baruch provides another example of a messianic reign of limited duration, and it is at the end of it that the new world comes. Messiah's principate lasts for an age, "until the world of corruption is at an end" (40:3). The Messiah is a warrior; some of the nations he shall spare, "and some of them he shall slay" (72:2); "all those who have ruled over you ... shall be given up to the sword" (72:6). This fits conventional Jewish teaching and does not correspond to "the late Jewish view" as Schweitzer had defined it. Incidentally is it conceivable that Jesus would have had any sympathy with the militant passages just quoted?

So far we have seen that three out of the four authorities which Schweitzer adduces are quite inconsistent with the view he ascribes to them. The Messiah belongs to this world, he is an earthly king ruling over a victorious nation, and it is at the close of his reign that the new creation supervenes. These writers give the exact opposite of what Schweitzer and his followers state.

The remaining work of the four selected is the *Book of Enoch*. This, as is well known, is in reality a collection of five works of varying date and teaching. J. T. Milik in a recent discussion dates the earliest part in the third century B.C. (Book of the Watchers, 1–36; a part of this section he would put earlier still); the latest part, the Similitudes (37–71) he puts in the third century A.D.[7] But apart from the period covered, it is important to notice that different conceptions of the future are set forth: (*a*) The Book of the Watchers (1–36) describes an earthly kingdom in rather materialistic terms but no Messiah is mentioned. Those who share in the kingdom live long lives and have many children. (*b*) The only section which mentions a Son of Man, more frequently called the Elect One, is the Similitudes (37–71). Here we have a figure of a distinctive kind, pre-existent and associated with God in the judgement. Nowhere is he described as coming with clouds, or even as coming; one has to read between the lines to obtain a picture of any definiteness. But there is something here which, far from being representative, is unique in Jewish teaching. Moreover, it is the one part out of the five which is almost certainly not of pre-Christian date. (*c*) The Book of Luminaries (72–82) is mostly concerned with questions of astronomy and makes no mention of a Messiah. (*d*) The Dream Visions (83–90) speak of a Messiah in one passage (90:37f.), which begins: "And I saw that a white bull was born." He comes forth from the bosom of the community, apparently after the resurrection of v. 33. As R. H. Charles suggests, "the new form of existence is an eternal one". (*e*) In the Epistle of Enoch (91–108) there is no reference to a Messiah, but there is a kingdom era of limited duration in the eighth week (91:12).

If we take these five works in conjunction with the other three which Schweitzer mentions (*Ps. Sol., 4 Ezra, 2 Bar.*) it will be seen that we have eight different types of teaching. They do not present anything which can be summarized as "the late Jewish view". Several of them do not mention a Messiah at all, and those which do so describe him generally as a human king; the only one out of the eight which gives a transcendent figure as judge (*Enoch* 37–71) is almost certainly not of pre-Christian date and quite apart from this cannot be regarded as representative on account of its unique character.

It is sometimes said that the absence of the Similitudes from the Qumran caves has reopened the question of their date. But long before Qumran was heard of, many scholars dated the Similitudes within the Christian era. I may be permitted to mention that in my book *The Second Advent* (1945) a chapter on "The Date of the Similitudes" showed that Charles' arguments for a pre-Christian date were quite unconvincing. The Qumran evidence was not a surprise to those who already on internal evidence favoured a later date. About a dozen manuscripts of various parts of Enoch have been found at Qumran, some of them substantial; and although the other four parts are well represented not a line of the Similitudes has been found.[8]

What now becomes of Schweitzer's confident description of "the late Jewish view" which is alleged to have had such a profound effect upon the mind of Jesus? Not a single relevant document is left of those to which he appealed. The mystery is the astonishing way in which this baseless theory had dominated the interpretation of the Gospels for seventy years.

To the end of his long life Schweitzer claimed that he adhered to the main lines of his original interpretation of the mission of Jesus. We must take into account not only his early statements of 1901 and

1906, but the 2nd edn of the *Quest, Geschichte der Leben-Jesu-Forschung* (1913). There is also *My Life and Thought* (German 1931, Eng. 1933) and the posthumous work, *The Kingdom of God and Primitive Christianity*, actually written in Africa 1950–1 and published in German in 1967 and in English the following year. He had died in 1965.

Right to the end he continued to speak of the late Jewish view as though there were a single generally accepted interpretation; but, very curiously, in some passages of his writings he recognizes that several views were extant in the first century A.D. The kingdom of limited duration, set forth in *2 Baruch* and 4 *Ezra*, he calls the scribal view. Jesus, however, dissented from this and held (so it is alleged) a view similar to the one set forth in the Similitudes of *Enoch*. At the same time there were original elements in the teaching of Jesus, and his eschatology was the product of a masterly mind, "a considerable intellectual achievement" (*The Kingdom of God*, 105; and *Leben-Jesu-Forschung*, chap. 17).

If there were several differing interpretations of the kingdom in the first century – the scribal view, the popular view, the view of the Similitudes, the masterly interpretation of Jesus himself – this makes complete nonsense of the passages where Schweitzer refers to the late Jewish view as so familiar and generally current that the bare announcement of the kingdom of God immediately brought the details to mind: "Jesus did not need to describe this future in closer detail. His hearers knew what it was all about, as soon as the sentence was spoken, 'The kingdom of God is at hand'."[9] It is also difficult to find consistency in what he says about spiritual interpretations of the kingdom. At times he declares that such views would have been unintelligible at that period:

> If Jesus had appeared with a fully spiritualized view of the Kingdom and its coming, his proclamation of it would never have been believed. The ancient world, Jewish, Greek and Roman, would have had no point of contact with such an announcement.[10]

He is most emphatic on this point. "Nowhere in the oldest sources ... is there any trace at all of Jesus intending to replace by a spiritualized expectation the realistic one, so widely spread among the people, of a supernatural kingdom which would come with glory" (*My Life and Thought*, 49–50).

Yet elsewhere he writes:

> In Jeremiah, Ezekiel and Deutero-Isaiah the Kingdom consists in a new everlasting covenant which God makes with his people, by which he gives them the strength to endure through imparting his Spirit to them ...

There was nothing to prevent Jesus, who continued and completed the ethics of the earlier prophets, from going back from the late Jewish conception of a completely supernatural and superethical Kingdom to the earlier idea of a spiritual and ethical Messianic Kingdom, and giving it new life and depth in accordance with his deeper ethical insight. This is not what he does; instead he accepts the late Jewish view (*The Kingdom of God*, 93–4).[11]

II

Were no dissentient voices raised at the time of the *Quest*? There were, but they were not sufficiently heeded. R. H. Charles, who knew more about the subject than anyone else in the world, said concerning the work that "Schweitzer's eschatological studies show no knowledge of original documents and hardly any of first-hand works on the documents."[12] Years before this, at a time when undue emphasis was being given to a transcendent interpretation of the king-dom, Dalman, the great Aramaic scholar, said that a picture of the messianic hope in the time of Christ ought never to have been given in these terms; and he pointed out that some of the alleged evidence had been manufactured (*The Words of Jesus* [1902] 131f., 248).

Nevertheless, the so-called apocalyptic view seemed to carry every-thing before it. According to Bultmann it is universally held on the Continent. How are we to explain this, if (as we have seen) it is clean contrary to the evidence and is riddled with inconsistencies? There were a number of reasons. There was the intimidating and masterful way in which Schweitzer had written. He implies that any-one who disagrees with him is evading the obvious. One of his chapters bears the title, "The Struggle against Eschatology". The important observations of Dalman were brushed aside as part of "the general resistance" to the new views. All this is in line with a strange principle which has come to be widely accepted: when alter-native views are open, the more unpalatable must be the true one.

Again, the First World War brought such shattering events that the dramatic "apocalyptic" interpretation seemed closer to reality than old views of progress which had become associated with tradi-tional Christian teaching. Admiration for the nobility of Schweitzer's life expressed in his medical work in W. Africa (an admiration which I wholeheartedly share) seemed to enhance the importance of his theological work; here was the ethic of Jesus in action, as Schweitzer had rediscovered it.

In Germany the alternative to the eschatological conception of the kingdom was the rather watery ethical interpretation of Ritschlianism. Schweitzer and those who followed him were right in rejecting this, but it was a misfortune that they did not take sufficient account of the kingdom as the era of redemption, inaugurated by the ministry, death, and resurrection of the Son of God and the gift of the Holy Spirit. British theologians were aware of the humanistic lives of Jesus rampant on the Continent since Strauss and had consistently rejected them together with the conception of the kingdom as an ethical improvement society inspired by a moral example from the distant past. Accordingly they were not carried away by the "apocalyptic" theory to the same extent as continental theologians, because they had as an alternative a sounder and more robust conception of the kingdom of God.

Again the apocalyptic interpretation was found to be compatible with various philosophies and theologies. Schweitzer himself was much influenced by such categories as world-denying and world-affirming, so prominent in the systems of Nietzsche and Schopenhauer. Jesus, in his view, was world-denying; and the idea that Jesus looked for an imminent destruction of the present world tied up neatly with this description. He also maintained that the sublime ethic of Jesus (apparently the only part of his teaching relevant to modern needs) was based upon the kind of "detachment from the world" which the apocalyptic outlook fostered. Later on the apocalyptic view was found to be congenial to systems of "crisis theology" and to various forms of existentialism. Once an interpretation becomes linked with some basic philosophy it is almost impossible to dislodge it by a discussion of individual texts.

Whatever the reasons may have been, the very wide influence of "the apocalyptic view" is undeniable. More than half a century after the initial works of Weiss and Schweitzer the same interpretation was put forward by Bultmann in his presidential address to the SNTS in 1953:

In later Judaism this hope for a prosperity on earth remained, a hope for a splendid future of the people ruled by the Messiah who will renew the kingdom of David, e.g. in the Psalms of Solomon and in the Eighteen Prayers. But besides this another hope arose, for a blissful future which is no longer of this earth and which shall not be realised by an historical crisis brought about by God, but by a cosmic catastrophe, the end of which will be the resurrection of the dead and the Last Judgment. The figure of the Davidic Messiah is superseded by the figure of the "Son of Man", as far as there is reflection at all on a Saviour apart from God Himself. This hope is connected with the conception of the two aeons which grew up in later Judaism (*NTS* 1 [1954/5] 6).

The latter view is ascribed to "the apocalyptic literature" (7) and it is stated that "in the New Testament (if we set aside Luke–Acts) the Old Testament view of history is preserved as well as the apocalyptic view, but in such a way that the apocalyptic view prevails".

In a little book which he published a few years later, *Jesus Christ and Mythology*, Bultmann put forward substantially the same view as Weiss and commended him for his epoch-making work of 1892. Bultmann wrote that although Jesus did not share the apocalyptists' love of detail he nevertheless "shared the eschatological expectations of his contemporaries". He looked for the inauguration of the kingdom of God in the immediate future and envisaged it as "a tremendous cosmic drama. The Son of Man will come with the clouds of heaven, the dead will be raised and the day of judgement will arrive." "God will suddenly put an end to the world and to history, and He will bring in a new world, the world of eternal blessedness" (12). This view of our Lord's expectations, said Bultmann, is now universally accepted in European theology.

It will be seen that Bultmann includes the usual messianic hope as existing side by side with the apocalyptic hope. He also sees quite correctly that the *Psalms of Solomon* belong to the former type, not the latter where Schweitzer had repeatedly placed them. But the interpretation of the hope expressed in "the apocalyptic literature" remains the same.

We have considered the four works to which Schweitzer appealed. Bultmann speaks more generally of the apocalyptic literature. But if we accordingly widen our examination and look at other items the same negative result emerges.

The book of *Jubilees*, for example, which is in reality a Midrash on Genesis and the early part of Exodus, has a few passages of a prophetic kind; these look forward to a gradual process by which a new era of peace will come to the world. Since patriarchal times, the term of human life has become shorter; at length "the heads of the children will be white with grey hair" (23:25). But now comes a turning-point: with the study of the Torah the tendency will be gradually reversed until at last primeval longevity will be restored, in accordance with Isa. 65 (see *Jub.* 23:26f.). No Messiah is mentioned; the prince of 31:18 is probably a reference to David.[13]

The *Assumption of Moses*, usually dated in the first half of the first century A.D., is one of the few writings of this class of literature to contain a reference to the kingdom of God, though here it is "his kingdom": "Then shall his kingdom appear throughout all his creation" (10:1). Chap. 10 gives a highly pictorial account of the coming of God to defeat evil, to exalt his people Israel after destroying their enemies. No Messiah is mentioned, but the agent of salvation is the angel of verse 2, probably Michael, the champion of Israel. The description of God coming forth to vindicate his people is similar to many passages of the Old Testament, where such imagery is used to express divine action and the Day of the Lord (e.g. Mic. 1:3; Isa. 42:13). This fragment is an expression of the "massianic" hope in nationalistic terms. God will "punish the Gentiles" and then Israel will "be happy". T. W. Manson regards the exaltation to the stars as a poetical description of an earthly possession of power and glory; it does not refer to eternal blessedness in heaven (*The Servant Messiah* [1953] 32). It should be noticed, however, that no military measures are encouraged, rather a passive waiting for God to intervene.

The *Testaments of the Twelve Patriarchs* is now thought to belong to the Christian era, though some sources were extant earlier. These writings have links with the Qumran community who looked for two Messiahs, a royal and a priestly. The Zadokite Fragment also can now be placed in its true setting with its reference to a Teacher of Righteousness. A Messiah is foretold who will put to rout the enemies of God's people.

It is unnecessary to explore in further detail the remaining works grouped together as apocalyptic writings. Messianic beliefs become more and more diversified, and there is nothing resembling the scheme put forward with such definiteness by the Schweitzer/ Bultmann school. When a Messiah is mentioned he is of the warrior type. There is no transcendent figure descending in glory to conduct the last judgement. Bultmann's statements are contrary to the evidence.

I am aware that discussions of the Son of Man are apt to be involved with the "history of religions" theory about the Man, with Anthropos and the Urmensch, Hermetic literature, Gnosticism, Mandaeism, etc. This does not alter the immediate point. A certain view is ascribed to the Jewish apocalyptic literature, and anyone who examines this literature with care will see that to summarize it in this way is a travesty of the facts. We saw that the works relied on by Schweitzer do not yield what he claimed; the remaining works of this class produce a result just as decisive.

III

This whole trend has had, in my opinion, a lamentable effect upon New Testament scholarship. The "Son of Man question" provides one example. This term occurs about seventy times in the Synoptic Gospels, but as a number of sayings occur in more than one Gospel the number of separate instances is reduced to forty. These may be distributed in three classes: (*a*) those which speak of the Son of Man's earthly life; (*b*) those which speak of his death and resurrection; and (*c*) those which speak of his future coming. One common method of approach is to say that the Son of Man was an existing term of Jewish eschatological teaching and that it implied a glorious parousia. Therefore only the sayings of group (*c*) have any claim to represent words actually spoken by Jesus. Groups (*a*) and (*b*) may be dismissed as church constructions. It is clear that instead of coming to the Gospels with an open mind to see what they say, this approach decides in advance what Son of Man means and then uses this as a criterion to discriminate between genuine and inauthentic sayings in the Gospels. One reason given for rejecting certain Son of Man sayings is "their dissimilarity from the authentic parousia sayings" (H. E. Tödt).[14] Hence what is so often presented today as the teaching of Jesus does not spring naturally out of what we find in the Gospels, but is largely determined by theories that are brought to the Gospels, theories which rest upon no solid foundation of evidence.[15]

Once Jesus is described as an apocalyptic preacher who was mainly concerned to warn his contemporaries of the rapidly approaching judgement and end of the world, any elements of his teaching which appear to conflict with this then have to be jettisoned. There are, for instance, a number of sayings in the Gospels which speak of a terrible fate which is to come upon the Temple and city of Jerusalem. These have to go, because if Jesus expected the end of all things as the immediate sequel of his death, no remaining time was available for such prophecies to be fulfilled. These passages are accordingly deleted by the apocalyptic school as non-genuine. Any suggestion that Jesus thought of a Church has also to go. The implication is that the rise of the Church was an undesigned accident.

It will be seen that by this kind of treatment the material of the teaching ascribed to our Lord in the Gospels is considerably reduced. And everything follows from a starting-point of apocalyptic theory which has no sound evidence to support it. Morna Hooker has well written:

> Too many commentators have approached the Synoptic material with fixed ideas about the meaning of the phrase [i.e. the Son of Man], and about where and how it could be used – ideas which have not only coloured their interpretation of the passages concerned, but distorted their judgement as to the genuineness of the various sayings, leading to the rejection of any which did not conform to the accepted pattern (*The Son of Man in Mark* [1967] 78).

But although the "apocalyptic" approach has been so dominant throughout this century there are signs of a more questioning mood. Thirty years ago in the book referred to earlier (*The Second Advent*) I dismissed as without evidence the view in question – a quarter of the book being devoted to this matter – and put forward a different solution for the origin of the parousia conception, and I am glad to see that in recent years others have come to question the dictum put forward with such confidence by Weiss and Schweitzer and their many followers.

E. Schweizer of Zürich contributed an article to *NTS* 9 (1963) in which he affirmed quite peremptorily, but with every justification, "The idea of a parousia from heaven is non-existent in Judaism" (260). Reference may also be made to N. Perrin (1967):

> A widespread assumption, especially in German language research, is that there existed in Jewish apocalyptic the conception of a transcendent, pre-existent heavenly being, the Son of Man, whose coming to earth as judge would be a major feature of the drama of the End time (164).

He rejects this. "No such concept of a coming Son of Man existed."[16] Similarly M. D. Hooker in the work cited above writes concerning the Jewish exegesis of Dan. 7:13: "There is no evidence that the 'coming' of the Son of Man with clouds was interpreted of the Messiah's arrival on earth in the time of Jesus."[17]

Attempts are made at times to find new evidence since all the old has evaporated. But it is surely unnecessary to reinflate this "frail and empty phantom" which has towered over the NT scene in such a menacing way. The Son of Man question is only one example of ways in which the approach pioneered by Weiss and Schweitzer has had a distorting effect on the interpretation of the New Testament.

How it came about that in the early Church a fixed belief in Christ's imminent parousia arose is a question we cannot embark upon here. Our immediate point is to expose the unsoundness of the answer which has been given so confidently throughout the present century, as a result of the wide acceptance of the main theme of Schweitzer's interpretation with its serious misrepresentation of the teaching of the apocalypses.

As we have seen, the apocalyptic writings to which he appealed present variety rather than uniformity. A number of them foretell an earthly messianic reign of limited duration followed by the new creation.[18] But this was taught also by the Rabbis and by other Jewish authorities, and it has been maintained up to the present time. There is no single view which can legitimately be described as "the apocalyptic view", and such terms should be dropped as meaningless and confusing.

NOTES

1 Cf. Billerbeck, i, 172–84; and J. Klausner, *The Messianic Idea in Israel* (1956) Part III.

2 For the various shades of meaning in the Gospels see Lagrange's analysis in his commentary on Matthew, clvi–clxvii.

3 According to the teaching of Jesus (affirms Weiss [1971] 130) when the kingdom comes "God will destroy this old world which is ruled and spoiled by the devil and create a new world".

4 "There did not exist at that time a political eschatology alongside the transcendental, and indeed it could not on inner grounds subsist alongside it. That was, after all, the thing which Weiss had shown most clearly" (*Quest*, 253).

5 *Quest*, 319 and elsewhere. In 1968, 42, he speaks of these writings as "the four works to which we owe our knowledge of the eschatological expectation of late Judaism".

6 G. B. Gray's translation in *The Apocrypha and Pseudepigrapha of the Old Testament*, ed. R. H. Charles (1913).

7 *HTR* 64 (1971) 333–78, "Problème de la Littérature Hénochique à la Lumière des Fragments Araméens de Qumran". J. C. Hindley argues for a date in the second century A.D. for the Similitudes *NTS* 14 (1967/8) 551–65. Some scholars have suggested that the messianic teaching of the Similitudes may be due to Christian influence upon Jewish thought (V. H. Stanton in Hasting's *Dict. of the Bible* iii. 356; cf. M. Black in *Bulletin of the John Rylands Library*, xlv [1947] 312 ff.).

8 For full details see J. T. Milik's *HTR* article referred to earlier and his more recent *The Books of Enoch: Aramaic Fragments of Qumran Cave 4* (1976). Cf. also his *Ten Years of Discovery in the Wilderness of Judaea* (1960) 33; and F. M. Cross, *The Ancient Library of Qumran* (1958) 150.

9 *The Psychiatric Study of Jesus* (1948) 49.

10 From the epilogue which Schweitzer contributed to E. N. Mozley's book, *The Theology of Albert Schweitzer* (1950) 105.

11 To the 3rd English edition of the *Quest* (1954) he contributed a new preface, actually written for the 6th German edition a few years earlier. Although he maintains that he still adheres to his original theory in its main lines, he continues with these remarkable words:

> It was Jesus who began to spiritualize the idea of the Kingdom of God and the Messiah. He introduced into the late-Jewish conception of the Kingdom, his strong ethical emphasis on love, making this and the consistent practice of it, the indispensable condition of entrance. By doing so he charged the late-Jewish idea of the Kingdom of God with ethical forces, which transformed it into the spiritual and ethical reality with which we are familiar ...
>
> Jesus is already the spiritual Messiah, as opposed to the Messiah of late-Jewish eschatology, in that he has the Messianic consciousness while living a human life in this world, and feels himself called to awaken in men the desire for the spiritual qualifications for entrance into the Kingdom ...

"As the spiritual Lord of the spiritual Kingdom of God on earth, he is the Lord who will rule in our hearts."

H. G. Wood, who quotes these words in his valuable book, *Belief and Unbelief since 1850* (1955), is surely justified in saying, "it seems to me that Dr Schweitzer does not realize how profoundly this modifies his original contention".

12 Preface to 2nd edn of *Eschatology* (1913).

13 For a recent study see G. L. Davenport, *The Eschatology of the Book of Jubilees* (1971). He thinks the book underwent several redactions and that differing eschatologies can be traced in the various strata.

14 *The Son of Man in the Synoptic Tradition* (1965) 125.

15 Some mention should be made of Daniel 7 since it is often brought forward in connection with "the celestial Messiah". Just as the four beasts represent pagan empires, so the man-like figure who is described as coming into the presence of God (v. 13) is interpreted later in the chapter as a symbol representing "the people of the saints of the Most High" who receive the kingdom (17). At a later stage, but only in the Christian era as far as our evidence goes, Jewish writers came to identify the figure with the Messiah; but, as Rabbi I. Epstein has written, "all Hebrew commentators take the words 'coming with clouds' as symbolic". (See *NTS* 7 [1960/1] 93.)

16 On the titular use of the term, see the article by R. Leivestad, "Exit the Apocalyptic Son of Man", *NTS* 18 (1971/2), 243–67.

17 169; see also the immediate sequel to these words, and the whole passage 163–73.

18 It is noteworthy that one of Bultmann's 'disciples', Eta Linnemann, strenuously disputes the thesis that Jesus taught the imminent end of the world. Similarly N. Perrin writes that "sayings which express an imminent expectation fail to stand up to serious investigation" (1967) 203.

7

*God in Strength**

BRUCE CHILTON

I *General*

Of the eleven passages singled out in the Introduction for analysis, we have uncovered five units (Mark 1:15; Luke 4:18, 19, 21; Matt. 8:11; Luke 16:16; Mark 9:1, all in modified form) which substantively record Jesus' announcement of the kingdom of God. While specific connections between this material and other logia in the Jesus tradition have been pointed out in the Exegeses, we have not appealed to an a priori conception of dominical theology or of *ipsissima vox* in order to isolate it. Rather, we have taken a *via negationis*, eliminating from each passage such diction, syntax and thematic emphasis as appeared to be characteristic of a given evangelist and of the transmitter of the logion to the evangelist. In each case, we have perceived Aramaic (or more generally Semitic) idioms, and the *Targum Jonathan* to Isaiah has been seen to be of especial importance as preserving material which seems to have been a formative influence on the thought and language of these announcements.

This finding is not in itself surprising; recent discussion has tended to confirm the consensus that Aramaic was Jesus' first language,[1] and P. Stuhlmacher has pointed out that it is precisely in the Isaiah Targum that the kingdom is identified as something which is to be preached.[2] Although this aspect of his contribution is often ignored, J. Weiss, referring to passages in the Targums which have been repeatedly cited in this thesis, agreed with G. Dalman that their kingdom diction achieved an avoidance of anthropomorphism and found in them the "transcendence ... which is so apparent in the preaching of Jesus". He concluded that the understanding of the kingdom as the "self-revelation of God" was an importantly common element in the Targums and the NT.[3] In the sense that it agrees with this conclusion, the present thesis does no more than emphasize an insight which has been widely neglected in the discussion which

* First published in *God in Strength* by Bruce Chilton (1979) 277–93.

has followed upon Weiss' work. This insight has now been put in centre stage on the basis of an empirical study of eleven NT passages which has led us to a primitive logia stratum with consistent linguistic traits and a distinctive theology. This route to Jesus is rigorous, but passable.

Along this way, the development of the synoptic tradition has been observed to have been one which was controlled by the desire to preserve dominical logia. Even the two most radical community formations (Matt. 8:12; Luke 12:32) appear to have been produced as an addendum to and an apocalyptic restatement of earlier material. To this extent, we should understand *Gemeindebildungen* ("community constructions") to have been formed in a milieu of exegetical, not substantive, innovation: the preaching of Jesus was interpreted, not invented. This process of interpretation was continued by the evangelists, who explicated logia by the conflation of similar traditions (Matt. 11:12f., cf. Luke 16:16; Matt. 16:28, cf. Mark 9:1), by innovative adjustments in diction, syntax and/or content (Luke 12:32; 13:28f., cf. Matt. 8:11f.; Luke 9:27, cf. Mark 9:1) and by the simple preference for one tradition over another (Mark 1:15, cf. Matt. 4:17, cf. Luke 4:18f., 21), each in the context of his own outline. In only two instances was a serious misinterpretation of Jesus' preaching the result of this process (Matt. 11:12f.; Mark 9:1), and in both cases the evangelists showed signs of familiarity with an earlier meaning of which their own work constituted a correction. Later exegesis (in the manuscript tradition and the Fathers) showed signs of a similar familiarity, so that the conservative handling of the synoptic tradition appears to have postdated as well as to have antedated the composition of the first three Gospels.

II *Methodological*

Redaction critical technique has been used as the only available linguistic tool for the analysis of three passages, and as the principal tool where source critical investigation was also possible. Particularly in the former case, this has proved to be a demanding method. It was necessary in the first place to note the frequency with which the diction, syntax and theme of a given logion occur in the Gospel which contains the saying.[4] This statistical observation was only the initial step in the analysis. It was then necessary to observe the meaning with which a parallel formation (if there was one) was used and the sort of material (e.g., logion, narrative, citation) in which it appeared. By exercising critical judgement in respect of the meaning and context of a formation, it was possible to decide (1) whether or not a language pattern was in force and, if so, (2) whether that pattern was redactional or traditional. In this way the editorial policy of the evangelists and their sources was distinguished from the material which they transmit.

This method is therefore both more and less than statistical notation in sentence form. It is more because statistical data provided the occasion upon which critical judgements regarding the existence and pedigree of patterns could be made. It is less because the critical observation of language patterns is less objective than the statistical observation of language formations. One mind might perceive a pattern which another does not, and this general *Gestalt* situation is more acute where language is concerned. There is no commonly accepted theory of language which classes all formations according to the ways in which they are used,[5] and no such theory of style which can reliably predict when a writer will prefer one formation to another. In the present study, the reasons for a given critical judgement were given when a previous position was challenged or an apparent pattern or pedigree discounted. But at other times the author has simply exercised his best judgement knowing that the perception of linguistic patterns is to some extent a subjective matter. Until language itself is more thoroughly understood, the objectivity of this method can only be measured functionally by the agreement and disagreement of subsequent investigators.

This caveat should guard against the tendency of crediting this method with certainty simply because it is based on statistical observation. In practice it relies on critical judgement, and is therefore subject to the ambiguity of a subjective procedure. That said, however, the fact remains that redaction critical discipline permits the researcher to make critical judgement on the basis of explicit instances of diction, syntax and thematic structures. No appeal to hypothetical forms has been necessary, nor to redactional motives not evidenced by the formation at hand.

Practically speaking, it must be admitted that the accuracy of the individual results obtained by this method is severely limited by the brevity of the Gospels[6] and more especially by that of the material isolated as traditional. We hear so little from the writers and speakers who contributed to the NT that one is only speculating when one speaks of the "characteristics" of a Gospel or a substratum thereof. The probability of error in an individual judgement, especially concerning a small traditional unit, is therefore high, and no single judgement can be called certain except within the limitations of the method.[7] But it was said at the outset of the study of Mark 1:14f. that when individual judgements combine to form what appears to be a redactional pattern, then the credibility of the total pattern should be held to exceed that of its constitutive judgements. So it is with tradition: when we see in five separate units of logia attributed to Jesus traces of targumic diction worked into an innovative assertion of the kingdom, it would be contrary to deny their reliability as examples of Jesus' preaching. Redaction criticism is a practicable method based on commonly observable phenomena which yields consistent results. Its inadequacy is a function generally of an incomplete understanding of language and specifically of its relative inability to cope with limited samples of diction. The present study is a victim of both of these, but it also exercises the means which can overcome them: the continued practice of the method in the knowledge of its limitations.

Consistent recourse to the Old Syriac manuscript tradition in instances in which evidence for a Semitic background was present has been the second guiding methodological principle in this study. It is admittedly an *ad hoc* procedure: in the absence of independent access to the Aramaic Jesus tradition, one appeals to the source which has the best chance of preserving at least traces of it. By this method, one avoids entirely hypothetical reconstructions of the tradition: if an Old Syriac reading appears not to be an intrusion from the post-synoptic tradition and leads us into the diction of the Targums, then the reading constitutes better evidence for a reconstruction of the pre-synoptic tradition than does the "re"-translation of any investigator. The possibility might be kept open that the OS has been generally influenced by targumic diction,[8] but at least at the logia in question we seem to be in the presence of innovative statements, not of the influence of a revered text form.

III *Substantive*

Given the understanding of the kingdom as it appears in the *Targum Isaiah*, i.e., as the saving revelation of God himself,[9] questions which have been perennially posed in our century with regard to the kingdom are cast in terms which offer, tentatively anyway, the prospect of answers.

If one thinks of the kingdom as a spatially conceived régime,[10] then it makes sense to ask if it is here yet, and if not, when it will be. Just this temporal question has haunted NT scholarship since J. Weiss, as the eschatology of Jesus has been described as "consistent", "realized", "self-realizing", and "inaugurated". But if the kingdom is taken as the self-revelation of God, then none of these schemes can claim exclusively to characterize the preaching of Jesus. God as kingdom can be viewed as acting now (*Tg. Isa.* 52:7; Mark 1:15; Luke 4:18f., 21), as moving towards a future, irresistible climax in which he will be fully revealed (*Tg. Isa.* 24:23; 31:4; Matt. 8:11; Mark 9:1), and as inaugurated by the strength with which he manifests himself (*Tg. Isa.* 40:9f.; Luke 16:16). Both *Targum Isaiah* and Jesus understood the kingdom in all of these dimensions; to assert one at the expense of the other two introduces a false systematization into their thinking.[11] More crucially, an exclusivist time scheme focuses so single-mindedly on when sovereignty is mechanically asserted over a territory that it does less than justice to the targumic and dominical insistence that the kingdom is a personal God revealed. When Jesus announced the kingdom, he made nothing less known than that God, who was and is and is to come (Isa. 41:4; Rev. 1:8).[12]

It has puzzled NT investigators that Jesus used the term "kingdom" to refer to the fruit of salvation.[13] N. Perrin observes that "he uses it in reference to God's decisive intervention ... and he uses it in reference to the state secured for the redeemed by this intervention."[14] This formulation is very useful in its emphasis on the first element, as this permits priority to be given to the personal revelation of God as the constitutive element in "the kingdom". But it introduces an unnecessary discontinuity into the sayings which have been treated here to refer to a "state" as distinct from the "intervention" itself. Jesus does speak of festivity in the presence of God (Matt. 8:11); he enumerates the blessing sent by God through his anointed (Luke 4:18f.); he urges his hearers to apprehend the kingdom, to grasp it with all of their strength (Luke 16:16). None of these passages describes states: they are all responses to a prior divine act. God gathers, men feast. God sends, men hear the one sent. God avails himself, men make this self-assertion their most prized possession. Only at Luke 12:32 of the sayings treated – where community interpretation was evident – does the kingdom appear as a static entity. At the dominical level, the kingdom refers in the first place to God's self-revelation and derivatively to the joy of men in his presence. There is no reason to posit a dichotomous kingdom diction on Jesus' part.

The step from joy in God's presence to the reward held ready of Luke 12:32 is not a great one, especially since Jesus himself could picture men's joy before God as a future response (Matt. 8:11). This ecclesial interpretation is therefore quite understandable in the context of the apocalypticism of the second half of the first century (cf. 1 Pet. 1:4). When the personal emphasis of the kingdom in Jesus' mind is appreciated, another ecclesial motif – that of the parousia[15] – is seen as a more understandable interpretation than it is when the kingdom is seen as a régime. Both the kingdom of God and that of

Christ (1 Cor. 6:9, 10; cf. Eph. 5:5) have a divine personality at their centre. Moreover, the incipient relation between the divine personality in the kingdom and Jesus' own personality is already operative in two dominical logia here analysed. Jesus seems to have been, even in his own preaching, the principal witness to God's reconciling act both now (Luke 4:18, 19, 21) and in the future (Mark 9:1).[16]

These three issues have been singled out because they have been repeatedly raised in reference to Jesus' preaching during this century. They have been raised again here because they are pivotal questions: any exegesis of the dominical use of "kingdom" which is inconsistent with Jesus' notion of the time of the kingdom, his flexible use of the term to refer both to divine act and human blessing, and the adaptation by the early Church of *basileia* terminology is simply inadequate. It is no coincidence that these questions are so repeatedly posed, for they are begged by the variety of kingdom diction in the NT as a whole. At the first two points, it has been suggested here that a targumic matrix of the kingdom diction offers a straightforward explanation of dominical usage and at the third point, that dominical diction in turn helps to explicate the parousia theology of the early Church. That is: precisely those questions which have occasioned the development of abstract views of eschatology can be replied to quite directly under the understanding that Jesus conceived of the kingdom as God come in strength. From this perspective he spoke of the present and of the climactic future of this revelation, he referred to its value for men, and the Church learned to treasure that personal aspect which she came to recognize in her Lord. With respect to each of these three issues, then, the results of our linguistic investigation can be seen to be tenable from a historico-critical point of view.

This study began by asking what Jesus meant by "the kingdom" in his initial proclamation. It ends by concluding that Jesus' concern was to announce: God in strength. At every point, Jesus' announcement directs our attention to God; the effects of the kingdom cannot be worked up into an entity separable from him. To do so results in a stereotyped scheme which can only by complicated exegesis be fitted into the flexible diction of Jesus' preaching. Attempts to see the kingdom as an apocalyptic régime, as a political movement, as a programme for social improvement, i.e., as anything other than the revelation of God, also run the risk of putting ideology in the place of faith. Such attempts are not only problematic as exegesis, they also ill accord with Jesus' refusal of self-will in favour of openness to a personal God. The basic stance of Jesus as well as his diction constrain us to do what we in so many ways resist: to apprehend God revealed in consummating strength.

Kingdom as "God in strength" is a formulation offered by the present analysis using redaction, source and tradition criticism. Historically, such a simple concept is necessary to explain the range of Jesus' diction.[17] Theologically, such simplicity is needed to preserve the God-centred focus of the kingdom against abstraction. Perhaps in some way, therefore, the conclusion here offered can be of use in coming to a historical and theological appreciation of Jesus' message.

IV *Tests of coherence*

The "criterion of coherence" has been used by N. Perrin as a second of two principles by which to isolate "authentic" Jesus tradition.[18] Material is favourably ruled upon if it "coheres" with material previously found to be dominical by the "criterion of dissimilarity". This second criterion is as problematic as the first in that it once again blunts the tools by which logia are analysed, reducing literary historical criticism to another rule of thumb. For this reason, valuable though Perrin's approach may be, it would not accord with the method of the present study to deem "authentic" all logia which agree with the kingdom theology here found to be dominical; "authenticity" in the present study is a function of linguistic analysis, not of *a priori* criteria. On the other hand, it would be ludicrous to argue for the central importance of the targumic conception of the kingdom in Jesus' theology if in fact other kingdom logia did not bear such a reading. We must therefore glance at the rest of the tradition of dominical kingdom sayings to determine, not if it is "authentic", but if the present thesis is useful to its interpretation.

Since we are not about to enter into a linguistic analysis of this material as we did in the case of the kingdom announcements, the categories developed in the Introduction are less convenient for the present purpose than is the thematic breakdown of the kingdom logia worked out by J. Jeremias.[19] We will also use his study of the parables – attending, however, only to those passages which explicitly refer to the kingdom[20] – to determine if they are coherent with the understanding of the kingdom here identified as dominical. As a final test of coherence, we shall ask if the present argument is useful to the understanding of some logia which do not refer to, but which were seen by A. Harnack to be immediately related to Jesus' proclamation of, the kingdom of God.

The "apocalyptic sayings" and "admonitions" accord with attitudes which we have seen in the announcements. Mark 9:47 asserts the value of the kingdom in terms as unequivocal as Luke 16:16, and the admonitions exhort their hearers to act upon just such an evaluation. Luke 17:20f. explicitly supports the conclusion that a rigid time scheme was not a feature of Jesus' eschatology. Also, whether on an interior or communal understanding, *entos hymōn* stresses the personal aspect of the kingdom which has been seen to be of importance in Jesus' proclamation of God's self-revelation.

Joy in the presence of God is the goal envisaged in the "entry" sayings; indeed, Matt. 25:21, 23, 30, when compared to 8:11f., show that at least one NT writer could see *hē chara* ("joy") and *hē basileia* as related terms. A treatment of the entry sayings would of course require that this relation be traced to its source, but for the moment it will suffice to indicate their thematic consistency with Luke 4:18f.; Matt. 8:11. Since Matt. 8:11f. was one of the logia analysed, we can say that the "feast" image fully coheres with our interpretation of the kingdom in Jesus' preaching, and of course the same can be said of "sayings about the nearness of the reign of God" and "mission sayings".

In the context of the preceding petition, the request for the kingdom at Luke 11:2 par. can be read as a plea for the self-revelation of God, and Matt. 6:10 further supports such a reading. Jeremias points out that "coming" is not posited of the kingdom in rabbinic sources, but that it is of God even at Isa. 59:20 and Mic. 1:3.[21] Even more to the point, the only exception found by Strack-Billerbeck to the rule that '*t*' is not posited of the kingdom appears in the *Targum Jonathan* (to Mic. 4:8).[22] The key kingdom saying in the Lord's Prayer can therefore be taken as evidence in favour of the present thesis.

The possession sayings cohere first of all (in Jeremias' list) with Luke 12:32, and, insofar as they share the inheritance conception of this passage, they do not fully share the point of view which has here been identified as dominical. There is no reason for which Matt. 5:3 par.; Mark 10:14f., 23–5 par.; Matt. 5:10; 21:31 must be taken in this sense, however, and if they are taken to assert that the kingdom influences those mentioned in the present, then these sayings are akin to the announcement logia. But even on such a reading, the limitation of the kingdom to a specific group is a departure from, perhaps even a contradiction of, the attitude preserved in Matt. 8:11, and this limitation is also encountered in the mystery logion (Mark 4:11 par.).[23] Similarly, the idea of ranks in the kingdom which is presupposed by Matt. 5:19; 11:11 par.; 21:31 has not been encountered before in this analysis of Jesus' preaching. This set of logia is therefore tantalizingly coherent and incoherent with what we have argued is dominical theology. Given a targumic base for Jesus' diction, there appears to be a variety within the kingdom sayings not treated in this thesis which remains to be traced and explained. Taken as a whole, however, such sayings do bear, and in some cases encourage, the interpretation of the kingdom as divine self-revelation.

Themes which we have perceived in Jesus' preaching also appear in the parables. Again and again, the personal aspect of the kingdom is underlined by its comparison to a man (Mark 4:26f. par.; Matt. 18:23; 20:1; 22:2). The parables of the mustard seed and of the leaven (Matt. 13:31f. par.) indeed "contrast the beginning with the end" but they also insist that "the end is *implicit* in the beginning",[24] so that their temporal understanding of the kingdom agrees with the interpretation which we have offered for Jesus' proclamation. Finally, the preciousness of the kingdom, a theme expressed in Mark 9:47 as well as in Luke 16:16, comes most vividly to expression in the "twin parables" of the treasure and the pearl.[25] The prominence given to each of these motives in the parables suggests that they are near to the centre of Jesus' theology.

As in the case of the other kingdom logia, however, kingdom parables also refer to the kingdom in an innovative fashion. Matthew has parables (13:24, 47; 18:23; 20:1; 22:2; cf. Luke 14:16f.; 25:1) which, in line with the two-stage eschatology of the first Gospel, present the kingdom as "Final Judgement".[26] This is not a theme which we have found in Jesus' preaching, although it did appear in the interpretation of the Q community (Matt. 8:12). This is another general category of material, then, whose relation to the tradition which we have isolated invites separate and detailed investigation.

It was suggested by Harnack that "I am come" sayings are implicitly connected to Jesus' kingdom theology.[27] To prove or disprove this assertion would (once again) require detailed analyses of the logia at issue, but the possible allusion to Zech. 14:9 (which in Targum form refers to the kingdom) at John 17:21; 11:52 raises the possibility that the dominical kingdom teaching, understood in the context of the Targums, was a root of Jesus' self-consciousness.[28] This would explain how Luke could see 4:18f. as in some way analogous to Mark 1:15. Some form of personal pretension would be a probable co-ordinate of any announcement of the kingdom insofar as such an announcement was, "almost without exception" (in the words of Strack-Billerbeck) understood to be a feature of "the messianic time".[29] Of course, the question of Jesus' self-consciousness is an open one, and these comments do not constitute arguments, only possible leads in developing some response to this question.

It therefore appears that, while the idea of the kingdom in logia ascribed to Jesus is not to be limited to the targumic paradigm, the themes which we have linguistically isolated in a very small selection of sayings form a tenable working hypothesis for the investigation of other traditions about Jesus.

NOTES

1 See J. A. Emerton, "The Problem of Vernacular Hebrew in the First Century A.D. and the Language of Jesus", *JTS* 24 (1973) 1–23.

2 Stuhlmacher, *Das paulinische Evangelium* (1968) 142–51. Stuhlmacher's observation becomes all the more significant when it is noted that in none of the kingdom material collected by J. Jeremias from the Apocrypha and Pseudepigrapha (see *Theology* [1971] 32 n. 2) and from the Agrapha (*Unknown Sayings of Jesus* [1964]) is the kingdom announced. In the Apocrypha, some of the uses of "kingdom" are predicative (Wis. 6:4; 10:10) and at Tob. 13:2 (as at Dan. 3:54 LXX; 4:34 Theod) "kingdom" occurs in a blessing. The latter usage does not fit in easily with the scheme developed in the Introduction, and is a type of diction which merits its own investigation. Such a use of the term in blessings does, however, support the argument that the kingdom and God are in some way identifiable (as they seem to be in the Lord's Prayer). In the Pseudepigrapha, predicative usage is also represented (*Ps. Sol.* 5:18), as is catechetical diction (*Ps. Sol.* 17:3; *Sib. Or.* 3:47:766; *As. Mos.* 10:1) and the blessing genre observed above (1 Enoch 84:2, see also 103:1, cited by J. Weiss [1900] 19f.) Two agraphic sayings treated by Jeremias are predicative (*Gos. Thom.* 82 with parallels and Tertullian, *De baptismo* 20:2), as is *Gos. Thom.* 27 (= *P. Ox.* 1:4–11) and *Barn.* 7:11. The other kingdom sayings ascribed to Jesus in *Thomas* and the *Oxyrynchus Papyri* are catechetical, consistent with and at least partially parallel to Luke 17:20f. (*P. Ox.* 654, 8–21 *Gos. Thom.* 3), Matt. 23:13/Like 11:52 (*P. Ox.* 655, but this is so fragmentary as to make identification speculative) and the parables (*Gos. Thom.* 97; 98). Insofar as this survey – based upon the collection of the material by Jeremias – is a full representation of the known evidence, we may say that kingdom announcements (as distinct from announcements of salvation, destruction, Messiah, etc.) are *sui generis* to the Targums and the NT. (The implications of this for form-critical analysis are discussed in Appendix IV.) Two further considerations may be noted here, however: (a) passages such as *Tg. Isa.* 40:9; 52:7; *Nah.* 1:15 are closest to the mission sayings among the NT kingdom logia and (b) it is possible that kingdom announcements lie behind the announcements of other entities in the literature surrounding the NT.

3 J. Weiss (1900) 16. It must be admitted that Weiss encouraged his followers to overlook the significance of this insight by interpreting the targumic view of the kingdom in the categories of Jewish apocalyptic.

4 Where a formation was rare or so ubiquitous as to suggest it was indigenous to NT Greek, statistical investigation was broadened to include the NT as a whole.

5 Not to speak of one which can take into account the complex linguistic background of the NT. For this and related matters, see Güttgemanns, *Candid Questions concerning Gospel Form Criticism* (1979).

6 One is particularly aware of this when Acts has a significant number of parallels to a formation which is rare in Luke alone.

7 The analyses of Luke 16:16 and Mark 9:1 might be singled out here as running counter to widely current interpretations.

8 Although the work of other researchers has shown the influence of Targums on the Koine NT, so that targumic influence cannot be said to be limited to the OS. See McNamara, *Targum and Testament* (1972); Kuiper, *Targum* (1972); Lentzen-Deis, *Die Taufe Jesu nach den Synoptikern* (1970).

9 See K. L. Schmidt, "*Basileia*", in *TDNT* 1. 579–90, 583; and K. G. Kuhn, *mlkūt šmym* in Rabbinic Literature", in *TDNT* 1, 571–4, 571.

10 Aalen (1961–2) 229, cf. Kuhn; J. Weiss (1900) 5, 6, 79; Manson (1931) 131.

11 Similarly, W. Michaelis, *Täufer, Jesus, Urgemeinde. Die Predigt vom Reiche Gottes vor und nach Pfingsten* (1928) 84; Kümmel (1957) 141; Percy (1954) 224 n. 1; H. W. Kuhn, *Enderwartung* (1965) 200–1, 203; Ladd (1964) 134f.

12 See H.-D. Wendland (1931) 106; Manson (1931) 135, 140; Schnackenburg (1963) 128f.; Perrin (1967) 55.

13 Percy (1954) 22, citing P. Billerbeck and G. Dalman.

14 Perrin (1967) 60.

15 See J. A. T. Robinson, *Jesus and his Coming* (1957).

16 See Vielhauer (1957) 51–79, 77 and more especially Manson (1931) 129f., 132, 161. Manson emphasized the personal dimension of the kingdom and the identity of this dimension with Jesus himself. When he called the kingdom a "paternal government" (163f.) and "divine authority" (132), however, an abstract tendency was posited with which the preaching here analysed does not agree. This is close to the *theokratia* idea which J. Weiss refuted, and is probably a result of Manson's over-reliance on later Jewish literature in order to define the kingdom. For a more recent emphasis on the personal dimension, see Kretzer, *Die Herrschaft der Himmel und die Söhne des Reiches* (1971) 171.

17 The present thesis also avoids the self-contradiction encountered in the argument that the kingdom is to be seen apocalyptically. Perrin (1963) 158, for example says unequivocally, " 'The Kingdom of God' is an apocalyptic conception in the teaching of Jesus"; twenty pages later, he is just as certain that "Jesus rejected the apocalyptic conception of history".

18 Perrin (1967) 43.

19 As cited in the Introduction to *God in Strength*.

20 This is the procedure commended by J. Weiss (1900) 47. Although Dodd and Jeremias are without doubt correct in asserting that there are parables of the kingdom which do not use the term *he basileia*, for the purpose of general discussion it is best to stick to explicit uses of the term.

21 Jeremias, *Theology of the New Testament* (1971) 102 n. 5.

22 Str-B I, 418.

23 Although Matt. 12:28 par. is fully coherent with Luke 4:18–19, 21; and Mark 9:1.

24 Jeremias (1963) 152.

25 Jeremias (1963) 198f.

26 Jeremias (1963) 226, 210, 213, 136 n. 18, 176, 51–53.

27 A. Harnack, "Ich bin gekommen", *ZTK* 22 (1912) 1–30, 24.

28 If the *ego eimi* ("I am") sayings are taken to be another articulation of the unity motif expressed in the Johannine passages, then this complex may also be associated with the kingdom announcement.

29 Str-B III, 282; see also III, 9 for the connection of Isa. 52:7 to the expectation of

Elijah, a point pressed further by Stuhlmacher, *Das paulinische Evangelium* (1968) 145. For the formative influence of Isa. 61:1 elsewhere in the NT, see Stuhlmacher, 116–122; Percy (1954) 108; and Guilding, *The Fourth Gospel and Jewish Worship* (1960) 10.

8

*Eschatological or Theocentric Ethics?**

Notes on the Relationship between Eschatology and Ethics in Jesus' Preaching

---

HANS BALD

I

To discuss the relationship between eschatology and ethics[1] in the preaching of Jesus prior to the resurrection[2] is at the same time to seek the unity of his preaching. The task of determining this relationship arises from the characteristic structure of the synoptic tradition, the frequently demonstrated presentation of different blocks of tradition in close proximity which seem to have no actual connection with one another. Conzelmann and Lindemann (346–8) have recently summarized the latest attempts to characterize the whole of Jesus' preaching; along with his understanding of God and his understanding of himself, eschatology and ethics are consistently regarded as "particularly important themes in the teaching of Jesus" (347). The special difficulty in determining the relationship between eschatology and ethics arises from the fact that in the synoptic tradition statements are to be found alongside Jesus' eschatological preaching of the coming kingdom of God which are not easily categorized under the heading, "eschatological". Jesus' ethical directions constitute the most significant example of this.

The problems presented by the structure of the tradition have been described with enviable clarity by Rudolf Bultmann:

> It is really not easy to say how an eschatological prophet, who thinks the end of the world is around the corner, who feels that the kingdom of God is already breaking in and therefore calls blessed those of his contemporaries

* First published in *VF* 24 (1979) 35–52. Translated by M. Rutter.

who are ready for it ... – how such a man can argue questions of law and coin wisdom sayings as a Jewish rabbi ... statements, which have nothing of this eschatological tension ...[3]

The attempt to solve this problem basically runs up against a simple alternative, assuming we ignore attempts to eliminate one of the two types of sayings in favour of the other on tradition-historical grounds. Either we call the whole of Jesus' teaching "eschatological", and subordinate theological and ethical teaching to eschatology, or we regard the whole of Jesus' teaching as "theocentric", and derive both his eschatology and his ethics from Jesus' conception of God. In the end, the question is whether we are dealing with theocentric eschatology or eschatological theocentrism, and – as applied to ethics – whether theocentric or eschatological ethics are at issue.

It is not our task here to summarize previous treatments of the question in detail,[4] or even to note the wealth of the usually brief remarks made recently on this topic within the context of works dealing with the whole or part of Jesus' teaching. Rather, we wish to attempt a short survey of the present state of discussion with reference to several recent proposals. We hope to work out the most essential lines of argument, and to identify the possibilities, dead-ends, and tasks which confront those who wish to pursue the topic.[5]

II

An obvious way to avoid all the difficulties of trying to find substantial unity among the divergent elements would be to offer a tradition-critical solution – that is, to divide the two classes of sayings into layers of tradition that have differing dates and origins. One could thereby, for example, explain the eschatological or apocalyptic components of the Jesus tradition as the consequence of a "re-Judaizing" of Jesus' message, which began in his lifetime and was completed by the post-resurrection Church; this programme has been carried out by Ethelbert Stauffer (*Jesus and his Story* [1960, German 1957] especially 127ff.; *Die Botschaft Jesu damals und heute* (1959) 9ff. and elsewhere). However, "the non-apocalyptic sections of the Jesus tradition" can also be "ascribed exclusively to the later Church", which may be understood to have added "an ethic of love within the circle of believers" and "comforting insights of a wisdom-type origin into God's saving management of creation" to the eschatological and apocalyptic message of Jesus; for such an explanation, see Walter Schmithals, *Apokalyptic* (German 1973); also "Jesus und die Apokalyptik", in G. Strecker (ed.), *Jesus Christus in Historie und Theologie* (1975) 58–85, especially 66f.

III

Bultmann himself, followed by most of his followers, with the exception of Schmithals, rejected a tradition-critical elimination of the non-eschatological sayings, despite the difficulties posed by the disparity discovered in the tradition for understanding Jesus as the "eschatological prophet". In Bultmann's view, the tension presented by the tradition should itself be a matter for interpretation. It is important to note from the outset what Bultmann means by the "moral" teaching of Jesus. It is a blanket term for non-eschatological elements of the Jesus tradition. This includes, not only ethical instructions (e.g., Mark 2:27; 7:15; 10:11–12), but also sayings which Conzelmann (see below) calls "cosmological" (e.g., Matt. 5:44; 6:25–34; 10:29).[6]

As is well known, Bultmann adopts Johannes Weiss' judgement on the religious concepts which formed the context of Jesus' teaching: God's kingdom was for Jesus a concrete, supernatural entity and the coming of the kingdom was a cosmic event of devastating proportions.[7] This historical finding is, according to Bultmann ([1952] 9) to be interpreted existentially, so that reference to the breaking in of the kingdom of God functions as an urgent demand to the individual to come to an immediate decision: "Jesus' call is the call to decision".

This radical reduction of Jesus' preaching in terms of the individual's necessity to make a decision, which is the key to an existentially interpreted eschatology, enables Bultmann to resolve the tension in the tradition between the "eschatological prophet" and the "teacher of wisdom" (19) by means of an eschatological interpretation of Jesus' ethics: "There is an inner connection: both things, the eschatological proclamation and the ethical demand direct man to the fact that he is thereby brought before God, that God stands before him; both direct him into his Now as the hour of decision for God" (21). It is then only logical to define Jesus' ethics as "eschatological ethics" (19). When seen in this way, the seemingly strained, unrelated juxtaposition of eschatology and ethics reveals itself to be merely an apparent contradiction. The timeless, existential interpretation of eschatology makes it possible to subsume ethics under eschatology and thereby to comprehend it existentially, "concentrated on the meaning of existence", because this concentration is the characteristic of the idea of God operative in eschatology. In this way, existential eschatology becomes the actual point of unity, and ethics can be formulated in terms of (*i.e.* reduced existentially to) the imperative to love.

The interpretation of Jesus' message among the liberal theologians had followed a formally similar course to that of Bultmann. The problem of the disparity in the tradition as manifested in the tension between sayings about the present and sayings about the future was solved by eliminating for all practical purposes one of the alternatives, and by subsuming all factors under the other, which was left as determinative. In this case, however, the eschatological elements were interpreted from "a religious and moral view of God" (e.g., H. J. Holtzmann, *Lehrbuch der Theologie des Neuen Testaments I* [1911²] 222). Both expositions – the existential-eschatological on the one hand, and the immanent-moral version of the liberals on the other – are concerned with producing a timeless interpretation. The actual contents of the eschatological and the non-eschatological sayings are regarded only as ways of expressing timeless truths, and the two categories are blurred.

By his existential interpretation of the eschatological expectation of Jesus, Bultmann avoids the dilemma of an univocally eschatological interpretation of Jesus' teaching. Such an interpretation would have to uphold the validity of an eschatologically oriented system of ethics in face of the fact that, from a historical point of view, the expectation of an early apocalypse turned out to be false. That was the difficulty with A. Schweitzer's interpretation of Jesus, previously outlined by J. Weiss. Schweitzer maintained: "Jesus thought in either eschatological or non-eschatological terms – but not in both."[8] If eschatology is the all-embracing horizon of Jesus' teaching, and if this eschatology is not to be divested of its temporal character, then Jesus' ethical imperative must in fact be regarded as a limited "interim system of ethics" valid only for the time being until an early end. As Jack T. Sanders said in connection with Schweitzer, the logical conclusion of this is that, in discussing contemporary ethics, all reference to Jesus is to be abandoned.[9] This seems more logical than the viewpoint of H. Braun[10] who adheres – despite that fact that both "quantitatively" and "qualitatively" Jesus' eschatology is seen to be mistaken[11] – to the ethical relevance of Jesus' teaching.[12] Bultmann himself criticizes Schweitzer on the grounds that a form-critical disparity between prophetic and wisdom-like texts in the tradition can be observed, and that it can be shown that Jesus' ethical demands are not based on the conviction that the End is near.[13]

IV

It seems, on the face of it, that Bultmann's eschatological interpretation of Jesus' ethical teaching, as finally expounded in his *Theology of the New Testament*, has not been taken up in the only textbook on NT theology to be written (so far) by one of his followers.

Both in his description of Jesus' teaching in his *Outline* (1969), and in the summary in the *Arbeitsbuch* (cf. n. 1) (325–81),[14] Hans Conzelmann criticizes Bultmann's analysis of the structure of Jesus' teaching and his treatment of the question of the relationship between eschatology and ethical teaching. Taking up the findings of liberal theology, he regards as rash the willingness to give eschatology the fundamental and all-embracing priority which it enjoys in Bultmann's view of Jesus' preaching; neither Jesus' ethical nor his theological teaching should be described simply as eschatological. In Conzelmann's view the ethical demands of Jesus are not eschatologically based as regards their content, and "the prospect of an imminent end of the world" does not appear "in the context of his conception of God" ([1969] 124, cf. 99). All that is eschatological is "the general call to repentance . . . not each concrete commandment" (119). In the cases of both ethical and theological teaching, "there is no limit to the duration of the world" (125). Thus, in Matt. 6:25ff. – a difficult passage for those who would represent Jesus as altogether eschatological in outlook – "the world (is) not seen as racing toward its end, but simply as creation, as space for God's dominion and care" (124). The obvious tension between eschatological and "cosmological" (as Conzelmann calls them) sayings is not to be explained "by speaking of the dialectic between God as far and near" as Bultmann does,[15] because this solution "associates too closely general reflection on the world . . . and eschatology", which in the tradition are distinct (124, 126).

The situation is no different in respect of ethical teaching. In interpreting eschatology existentially and ethics eschatologically – both categories expressing the same human predicament of decision before God – Bultmann eliminates too quickly the very disparity in the complexes of sayings which poses the "exegetical problem" (100, 126). Conzelmann argues for the "indirect Christology" of Jesus as the "common point of departure for all three schemes (*sc.* theological teaching, ethical teaching and eschatology)", and against Bultmann's idea of the unity of the conception of God, ethics and eschatology in an (eschatological) understanding of existence (126f.).

The key to understanding the "indirect Christology" of Jesus in Conzelmann's view probably lies in his concept of eschatology, which is essentially the same as that of his teacher and his tradition. Eschatological preaching is the proclamation of the future coming of the kingdom. The eschatological premise is that "the evil world will soon come to an end" (99). The indirect Christology of Jesus is also defined eschatologically in this sense. It is established "by the manner in which Jesus connected proclamation of God's kingdom with himself as the sign of the kingdom" (140). He is the sign of the kingdom which is to come in future. Eschatology seems to have returned here as the really determinative factor in Jesus' teaching and as its hermeneutical key, even though Conzelmann himself criticized Bultmann for the one-sidedness of this approach. Precisely in this sense, Bultmann (according to whom Jesus understands himself "as, so to speak, an eschatological phenomenon"),[16] agrees with Conzelmann's formulation of indirect Christology.

Of course, the relationship between Christology and Jesus' conception of God has still not been explained satisfactorily by Conzelmann. In the same way as Jesus' conception of God, as he understands it, also includes cosmology (118f.) – more exactly, God's action in history and at the present, which accordingly must be characterized as non-eschatological, given Conzelmann's definition of eschatology – so Christology does not mean just the authority to call the world to eschatological decision, but also the authority to reveal God's already evident power and creative will. But the description of Jesus' conception of God as cosmological is not developed by Conzelmann, either as regards its range of meaning, or its concrete importance for an exposition of Jesus' teaching as a whole. In the final analysis, even Conzelmann adopts the division of Jesus' teaching into ethical teaching and eschatology – despite his protests against his teacher. The hermeneutical key of indirect Christology, which is said to disclose the structural unity of Jesus' teaching, makes it possible for Conzelmann to ignore the question of the substantive relationship between eschatology and ethics.

Some important points for our enquiry nonetheless arise from Conzelmann's criticism of Bultmann's view of Jesus' teaching. We should make positive use of his observation that cosmological statements about God are to be found in Jesus' teaching, statements which, with the ethical ones, cannot be interpreted eschatologically. We can overcome the difficulties which, in my opinion, lie in Conzelmann's scheme by adopting a second of his observations and joining it with the first: in the common ground of a conception of God oriented towards the present state of creation the connection between the cosmological and the ethical teaching is established. It is advisable not simply to equate the terms "doctrine of God" and "cosmology" (118). It would do better justice to the material to make a distinction within the Jesus tradition first of all between those statements which are eschatological, oriented towards the kingdom, and non-eschatological sayings, referring to God's power and will as present since the creation (Conzelmann's categories of cosmology and ethics).

If a "non-eschatological" conception of God, one oriented towards the present, can be traced as the common background of both cosmological and ethical sayings, then the possibility emerges of taking up the question of the relationship of this "conception of God" to the understanding of God which can be seen in the eschatological teaching of Jesus. From the point of view of a concept of God which includes ethics and eschatology, it may be possible to regard these, not as unconnected antitheses, but as the explication of a theological conception which involves both and which cannot be interpreted as simply eschatological. Presentations which attempt just that are our concern in the next section.

V

The essay by Heinz Schürmann on the mutual relationship between eschatology and theology first appeared in 1964. Until now there has hardly been a single critical study of it. Anton Vögtle's comment seems to sum up the situation accurately: "This original hypothesis was described repeatedly in the literature as 'remarkable', 'important', and so on. But there is hardly any indication of what exactly made it so significant."[17] The reason for this reticence lies partially in the not completely straightforward terminology and argumentation of the author; but principally – and especially from the Protestant standpoint – the (Catholic) Schürmann's explicitly immanentist approach (that is, his view of God as revealed in the world, rather than as disclosing himself from outside it) has stood in the way of readiness to enter into serious discussion with him. This deficiency in explicit discussion justifies devoting somewhat more space here to Schürmann's views.

Schürmann's study is explicitly directed against Bultmann and his followers, that is, against "pan-eschatology" and the existential interpretation (16 n. 20, and 20). He starts from the observation that an exclusively eschatological understanding of Jesus' teaching is not supported by the source material; as against the specifically eschatological sayings, there are also those in which the "eschatological tension is missing" (passages such as Matt. 6:25ff.; 7:1f.; 10:29; Mark 2:27, etc.) (16). Further, it is impossible to eliminate the disparity within the sayings by subordinating the non-eschatological sayings to eschatology.

If we take account of his exposition in a paper on eschatology and the service of love in Jesus' preaching (1959, reprinted in *Vom*

Messias zum Christus, ed. K. Schubert, 1964), Schürmann's theories, precisely because they are polemically expressed, take definite shape, particularly as regards the position of ethics in Jesus' teaching. Here Schürmann concludes against Bultmann "that Jesus' commandment to love is motivated not only by eschatological considerations ... but that in and behind all the expressly designated 'themes', it is also theocentric – determined at base by God as the Lord and Father" (211). From this there follows for Schürmann an important distinction: "The nearness of the end has only an incidental effect on behaviour as required by Jesus; it only motivates it on a practical, parenetic basis; it has no intrinsic or ultimate role" (212). Methodologically, this means that a distinction must be made "between secondary themes, incidentally motivated, which have been employed to serve as practical parenesis, and primary themes which are more deeply embedded in the substance of the teaching" (226 n. 37). If one accepts this distinction, then eschatology is "incidental" while theology is "central". By this route "eschatology is 'qualified', subordinated to a greater whole", certainly not "set aside and explained away ... But 'theocentrism' is not reduced to eschatology, as by Bultmann and his students" (230 n. 50). Elsewhere (13), Schürmann calls this procedure "de-eschatologizing".

Instead of "de-eschatologizing", talk of a timeless, existential view of eschatology would correspond more closely to Bultmann's concerns; Bultmann sees the requirement to make a decision as itself the eschatological situation, and for him Jesus' moral imperative has the same meaning: it forces a decision. This is how Bultmann can indeed speak logically of Jesus' eschatological ethics.

Just as Bultmann and Conzelmann, Schürmann also tries to determine the unity of Jesus' message, or, as he puts it himself, to demonstrate that the "uneasy juxtaposition" of the sayings is really a "centred co-ordination" (15). While Bultmann is at least structurally correct in dividing Jesus' teaching into two extremes (even though his analysis of the content is incorrect), Conzelmann does not realize that ethical teaching is not on the same level as eschatology and theology. For Schürmann, on the other hand, ethics are motivated by both eschatology and theology: "One must ... attempt to interpret Jesus' moral precepts against the background of both his proclamation of the kingdom and his view of God's revelation" (22).

For Schürmann, as was also the case for Conzelmann, the reference point for this co-ordination is Christology. However, there is no cautious understanding here of an "indirect" or "implicit" Christology: rather, Jesus' consciousness of himself is expressed as consciousness of being the Son of God, and is derived directly from the fact of his sonship (33). Sonship is the point where "all eschatological sayings are rooted and where they all come together". What is not explained is how Jesus' sonship is to be seen in relation to the Father. The reference to the "christological dogma of the Church" (35), however, gives an indication of the general direction in which an answer would lie. The connection between theocentrism and – if we can so call it – Christocentrism is given in the "foreknowledge" of Jesus, which is grounded in the Son's essential knowledge of the being and essence of the Father. Behind his promise of salvation and his summons is Jesus' "familiarity with the 'heavenly' Father" ("*Liebesdienst*", 217). Schürmann describes Jesus' words as a "communication of a personal moment of revelation and an ontological fact of revelation" which, in essence, are more than a matter of praising God (26f.). From this there follows the rather pointed statement:

> If God's essence is not to be reduced, and the series of ontological sayings not sacrificed to the eschatological, then we must further add that it is not because he has revealed himself as the eschatologically far and near God that God is "Lord" and "Father", but because he is both of these essentially, before and after every eschatological revelation.

He therefore goes on:

> Only a theology which dares to give God's Fatherhood and Lordship radical precedence over his future "coming" (or "having come") and which interprets the latter in the light of the former will be true to what shines forth in Jesus' words (32).

Although Schürmann's advance in the area of the ontological sayings is worthy of consideration, the categories he uses are still too heterogeneous when judged against the biblical text. Schürmann himself is perfectly clear that his "view of the problems raised, and the attempt at a solution ... (are) both determined by philosophical and dogmatic presuppositions ... The idea of Jesus' sonship precedes ... (and) informs the way the problem is posed and solved" (34). In any case, Schürmann is right in insisting on the independent value and importance of the statements about God's creative activity and, in this connection, in warning against an uncritical eschatologizing of Jesus' teaching. However, he does fail to appreciate the character of the biblical faith in God by maintaining the distinction between ontology and eschatology. To acknowledge God as the creator and Lord is first and foremost an acknowledgement of God's creative activity in the past, present and future, and not an ontological statement. Just how far this faith implies an ontological perception is a question that must be posed and answered separately.

As already mentioned, Anton Vögtle was the first to make a comprehensive criticism of Schürmann's account. We shall now take a short look at his arguments, with special regard to the question of the relationship between eschatology and ethics. First, Vögtle makes critical observations about Schürmann's terminology (372–5) and shows that the concept of revelation used by Schürmann is questionable. As for the latter's evaluation of the content of the "series of 'eschatological' sayings" (375), he feels it is ambiguous that "God's present and future eschatological action are both designated under the same heading as the 'coming' of God" (377).

But Vögtle's main objection is to Schürmann's formulation of the problem. For, he believes, the "sayings about God" are always concerned with a "totally existential application", so that to describe the non-eschatological ethics as a "series of ontological sayings" constitutes a "distorted perspective". The existence of a series of expressly non-eschatological sayings in Jesus' teaching cannot be inferred from the reference to God's present power in his creation. Such a reference only makes sense from an eschatological viewpoint (384f.), even if the eschatological motivation is not made explicit in every case (387). Then, too, we are fully justified in doubting the assumption of a juxtaposition of eschatological and theological statements:

> What would happen if the "uneasy juxtaposition" of both strands of sayings could not be established? Then there would be no reason at all to search for some point of reference which would make this juxtaposition comprehensible, or to fix "the strained unity (of Jesus' sayings) in an overarching principle", namely in the sonship of Jesus ...

Schürmann's formulation of the problem can be explained in the final analysis "as an attempt to legitimate 'theological' and 'christological' statements of an ontological sort ..." (389).

Vögtle does not dispute the legitimacy of this attempt, but he considers impossible Schürmann's belief that Jesus substantiated his preaching "on the basis of his sonship" (391). The "really problematic point" for Vögtle of course, is the distinction between "present and future eschatology", that is, the attempt to impute to Jesus an emphasis on "God's being in itself" and a distinction "between a non-eschatological and an eschatological application in his words about the Lordship and Fatherhood of God" (393). The problem of Jesus' expectation of an imminent End cannot be resolved christologically with the argument that "Jesus' eschatology is primarily a 'present eschatology' rather than a 'future eschatology', and that the 'nearness' of the eschaton is not 'primarily' a temporal phenomenon but a matter of revelation in which God himself – in Christ – comes near". Vögtle thinks it ludicrous to combine "the present and future eschaton under the heading of the 'nearness' of the eschaton" and then to subdivide this nearness within the categories "matter of revelation (the present 'nearness' of God in Jesus)" and "temporal phenomenon (the nearness of the kingdom which has not yet arrived)", and to explain the latter away (396). The contrary is in fact the case, for the presence of salvation – "the present 'nearness of God' in Jesus" – is determined "by the coming of God's rule . . . and not by the fact that the Son has come and is present" (397). Vögtle's final assessment is harsh: we must come to the conclusion that even the formulation of the problem "was inspired by its own, preconceived solution", and "that neither the formulation nor the solution can be reconciled with Jesus' teaching about God and God's kingdom" (398).

We can in no way dispute the fact that there are doubtful points in Schürmann's analysis, for example the ambiguous and doubtful categories he uses, the elaborate christological conception and the problematic emphasis on ontology. It nevertheless seems to me that his discussions contain a number of important insights which might be useful in solving our question of the relationship of eschatology and ethics in Jesus' teaching. The most important observation is that the tension in Jesus' teaching between statements oriented towards the future (temporally) and non-eschatological (e.g., ethical) statements oriented towards the present cannot be reduced and removed in some timeless, existential interpretation by eliminating the time factor. In my opinion, the idea that Jesus' concept of God is to be regarded as the basis of both ethical and (in the final analysis) eschatological teaching is just as important.

Vögtle's criticism of Schürmann's formulation of his topic is indeed justified. Within the biblical text itself there are statements in which the eschatological action of God is differentiated from his constantly present action. Accordingly, it is not possible to compare eschatology and theology in such a way that each has the same value as the other. Even Schürmann does not attempt to do so; rather, he finally subordinates the eschatological statements to the theological statements.

The decisive methodological weakness in Schürmann's reconstruction, as it seems to me, is that he almost completely ignores the difficulties his scheme poses from the points of view of the history of tradition and the history of religion.[18] We really cannot determine the relationship between Jesus' self-understanding and the ideas and traditions of his time if these conceptions are taken to be mere forms of expression for an alleged consciousness of being the Son. The faith in God which scholars now believe Jesus shares with his contemporaries is a belief in the creator and Lord of history.[19] On the basis of this faith in the creator, statements in Jesus' preaching concerning future eschatology and those concerning present ethics are to be joined into a single unit, while their own individual character is preserved.

VI

Leonhard Goppelt's contribution is an important attempt to overcome the dichotomy between the timeless and the eschatological which arises in defining the relationship between eschatology and ethics: for him, the answer lies in an emphasis on the idea of God, or, to be more precise, on the OT Jewish faith in the creator and Lord of history. He has summarized and developed his position, which is represented in a series of publications,[20] in *Theology of the New Testament*, vol. i (ET 1981).

Both when dealing with Jesus' teaching as a whole and when defining his ethical teaching in particular, Goppelt starts from the argument that Jesus thinks "theocentrically" (70). In other words, each individual demand of Jesus intends "in essence only one thing, namely complete repentance" (107). This is developed in three directions, (1) "Jesus calls men away from human precepts to the commandments of God in the Old Testament . . ."; (2) "at the same time, Jesus goes beyond the OT commandments, even against them, in calling men back to the original order of creation"; (3) in tension with this, Jesus demands that "for the sake of discipleship" men should do away with the shackles that tie them to the present world (108). These instructions, understood within Jesus' theocentric approach, cannot be developed "into a static system of ethics". "They can only be grasped as a unity when their goal is seen, not as a worldly organization, but as the reconciliation of man with his God." From this there follows an important observation: "God's will confronts us now in a distinctive way. Because his eschatological rule is established secretly in history, his will now confronts us both as a demand of the eschatological rule and also as a demand of the original creation." It is also necessary to add that we are confronted by this will "as a demand of the law, which has been provided because of people's 'hardheartedness', for a creation marked by evil" (108). In the face of the coming kingdom one can therefore point to the evident loving care of the Father as a motivation for taking no care for the morrow (73f.), to the creator who evidently makes the sun shine and the rain fall on the just and the unjust as a motivation for loving one's enemies, and to the will of the creator who made man and woman for one another as the basis of indissoluble marriage (111).

The eschatological call to repentance and his ethical instruction find their unity in Jesus' conception of God and, to that extent, Jesus' ethical teaching could be described as *theocentric ethics* in Goppelt's sense of the word. The God who is now coming in a new form is none other than the creator. "The claim of God's eschatological rule is foremost and decisive." "In the face of the demand of God's rule, obligations vis-à-vis creation and the law are not irrelevant; they are, on the contrary, revealed as what they are, but they occupy only a secondary position" (108). Only from the standpoint of the coming rule of God can we really know "what God's creation is" (73). God's activity as creator becomes clear in the light of his eschatological activity, just as the original will in creation becomes clear in the light of his eschatological demand. But it becomes clear as the will of God which is always valid, independent of his eschatological coming.[21] The reference to the creation in Jesus' ethical instructions therefore reflects his view of God's rule as breaking in on a world which is God's creation, even though affected by evil (67–76); it is put seriously in question, but not abolished.

God's kingdom comes both in the future and now (70, 112). At the same time, Jesus viewed "the coming of the kingdom ... (as) independent at base of an alteration in world conditions" (68f). Jesus' precepts are concerned with the conduct of the individual in a world which goes on for the moment as God's creation, but in which the *eschaton* is always present. For this reason, Jesus' summons, summarized in the commandment to love, is aimed not only at "the individual's relationship with his neighbour", but also at conduct within the framework of "social relationships provided by society's institutions", which are "not to be reduced to love of one's neighbour" (109). The eschatological summons to repentance, and Jesus' instructions which refer to behaviour in the world as it is, correspond to an image of God which includes past, present and future.

From the standpoint of this understanding of God, Jesus explains "the concrete demands of real life and at the same time conducts us into the eschatological distance" (110). Goppelt instances this in Jesus' words "on society's institutions", marriage and government (110ff.). At this very point eschatology and ethics are connected under the signature of faith in the creator whose activity shows itself as saving, both in his life-giving care and in his renewed eschatological concern for his creation. The certainty that God acts salvifically in the institutions and structures of the present world, and is concerned with them, is grounded in the soteriological dimension of the doctrine of creation. The world, even in its present, distorted condition, is still God's creation when seen from the viewpoint of a faith that includes confidence in God's creative activity, both present and future. Creation can neither be devalued in the apocalyptic manner, nor made absolute.

Only in discipleship do eschatology and ethics come together to form a unity in the conditions of actual history. The conduct of a disciple is, in principle, expected of everyone, but it is only possible to the believer. This behaviour is a sign, as in Jesus' ministry, and it is only by means of it that the new reality of the kingdom becomes effective and that the eschatological event succeeds in breaking through present world conditions (110ff.). Discipleship is the way in which the yet unknown future of the kingdom can be realized as a sign in the present world. It accordingly points beyond the present creation to God's new creation, where God the creator's saving will, which maintains and keeps the world as we know it, will come to perfection.

To clarify this position, we should make reference to the explanations of Goppelt's pupil, Jürgen Roloff. For Roloff the unity of eschatology and ethics can be found in "the uneasy unity between the will of the creator and that of the saviour". This tension is "the real driving force" of Jesus' ethical teaching. It is "the tension between God's will as creator, on which basis Jesus teaches us to see the structures of society and of human communal life anew, and his will as directed towards the final consummation, which should become the yardstick for the behaviour of those called by Jesus". "The transgression of established norms", even in respect of institutions and structures, becomes possible, because that which is promised for the future is already present by anticipation in faith. (J. Roloff, "Jesu sittliche Forderung", in W. Lohff and B. Lohse, ed., *Christentum und Gesellschaft* [Göttingen: 1969] 98–116, especially 110–13).

VII

Helmut Merklein has vehemently contested the argument that Jesus' ethics must be assessed on the basis of his conception of God; his analysis of Jesus' ethics appeared under a programmatic title, which designated the rule of God as "a principle of action". This splendidly written book renews the attempt to explain "the theological teaching of Jesus" (and therefore his ethics, which are largely developed on a theological basis) as "an implication of his message about the rule of

God" (173). This approach opposes other reconstructions, especially Schürmann's theocentric model.

The starting point of Merklein's reflections is the tension between the eschatological and non-eschatological sayings of Jesus which has been confirmed again and again by scholars. It is especially important that "precisely the moral precepts of Jesus are largely motivated ... not by eschatology, but by reference to wisdom or theology". An investigation of the ethics cannot, therefore, disregard the hermeneutical question of what Merklein calls "the relationship between eschatology and ethics, or rather between eschatology, theology and ethics in Jesus' teaching" (14).

Proceeding from the generally recognized central significance of Jesus' eschatological teaching, which is summed up in Mark 1:15 as the proclamation of the coming of God's rule, Merklein poses "the question of the status of the kingdom preaching within the framework of the whole of Jesus' teaching" (31). The mere existence of a "juxtaposition of different themes" can, in his view, be established "on a purely literary level", and can be analysed by tradition criticism or redaction criticism "into different form-critical or thematic categories". But such an analysis of the "juxtaposition between eschatological and non-eschatological sayings should not be made into the starting point of investigation, for this would mean having to search for some superior point of reference" from which "both categories derive their unity in Jesus' preaching" (37). On the contrary, he insists, we should look for "the saying which is hermeneutically central to this juxtaposition", "on the basis of which the juxtaposition can be seen to be a sensible combination" (31). In more concrete terms, we should "start, hermeneutically speaking, from the proclamation of the kingdom (Mark 1:15) as the overarching perspective and integrating value for the whole of Jesus' teaching". Within this preaching it is possible for Jesus "to make non-eschatological (theological and ethical) statements along with eschatological ones, without the kingdom announcement losing any validity in its character as the integrating value, or requiring clarification with some further statement" (37).

Merklein adopts positions similar to those developed in the work of Heinz-Dietrich Wendland[22] and, to a certain extent, of Erich Grässer ([1959] 38f.). But he especially criticizes the attempt to interpret Jesus' teaching, which formally juxtaposes "eschatology" and "theology", from what is in the final analysis a theological standpoint, and thereby to "explain" eschatology "as a function of theology" (40). In his view it is even more suspicious to attempt to define the unity of Jesus' teaching by means of the hermeneutical key of an explicit (Schürmann) or implicit (Conzelmann, Fuchs, Jüngel) Christology (40f.). Jesus' self-understanding is to be derived from his eschatological message, and not the reverse. "The question of Jesus' self-understanding does not [override] the question of the relationship between Jesus' eschatology, theology and ethics" (42).

In respect of ethics, this means "that Jesus' moral message is to be interpreted both formally and substantially (at least in its main features) from the point of view of his eschatology" (42). As his analysis proceeds Merklein attempts to develop his hermeneutical approach by describing how "the message of God's rule demands a new orientation in behaviour" (47).

To say that Jesus' ethical teaching is eschatological is in the first place a formal statement. Even Schweitzer and Bultmann came to this conclusion. For both of them, Jesus' eschatological expectation was, historically considered, the expectation of a future apocalypse. Schweitzer believed that Jesus' eschatology looked to the near future for fulfilment; for him, eschatological ethics are ethics which are valid for the "interim" period until the inception of God's rule. Bultmann interprets the temporal imminence of the kingdom in terms of his timeless existentialism as an expression of the urgency of the demand to make a decision here and now. Conzelmann makes a distinction between the motivation for a general call to repentance by means of an eschatology oriented towards the future and the non-eschatological (theological) motivation of Jesus' individual precepts. Against these attempted solutions, Merklein stresses the central function of eschatology even in the theological – or primarily non-eschatological – sayings in Jesus' teaching.

According to Merklein, "the eschatological message of Jesus is only formally characterized by a juxtaposition of sayings referring to the future and those referring to the present". "God's rule", therefore, is "primarily future, something still to be expected", which means that "statements about its present existence are determined by its future aspect, and not the reverse" (165). The point of the statements in Mark 1:15, which sum up Jesus' message of the kingdom, is "not the moment in time, but the proclamation of the eschatological resolution, which God has already made, to save mankind" (167). This substantive (rather than temporal) interpretation of Mark 1:15 and of the eschatological teaching of Jesus as a whole unmasks our great difficulties in regard to Jesus' imminent expectation as a pseudo-problem. "The reason that statements are directed towards the present time is not that the end is near in time, but that God has already resolved to save" (166). This means: "For God the great turning point has already been reached: God has conclusively made

148

up his mind in favour of salvation. Even now this salvation is making its influence felt in the present and on this basis it encourages anticipation of the great turning point for man and the world as a whole" (170). Therefore, Jesus' ethics are "eschatological ethics directed towards the eschaton's imminence, but made possible by means of its inception in God's mind" (168). In other words, "the man who ventures on the kingdom can live in the conviction that God has now already decided for his salvation, that he will keep to this decision, and that he will therefore establish this salvation in a comprehensive way" (182). Jesus' ethics primarily concern "action based on the experience of God's goodness" (205). This experience of God's action is, however, experience of a God who acts eschatologically. Jesus' moral instructions are "individually nothing other than specific expressions of the radical devotion of man to man, which must correspond to the radical devotion to man of a God who acts eschatologically" (295).

"In saying this we have already covered the essential aspect of the relationship between theology and eschatology in Jesus' teaching. The particular characteristic of Jesus' theology ... is, in terms of its content, an implication of eschatology ..." (206). However, all attempts to discover "in his concept of God the basic unity of Jesus' form-critically and thematically heterogeneous teaching" are to be rejected. "God's radical goodness is nothing other than the goodness of a God who acts eschatologically." A reconstruction which derives eschatology from theology

> overlooks the fact that for Jesus eschatology is not a theological treatise which is to be evolved from belief in God, but rather a proclamation of the eschatological resolution, now made and already manifesting itself in Jesus' ministry in a presently effective way. By taking this "now" seriously we can understand Jesus' theology as essentially an implication of his eschatology ... If God is resolved to save sinful man, then it is only "logical" that he should come into the picture as a radically merciful God ... The reverse explanation does not work: it does not follow from God's radically intentioned mercy that he has now resolved in favour of eschatological salvation ... (213f.).

If we accept this assumption, we can see that even the at first sight non-eschatological ethics have an eschatological orientation, despite their theological base. Jesus' proclamation of the coming of God's rule is "the point which demonstrates an internal order within the themes of Jesus' teaching and raises eschatology to the status of the point of reference for the other themes" (214).

There is still the problem that within the synoptic tradition the subject areas of ethics, eschatology and theological teaching are set side by side and not joined together into a literary unit under the heading of eschatology. Merklein explains this by pointing out that the primitive Christian tradition consisted of individual units of tradition, as has been shown by form criticism. "Given this characteristic of the method of transmission it must be considered significant that there still remain some pericopae (e.g., the passage on care in Matt. 6:25–33 and parallels) which exhibit a strong literary connection between eschatological and theological sayings" (214).

Needless to say, some critical reservations do arise concerning the impressively complete view of Jesus' teaching developed by Merklein. One might wonder whether passages such as Matt. 6:25f.; Matt. 5:43ff.; Mark 10:1ff., etc. are really to be interpreted in such a way that the theological motives they contain become no more than implications of eschatology. Perhaps it is rather a case of theology being used eschatologically, with creation as the "basis of perception" for eschatology.

Further, we should ask whether Mark 1:15 can in fact be interpreted in the way he suggests, and made into the hermeneutical key for the whole of Jesus' teaching. Can the problem of the time factor in Jesus' teaching be solved by interpreting temporal imminence as actual experience of the eschatological mercy, of God's already formed resolution to save? Is it not, as Conzelmann has explained, that Jesus' whole teaching is concerned finally with the one God, who is the same in the past, present and future? Doubtless, God now approaches mankind in Jesus' ministry and teaching in a new – one can even say eschatological – way. But must we not agree with Schürmann that this God is more than his eschatological activity?

VIII

The question of the relationship of eschatology and ethics in Jesus' teaching is a specific form of the hermeneutical question of the substantive unity of his message in the face of its form-critical variety. The question can also be formulated as that of the relationship of eschatological and non-eschatological (predominantly ethical) components of the Jesus tradition, or as the question of the relationship of eschatology, ethics and theology. The largely theocentric motivation of ethics is apparent. Can these questions be reduced to the simple choice between eschatological theocentrism and theocentric eschatology? Or are these only apparent alternatives?

Our review has shown how much each view of the problem and of its solution is fundamentally handicapped by a series of uncertainties related to the tradition of Jesus' ministry and preaching. First of all there is the problem of appreciating Jesus' "eschatology". The debate surrounding the determination of the relationship of eschatology and ethics is hindered by an insufficiently precise definition of what eschatology is supposed to mean in this context. The positions adopted are still very far apart, even if hardly anyone proposes equating eschatology and apocalyptic any longer.[23] The debate about the relationship of eschatology and ethics can scarcely lead to convincing conclusions without detailed criticism of the phenomenon of Jesus' eschatology, starting once more at the historical level.

E. Grässer has taken up some of K. Rahner's thoughts in summarizing the position as follows: "It will be the task of theology to find a path between the incorrect, apocalyptic understandings of eschatology as either an anticipatory commentary on later events or an absolute, demythologized existentialism, 'which forgets that man lives in true, altogether future-directed, temporality, in a world which is not just abstract existence, and that he must strive for salvation within the dimensions (including the ordinary temporality) of that world'."[24]

After all, it is impossible historically to trace Jesus' teaching back to a single tradition or religious influence. There are indisputably apocalyptic elements in Jesus' teaching, but then too we have his emphasis on the theology of creation and the present action of God, and his reference to the function of contemporary structures which make on-going life possible, even if only temporarily: the latter elements make it improper to classify Jesus as an "apocalyptist".[25] In the context of a conception of God in which the theology of creation and soteriology are locked together apocalyptic elements also find their place. This raises the question once more of how we define the concept of God which is the point of union between eschatology and ethics. In my opinion, Schürmann's observations should be taken up, but also corrected and made more precise by tradition-historical and history of religions investigation. Space remains here for only a few hints for further enquiry.

Scholars are generally agreed that Jesus introduces no new concept of God,[26] but proclaims the God of Israel, the creator and the Lord of history, as the one who is now coming. He bases his ethical demand on this God; even his eschatological message would be without content but for its reference to the already recognized God of creation. Jesus' eschatological message acquires its intelligibility from faith in the creator and Lord of history: God's activity in creation is not deduced from his eschatological activity, but the certainty of his present and future activity is derived from his creative activity (Matt.

6:25ff.). In fact, as Ulrich B. Müller pointed out quite rightly, "Jesus is reminiscent in a certain sense of Deutero-Isaiah",[27] not in the sense that he stresses the "boundless breadth of God's activity", but in the sense that eschatological hope in the new activity of the creator grows from faith in the creator.

Even in literature contemporary with the New Testament, the expectation of the new creation stands unreconciled side by side with confidence in God's saving care for the present creation. Both views of the world, however, are – insofar as they are kept separate – only partial explanations of the concept of creation. In Jesus' teaching, both aspects are brought together in a rather strained union on the basis of the concept of the all-embracing lordship of the creator and Lord of the world who is now establishing his dominion.

Eschatological theocentrism or theocentric eschatology? Jesus' theology is eschatological, because he preaches the coming of God "now"; but his eschatology is theocentric, because it is based on a conception of God which includes eschatology. Jesus' ethics are eschatological and non-eschatological at the same time. This can be the case because Jesus now proclaims the will of God, who is more than his eschatological coming.

NOTES

1 Clearly the phrase "Jesus' ethics" does not mean an ethical system in the formal sense, but is used as an abbreviation for his ethical precepts. On this question, cf. Conzelmann and Lindemann, *Arbeitsbuch zum NT* (1976²) 360; Goppelt, *Theology of the New Testament*, vol. I (1981) 106; H.-D. Wendland, *Ethik des Neuen Testament* (1977³) 2–5.

2 On the question of terminology: F. Hahn, *Historical Investigation and New Testament Faith* (1983) 72–5.

3 R. Bultmann, *Form Criticism* (1934) 24.

4 On this cf. R. H. Hiers (1968); Jack T. Sanders (1975) 1–29; Merklein (1978) 38–41 and *passim*.

5 I will be taking up observations made in my unpublished dissertation, *Eschatologie und Schöpfung: Untersuchungen zum Problem des Gottesverständnisses Jesu* (Munich: 1976).

6 Bultmann (n. 3) 24, 58; see also (1952) 11–22; *Jesus and the Word* (1934); cf. Conzelmann (1969) 122, 146.

7 J. Weiss (1971) 114; cf. Bultmann (1952) 4, 23 and elsewhere.

8 A. Schweitzer, *Das Messianitäts- und Leidensgeheimnis* (Tubingen: 1956³) 15; cf. 15–19.

9 Sanders (1975) 29.

10 H. Braun (1979) 44ff., 116ff.

11 So G. Klein (1970) 642–70, 645.

12 Cf. Sanders (1975) 23–8; further, E. Güttgemanns, *VF* 15 (1970) 41–75, 59–61.

13 (N. 3) 24, 73; cf. H.-D. Wendland, *Ethik*, 18.

14 In addition, H. Conzelmann, *Jesus* (1973, German 1959) is important. Also his "Method of the Life-of-Jesus Research", in Braaten and Harrisville (ed.) *The Historical Jesus* (1964, German 1959), and *Theologie als Schriftauslegung* (1974) 30–41.

15 Conzelmann, "The Historical Jesus ..." 65f.

16 Bultmann, "The Primitive Christian Kerygma and the Historical Jesus", in Braaten and Harrisville (1964) 30.

17 A. Vögtle (1974) 371.

18 It is not by chance that Schürmann ("Eschatologie", 27f.) refers in his argumentation to the phenomenologically characterized conception of the "holy" in R. Otto (1934).

19 Cf. most recently, J. Becker, "Das Gottesbild Jesu und die älteste Auslegung von Ostern", in G. Strecker (ed.), *Jesus Christus in Historie und Theologie* (1975) 105–26.

20 In this connection see also L. Goppelt, *Christologie und Ethik* (1968) 28–43, 106–36, 190–219.

21 Cf. F. Hahn (n. 2) 62: "Thus the divine activity in creation becomes the explanation for God's will."

22 H.-D. Wendland (1931).

23 Cf. G. Klein's (1970) 658f. criticism of W. Schmithals.

24 E. Grässer, *Die Naherwartung Jesu* (1973) 140, citing K. Rahner in *Lexicon für Theologie und Kirche* III² 1096.

25 In any case, Jesus set aside the motif of the two ages which was constitutive for his religious background. Cf. H. Leroy, *Jesus* (1978) 71.

26 Cf. Conzelmann–Linnemann, *Arbeitsbuch*, 350–2.

27 U. B. Müller, "Vision und Botschaft. Erwägungen zur prophetischen Struktur der Verkündigung Jesu", *ZTK* 74 (1977) 416–48, 445 n. 78.

Select Bibliography

Aalen, Sverre, " 'Reign' and 'House' in the Kingdom of God in the Gospels", *NTS* 8 (1961–2) 215–40.

Bald, Hans, "Eschatologische oder theozentrische Ethik?", *VF* 24 (1979) 35–52. See 133–53 in this volume.

Berkey, Robert F., "*Engizein, phthanein* and Realized Eschatology", *JBL* 82 (1963) 177–87.

Bornkamm, Günther, *Jesus of Nazareth.* (German 1956) London: Hodder & Stoughton, 1960; New York: Harper, 1960.

Braun, Herbert, *Jesus.* (German 1969) Philadelphia: Fortress, 1979.

Buber, Martin, *Kingship of God.* (German 1932, 1956³) London: Allen and Unwin, 1967³.

Bultmann, Rudolf, *The History of the Synoptic Tradition.* (German 1921, 1931²) Oxford: Blackwell, 1963, rev. 1968; New York: Harper & Row, 1963, 1968.

—*Jesus and the Word.* (German 1926) New York: Scribner, 1934; London: Collins, 1958.

—*Theology of the New Testament* Vol. I. (German 1948) London: SCM, 1952; New York: Scribner, 1952.

Cadoux, Arthur Temple, *The Parables of Jesus.* London: Clarke, 1930; New York: Macmillan, 1931.

Campbell, J. Y., "The Kingdom of God has come", *ExpT* 48 (1936–7) 91–4.

Chilton, Bruce David, "An Evangelical and Critical Approach to the Sayings of Jesus", *Themelios* 3 (1978) 78–85.

—*The Glory of Israel*, JSOTSup 23. Sheffield: *JSOT*, 1982.

—*God in Strength, SUNT* 1. Linz: Plöchl, 1979. See 121–32 in this volume.

—" 'Not to taste death': a Jewish, Christian and Gnostic Usage", *Studia Biblica 1978, JSNTSup* 2(Sheffield: *JSOT*, 1980) 29–36.

—"Regnum Dei Deus Est", *SJT* 31 (1978) 261–70.

Clarke, Kenneth W., "Realized Eschatology", *JBL* 59 (1940) 367–83.

Colpe, Carsten, *Die religionsgeschichtliche Schule*, *FRLANT* 60. Göttingen: Vandenhoeck und Ruprecht, 1961.

Conzelmann, Hans, *An Outline of the Theology of the New Testament.* (German 1968) London: SCM, 1969; New York: Harper & Row, 1969.

—"Present and Future in the Synoptic Tradition", (German 1957) *JTC* 5 (1968) 26–44.

Dalman, Gustaf, *The Words of Jesus*. Edinburgh: Clark, 1902, from the German (Leipzig: Hinrichs, 1898).

Dodd, Charles Harold, *The Parables of the Kingdom*. London: Nisbet, 1935; Collins, 1961; New York: Scribner, 1936.

Fascher, Erich, "Gottes Königtum im Urchristentum", *Numen* 4 (1957) 85–113.

Flender, Helmut, *Die Botschaft Jesu von der Herrschaft Gottes*. Munich: Kaiser, 1968.

Fuller, Reginald Horace, *The Mission and Achievement of Jesus*, SBT 12. London: SCM, 1954; Chicago: Allenson, 1954.

Funk, Robert W., *Parables and Presence*. Philadelphia: Fortress, 1982.

Galling, K., Conzelmann, H., Wolf, E., Gloege, G., "Reich Gottes", *RGG*[3] 5 (1961) 912–30.

Glasson, Thomas Francis, *Jesus and the End of the World*. Edinburgh: St Andrews, 1980.

—"The Kingdom as Cosmic Catastrophe", *Studia Evangelica* III (Berlin: Akademie, 1964) 187–200.

—"Schweitzer's Influence – Blessing or Bane?", *JTS* 28 (1977) 289–302. See 107–20 in this volume.

—*The Second Advent*. London: Epworth, 1945.

—"What is Apocalyptic?" *NTS* 27 (1980) 98–105.

Gloege, Gerhard, *Reich Gottes und Kirche im Neuen Testament*. Darmstadt: Wissenschaftliche Buchgesellschaft, 1968, from the 1929 edn.

Grässer, Erich, *Das Problem der Parusieverzögerung in den synoptischen Evangelien und in der Apostelgeschichte*, BZNW 22. Berlin: De Gruyter, 1959, 1960[2].

—"Zum Verständnis der Gottesherrschaft" *ZNW* 65 (1974) 3–26. See 52–71 in this volume.

Hengel, Martin, *Was Jesus a Revolutionist?* (German, 1970) Philadelphia: Fortress, 1971.

Hiers, Richard Hyde, *The Historical Jesus and the Kingdom of God*. Gainesville: University of Florida Press, 1973.

—*Jesus and Ethics*. Philadelphia: Westminster, 1968.

Jeremias, Joachim, *The Parables of Jesus*. (German editions since 1947) London: SCM, 1954, rev. edn 1963[2], 1972[3]; New York: Scribner, 1972.

Klein, Günther, "'Reich Gottes' also biblischer Zentralbegriff", *EvT* 30 (1970) 642–70.

Knoch, Otto, "Die eschatologische Frage", *BZ* 6 (1962) 112–20.

Koch, Klaus, "Offenbaren wird sich das Reich Gottes", *NTS* 25 (1979) 158–65.

Kümmel, Werner Georg, "Jesusforschung seit 1965: Nachträge 1975–1980", *ThR* 47 (1982) 136–65.

—"Die Naherwartung in der Verkündigung Jesu", *Zeit und Geschichte*, ed. E. Dinkler (Tübingen: Mohr, 1964) 31–46. See 36–51 in this volume.

—*The New Testament, The History of the Investigation of its Problems.* (German 1958) Nashville: Abingdon, 1972; London: SCM, 1973.

—*Promise and Fulfilment*, SBT 23. (German 1945) London: SCM, 1957; Naperville: Allenson, 1957.

Kuhn, Karl Georg, "*Malkuth shamayim* in Rabbinic Literature", *TDNT* I (1978⁹) 571–4.

Ladd, George Eldon, *Jesus and the Kingdom* (New York: Harper & Row, 1964; London: SPCK, 1966; Grand Rapids: Eerdmans, 1974²).

Lattke, Michael, "Zur jüdischen Vorgeschichte des synoptischen Begriffs der 'Königsherrschaft Gottes'", *Gegenwart und Kommendes Reich*, ed. P. Fiedler and D. Zeller (Stuttgart: Katholisches Bibelwerk, 1975) 9–25. See 72–91 in this volume.

Linnemann, Eta, *The Parables of Jesus*. (German 1961) London: SPCK, 1966; New York: Harper & Row, 1966.

Lundtröm, Gösta, *The Kingdom of God in the Teaching of Jesus. A History of Interpretation from the Last Decades of the Nineteenth Century to the Present Day*. Edinburgh: Oliver & Boyd, 1963; Richmond: John Knox, 1963.

Manson, Thomas Walter, *The Teaching of Jesus*. Cambridge: University Press, 1931.

Marshall, I. Howard, "Palestinian and Hellenistic Christianity: Some Critical Comments", *NTS* (1972–3) 271–87.

Merklein, Helmut, *Die Gottesherrschaft als Handlungsprinzip*. Wurzburg: Echler Verlag, 1978.

Otto, Rudolf, *The Kingdom of God and the Son of Man*. (German 1934) London: Lutterworth, 1938, rev. 1943; Grand Rapids: Zondervan, 1951; Boston: Starking, 1938, 1957. See 27–35 in this volume.

Pannenberg, Wolfhart, *Theology and the Kingdom of God*. (German 1971) Philadelphia: Westminster, 1969.

Percy, Ernst, *Die Botschaft Jesu*. Lund: Gleerup, 1954.

Perrin, Norman, *Jesus and the Language of the Kingdom*. Philadelphia: Fortress, 1976; London: SCM, 1976. See 92–106 in this volume.

—*The Kingdom of God in the Teaching of Jesus*. Philadelphia: Westminster, 1963; London: SCM, 1963.

—*Rediscovering the Teaching of Jesus*. New York: Harper & Row, 1967; London: SCM, 1967.

Ritschl, Albrecht Benjamin, *Justification and Reconciliation*. Vol. III. (German 1874) Edinburgh: T. & T. Clark, 1900; New York: Scribner, 1900.

Robinson, James McConkey, *The Problem of History in Mark*, SBT 21. London: SCM, 1957; Naperville: Allenson, 1957.

Robinson, James M., and Koester, Helmut, *Trajectories through Early Christianity*. Philadelphia: Fortress, 1971.

Sanders, Jack T., *Ethics in the New Testament*. London: SCM, 1975; Philadelphia: Fortress, 1975.

Schmidt, Karl Ludwig, "*Basileia* (*tou Theou*) in Hellenistic Judaism", *TDNT* I (1978⁹) 574–6.

Schmithals, Walter, "Jesus und die Weltlichkeit des Reiches Gottes", *Jesus Christus in der Verkündigung der Kirche* (Neukirchen-Vluyn: Neukirchener, 1972) 91–117.

Schnackenburg, Rudolf, *God's Rule and Kingdom*. (German 1959) London: Nelson, 1963 and Burns & Oates, 1968; New York: Herder, 1963.

Schulz, Siegfried, "Die Neue Frage nach dem historischen Jesus", *Neues Testaments und Geschichte*, ed. H. Baltensweiler and Bo Reicke (Tübingen: Mohr, 1972; Zürich: Theologischer Verlag, 1972) 33–42.

Schürmann, Heinz, "Das hermeneutische Hauptproblem der Verkündigung Jesu", *Traditionsgeschichtliche Untersuchungen zu den synoptischen Evangelien* (Düsseldorf: Patmos, 1968) 13–35.

Schweitzer, Albert, *The Kingdom of God and Primitive Christianity*. (German 1967) London: Black, 1968; New York: Seabury, 1968.

—*The Mystery of the Kingdom of God*. (German 1901) London: Black, 1914.

—*The Quest of the Historical Jesus*. (German 1906, 1913²) London: Black, 1910, SCM, 1981; New York: Macmillan, 1922.

Via, Dan Otto, *Kerygma and Comedy in the New Testament*. Philadelphia: Fortress, 1975.

—*The Parables*. Philadelphia: Fortress, 1967.

Vielhauer, Philipp, "Gottesreich und Menschensohn in der Verkündigung Jesu", Festschrift für Günther Dehn, ed. W. Schneemelcher (Neukirchen: Moers, 1957) 51–79. Repr. in his *Aufsätze zum Neuen Testament* (Munich: Kaiser, 1965) 55–91.

Vögtle, Anton, "'Theo-logie' und 'Eschato-logie' in der Verkündigung Jesu?", *Neues Testament und Kirche*, ed. J. Gnilka (Freiburg–Basel–Wien: Herder, 1974) 371–98.

Volz, Paul, *Die Eschatologie der jüdischen Gemeinde* (Tübingen: Mohr, 1934, 1954). 1st edn, *Jüdische Eschatologie* (Leipzig and Tübingen: Mohr, 1903).

Weiss, Johannes, *Die Predigt Jesu vom Reiche Gottes*. Göttingen: Vandenhoeck und Ruprecht, 1892, 1900², 1964; ET of the 1st edn, Philadelphia: Fortress, 1971; London: SCM, 1971.

Wendland, Heinz-Dietrich, *Die Eschatologie des Reiches Gottes bei Jesus*. Gütersloh: Bertelsmann, 1931.

Wheelwright, Philip Ellis, *Metaphor and Reality*. Bloomington: Indiana University Press, 1962.

Wilder, Amos Niven, *Early Christian Rhetoric: The Language of the Gospel*. London: SCM, 1964; New York: Harper & Row, 1964, with the title and subtitle in reverse order; Cambridge: Harvard, 1971².

Yates, John Edmund, *The Spirit and the Kingdom*. London: SPCK, 1963.

Index of Modern Authors

Index of New Testament References